STRAI[illegible]

Essays on the Struggle of Blacks in America, 1934 - 1994

by
William H. McClendon

Edited and with an Introduction
by Robert Chrisman

THE**BLACK**SCHOLAR PRESS • Oakland, California

A Black Scholar
25th Anniversary Edition

ACKNOWLEDGEMENTS:
Some of these works have been previously published in *The Black Scholar* and *The Front Page.* "In Defense of Black Life," was written at the request of Bruce Broussard, Publisher of *The Portland Observer,* in the early 1980s.

The Black Scholar Press extends its thanks to Chalis Johnson, Ntombi Marrengane, Delores M. Mortimer, Laura Tyler and Maize Woodford for their research and editorial work. We extend special thanks to Ida A. McClendon, Jr. for her assistance.

A portion of this research was made possible by means of a faculty research grant from the Center for African and Afroamerican Studies, University of Michigan, Ann Arbor.

Robert Chrisman

COVER ILLUSTRATION:
William H. McClendon
Photograph by Robert Chrisman.

ISBN #0-933296-16-9

Printed in the United States of America.

Published by The Black Scholar Press.
P.O. Box 2869, Oakland, California, 94609.

To Ida,

In Memory of

Annie Mae and Jessie

Table of Contents

The People's Observer

The Observer

IV. THE FOUNDATIONS OF BLACK CULTURE

INTRODUCTION

I.
STRAIGHT AHEAD

Straight Ahead is a collection of editorials, articles and essays by William H. McClendon, one of the most important black authors, educators and community leaders in the Pacific Northwest region over the past 60 years. These essays reveal a remarkable consistency and integrity of vision and manifest his unflinching commitment to the struggle for liberation by black people in America.

Straight Ahead compiles, in chronological order, some of McClendon's major writings for six decades, commencing with "Which College — White or Negro," an essay he wrote as a freshman at Morehouse College in 1934. This essay received the Joel E. Spingarn Award and was published in the August 1934 edition of *Crisis* magazine. Additionally, ***Straight Ahead*** compiles McClendon's writings as editor and publisher of T*he Portland Observer,* a newspaper he founded with Charlie Garrett in 1938. These are followed by editorials from *The People's Observer* (1943- 1945), and *The Observer* (1945-1950), which were edited and published by McClendon. ***Straight Ahead*** concludes with critiques, position commentaries and analyses from the 1960s to 1990s. These are significant and distinguished illustrations of his work as an educator and political activist.

For the past 25 years, McClendon has been a Contributing and Advisory Editor to **The Black Scholar.** His essays on education and black culture have received wide acclaim. In 1995, McClendon was awarded The Black Scholar Lifetime Award for Excellence in Education and Culture.

II.
THE BLACK INTELLECTUAL TRADITION: THOUGHT, ACTION, COMMUNITY

BORN IN ATLANTA, GEORGIA on December 6, 1915, McClendon writes in the tradition of black activist intellectuals such as Richard Allen, Henry Highland Garnet, Frederick Douglass, Martin Delaney, Frances W. Harper, Ida B. Wells-Barnett, William Monroe Trotter, and W. E. B. Du Bois. This tradition has its origins in the black struggle against slavery, and first took collective political form with the slave revolts and conspiracies of the eighteenth and nineteenth centuries, and in the development of an oppositional vernacular tradition. Black intellectuals who were enslaved were confined by its strictures to black vernacular expressions and materials — folklore, songs, sayings and axioms — and the reformulation of Christian mythology and Biblical texts. Whether enslaved or non-enslaved, blacks viewed literacy and education as instruments essential for individual and collective liberation. Many black intellectuals have pointed out that their struggles to achieve these skills were themselves a political process that often has been regarded as a mode of opposition. As Frederick Douglass cites in his *Narrative,* slavemasters were perfectly well aware of their reasons for denying slaves literacy. In Master Auld's famous words, "A nigger should know nothing but to obey his master — to do as he is told to do. Learning would *spoil* the best nigger in the world." Douglass then extended this insight into a principle of dialectical opposition:

What he most dreaded, that I most desired. What he most loved, that I most hated. That which to him was a great evil, to be carefully shunned, was to me a great good, to be diligently sought; and the argument which he so warmly urged, against my learning to read, only served to inspire me with a desire and determination to learn.

THE DIALECTIC THAT ENSUED BETWEEN THE NECESSITIES of the black condition and the creative actions of black intellectuals in responding to those needs brought about many important antebellum Afro-American projects of the nineteenth century: the struggle against colonization, the formation of the black church, the launching of independent black periodicals, the formation of black schools such as the African Free School and the black convention movement.

In 1827, Samuel Cornish and John Russwurm, the editors of the first black newspaper in the United States, *Freedom's Journal,* issued a preamble for their first issue that has since served as a model for independent black expression and action:

We wish to plead our own cause. Too long have others spoken for us. Too long has the public been deceived by misrepresentations, in things which concern us dearly, though in the estimation of some mere trifles; for though there are many in society who exercised towards us benevolent feelings, still (with sorrow we confess it) there are others who make it their business to enlarge upon the least trifle, which tends to the discredit of any person of colour. . . .

This theme, of the necessity for the self-determination and vindication of blacks in America by their own independent, diligent and morally righteous efforts, is developed in the remainder of the editorial. The editors then go on to articulate their mission: liberal education; the "general principles and rules of economy"; civil rights and the independent use of the vote; technical and scientific knowledge;the nurture of children; an open discussion of ideas among blacks; knowledge of Africa; support for "our brethren who are still in the iron fetters of bondage"; an education of the general public against prejudice and the continuing advocacy of the interests of black free persons. Today, nearly one hundred seventy years later, this agenda persists in the thought and action of any black intellectual of significance.

These black intellectuals were also activists. They lectured against slavery, supported slave rebellion, fought pro-slavery mobs in the streets, worked in the Underground Railroad, petitioned for the right of blacks to fight in the Civil War and organized regiments, raised funds and recruited black soldiers. After the Civil War, intellectuals such as Ida B. Wells published and edited periodicals and led the fight against lynching. This struggle was waged subsequently by W. E. B. Du Bois and James Weldon Johnson. Several others devoted their energies to the black education movement.

Black intellectuals produced from this tradition of struggle must necessarily conduct continuing critiques of white racism, in their quests for collective social and economic justice for the black community. Black intellectuals and artists of this orientation, while both influencing and cognizant of metropolitan culture, find their primary criteria for value and meaning in the contemporary and residual reality of black life itself. They were not alienated from the black community; they were involved with it. Long before the term *engagé/e* became popular in twentieth century Europe, it was typical of the nineteenth century black intellectual . The moral and philosophical tenets of this tradition are that black intellectuals are the representatives of a people who, through their suffering, struggle and achievement, have demonstrated a moral position that is superior to the individual, institutional and structural racism of white America.

William H. McClendon is fully aware of this. At an early age he was taught by his mother of the many intellectual, social and political currents within the black community. He recalls in the 1920s that E. Franklin Frazier came to teach sociology at Morehouse College and to establish and develop the Atlanta School of Social Work. Frazier's arrival was believed to have resulted from the tireless campaign carried out by Jesse O. Thomas and others to make it possible for trained social workers to be able to provide services for black people in Atlanta and other parts of the South. During this same period, some black men had formed a social group that included John Hope, John Hill, William Holmes, Grant Carter, William Driskell, A. McClendon, J. W. Dobbs, several other members of the Prince Hall Masons and some members of the Letter Carriers Association. Infrequently they met, played whist and had lengthy discussions dealing with serious social issues of concern to Atlanta's black population.

In family conversations between his parents and grandparents, McClendon became familiar with many contemporary expressions, such as the Washington paradigm of industrial education, NAACP, Du Bois' vision of civil rights and liberal education, Frazier's pioneering work in black sociology. (While these informal pedagogies have no designation in Anglo-American education, they are known as "tertulias" in Spain and the Hispanic Caribbean, and called "groundings" in the Anglophone Caribbean. They serve to consolidate the community and distribute knowledge in a organic fashion.)

McClendon's essay, "Which College — White or Negro," in its depth and clarity of analysis, shows an unusual maturity and awareness. This renders "Which College" of contemporary value. McClendon's narrative of the black student's alienation from white students and from black students as well at the white college, is all too familiar on today's college campuses. McClendon's profile of the alienated black is prophetic of many of today's black intellectuals and careerists:

He is not prepared for life among his people or among any people because he is unsympathetic with their aims and shortcomings, never having experienced the same group ambitions or despair. He cannot lead the people because he has not the initiative and he cannot follow a leader because he feels he is too superior. There is only one thing he can do successfully and that is to deride and criticize his associates who have been 'victims' of a segregated school system.

In concluding that "the type of training that [the black student] needs to sharpen his innate faculties, to increase his self- respect, and to make him more companionable with his own people is not to be found in the so-called 'white' schools of the country, but in the colleges designed for the training of Negro youth," McClendon is not endorsing a Jim Crow system. He , instead, recognizes the value of a liberal education for the black student, but asserts that such education can only be sustained in a supporting and nurturing environment, a theme that persists throughout his career and is indisputable.

III.
THE PORTLAND OBSERVER

COLLECTED HERE ARE MOST OF THE EDITORIALS McClendon wrote throughout the three stages of the *Observers.* Some are not available. But the fifty plus editorials published here represent some 80 percent of the total that were published. *The People's Observer* was the most influential black newspaper in the Portland area during World War II. As a militant voice of the black community, it consistently addressed issues of segregation, discriminatory labor practices, housing, police-community relations, and black community politics and education. *The Portland Observer* is mentioned in all the major bibliographies of black periodicals. ***Straight Ahead*** is the first book to publish from its archive.

McClendon writes with the sense of telling fact of the seasoned journalist. His editorials achieve distinction through his ability to locate the general social, political and cultural principles inherent within a local or national black issue and deliver a telling critique. The editorials are short, well- reasoned critical essays and their value and insight continue beyond the immediate occasion. McClendon's ability to perceive the general within the particular, imbues these editorials with a remarkable, sometimes even prophetic, freshness, and the contemporary reader is startled to find an analysis of present-day problems as they appeared some forty or fifty years ago.

In "The American Serf," McClendon succinctly outlines the grim conditions of black sharecroppers in 1939, who had become dispossessed refugees from their tenant farms due to New Deal policy: ". . . more than one thousand sharecroppers are now huddled around improvised shelters and non-warming campfires along highways 60 and 61 in Missouri," because "Any landowner who can show that he has no farmers living on the premises as sharecroppers, but instead is employing day labor at seventy-five cents a day, will receive government pay." McClendon raises the questions, ". . .can any nation that mistreats and exploits its own citizens effectively shelter and safely provide for the outcasts of another? And if such were possible, does it not seem that a rectification of atrocious conditions at home would be more in order before offering this nation as a haven for others who are distressed and oppressed.?"

The opening sentence of the editorial, "Socialized Medicine," "Negroes in America suffer more tuberculosis and syphilis than do the white groups; however, less is done for Negroes than for any other group," foreshadows today's lethal combination of AIDS and tuberculosis that occurs increasingly among blacks and other minorities. McClendon's call for a comprehensive public health system of clinics and hospitals dedicated to diagnosis, treatment and prevention, has still not been answered fifty-five years later.

These editorials express a continuing devotion to the cause of civil rights. The first editorial published here calls for a civil rights bill, and subsequent editorials in *The Portland Observer* urge the black community to join and support the National Association for the Advancement of Colored People. McClendon was aware of the limits of that organization, but he recognized its merit as the civil rights organization with the greatest potential for addressing black issues on a mass basis. Throughout these editorials one finds insightful, scathing, witty and at times very funny criticism directed toward opportunists within the black community who would sell out the collective black interest for individual gain. In "Remove the

Trojan Horse," McClendon observes, "The Negro who measures his own progress in terms of his ability to sell other Negroes down the river must be exposed and discarded." In "Political Reverses," McClendon comments on a persisting problem:

. . . Oregon's Negro populace is full of leaders, but there are not many followers. The would-be followers sit around envying the leaders who stand around denouncing the followers and no one gets any place. This is typical of the sudden flame and long dark side of which the Negro is so capable.

THE PEOPLE'S OBSERVER FOCUSED ON THE MAJOR CONTRADICTION bedeviling the United States during its participation in World War II. As the ostensible leader of the world's democratic forces, the U.S. was waging a war against fascism, yet it too endorsed white supremacy and practiced racial discrimination against its black population. Black workers in the Northern and Western shipyards and factories suffered racial humiliation, discrimination and segregation at the work site, in housing and in all social sectors. Claiming to defer to the wishes of migrant white southern workers and their northern cohorts, civic, business and social leaders of white America established Jim Crow structures for the rapidly expanding black populations newly drawn to the nation's industrial centers. This leadership thus chose to extend racist practices instead of using the occasion to eradicate them.

Blacks in America were the Achilles heel of the war effort: they were alienated from social and political processes of white America, yet essential for the industrial production needed for victory. Many blacks saw no reason to suppress their own anti- racist struggle to wage a freedom struggle on behalf of Europe and Asia; other blacks were willing to support such struggle provided that race relations improved in American society. Still others perceived that supporting an ideological struggle against racism in any form would inevitably advance the cause of black equality in the United States. But waging an anti-racist struggle within the United States during a time of war was a difficult and at times hazardous undertaking. The broad War Powers Act provided for suspension of Constitutional rights as necessary to suppress those organizations and individuals the Executive branch deemed as harmful to the war effort. The black press in particular was singled out for observation by the Post Office, the Justice Department, the FBI and intelligence agencies of the Armed Forces.

The People's Observer took the position that the battle against racism overseas required a battle against racism within the United States. In McClendon's view, the Four Freedoms enunciated by President Roosevelt in a speech to Congress on January 6, 1941 — freedom of speech and expression, freedom of worship, freedom from want and freedom from fear — as touchstones for global policy, also applied to blacks in the United States. In the editorial, "Background for Riots," McClendon observes, "No line of demarcation can be drawn to separate the philosophies of the white supremacists who foster poll-tax, lynching and Jim Crowism, from that of Hitler and his followers in Europe who are intent on enslaving the free people of the world and establishing Aryan superiority over the face of the globe." The editorial concludes that black gains during World War II, "have been realized because the Negro people are now awakening to the clarion call of Frederick Douglass, Negro leader of immense mental stature, who taught his people eighty-three years ago that men 'who would be free, themselves must strike the first blow.' "

McClendon also warned that, "the vast extension of Jim Crow policies throughout the armed services; flagrant discrimination by lily-white trade unions and industrial management," slurs in the white press and the vacillation of "so-called white progressives," could well "serve as conditioning instruments to maintain a system of outrageous subjugation for this [black]portion of America's population." Arguing against the idea that civil rights, "must wait until the war is finished," McClendon observes in "Another Complication":

This is a most absurd paradox when applied to the Negro's struggle. The Negro people in their efforts to acquire freedom and equality in America serve as the vanguard of all liberty-inspired movements. The success or failure of their attempts will determine whether or not there will ever be any practical application of democracy.

Of particular concern to *The People's Observer* was the struggle being waged at Local No. 72 of the Boilermakers' Union between white union officials and black shipyard workers residing and working in the Vancouver-Portland area. The union's leadership rejected blacks' petition for membership in the Local and, with the collaboration of the Portland Metal Trades Council and the government, proposed black "Auxiliary Unions" which would be under the direction of white leadership. Segregated auxiliaries were a common practice. With the inevitable reduction in labor force at the end of the war, they were dissolved and black workers lost their union membership. Characteristically seeing the larger picture, McClendon writes auxiliaries "prevent the emergence and rise of a militant rank and file Negro labor leadership which is now far more necessary for the advancement of the Negro people than the leadership which has been developed within the professional and middle class groups; they tend to subjugate completely Negro women and deny them adequate participation in the social, economic and political programs which are vital to the welfare of the whole group. . . ."

McClendon saw clearly in the "Crystallized Collaborations" editorials that, "The advent of the Negro upon the American industrial scene is in itself a significant economic and social development" and argued that their degradation by industrialists and union leadership, "is a challenge to the integrity of the progressive groups of both white and Negro workers in every quarter of our industrial and economic existence, because these workers have a materialistic understanding of the unconditional necessity for unity and equality in the American trade union movement." Without unity, McClendon argued, "victory over both foreign and American Hitlerism is an utter impossibility."

By the time World War II had ended, the black population in Portland had increased by ten times over that of 1938. McClendon observed that, "In Portland the Negro people are passively witnessing the development of a first-rate ghetto with all the potentials for squalor, poverty, juvenile delinquency and crime," brought about by restrictive covenants and other discrimination strategies. Quality housing, economic planning, capital punishment, police brutality, the need for black policemen became powerful issues for the postwar black community in Portland, and *The People's Observer* addressed these concerns.

In addition to McClendon's own efforts, *The Portland Observer, The People's Observer* and *The Observer* published a number of quality articles and graphics by other authors. We have included some of the editorial cartoons by Frederick Perry and cover designs by Ruby Wright.

IV.
THE SEARCH FOR QUALITY EDUCATION: THE STRUGGLE IN PORTLAND

THE ESSAYS IN THE THIRD SECTION OF ***STRAIGHT AHEAD,*** The Search for Quality Education: The Struggle in Portland, chronicle the complex struggle of blacks in Portland to achieve quality education for their children. The entitlement programs of the 1960s offered new hope to the black community, that the ghetto-bound gridlock of racial discrimination and poor education could be broken. But many career educators, administrators and bureaucrats in the City of Portland's Public School District resisted change in the 1960s, just as they had refused in the 1940s to adjust to the changes in the city's racial composition.

"Sanity, Silence and Social Justice," an address delivered to the Japanese-American Citizens League, asserted that, "The vast economic and social problems of today do not cause segregation, but segregation is in itself the cause of these colossal difficulties." McClendon here pursues a theme he had touched upon in *The People's Observer:* that the random and racially-motivated housing of black defense workers during World War II had created a ghetto in the region called Albina, formerly a deteriorating white neighborhood. Citing that less than two per cent of new homes insured by the Federal Housing Authority have been for non-whites, McClendon noted that:

"During the ten year span (1950 to 1960) there was a 400% plus influx of Negroes to take up residence in the Albina district. It is estimated that by 1960 more than 78% of all of Portland's Negro population had been herded into this area. Fifty two percent of all Negroes in the state were living in this district whose dimensions were one square mile. This population concentration was six times greater than that of the city of Portland and the density is believed to have exceeded that of any other area of the state."

McClendon wrote "The NAACP and The Model School Program: Community Problems Produced from Racial Segregation in Portland Public Schools" in 1968. He had become Chairman of the Education Committee of the Portland Branch of the NAACP in 1964. He also delivered this commentary as an address to a Jefferson High School Faculty and Staff Meeting. This critique of the Model School Program pointed out its essential contradiction — that within the rubric of integration, ninety percent of the black children in attendance were being segregated by tracking and streaming policies, "holding in careful, isolated containment ninety per cent of its black pupils so that they can stagnate and fester in the corruption of segregation and its accompanying intellectual shortfalls."

Integration, McClendon argues, is selective segregation, which "is no longer confined to arranging human body placements according to white racist color schemes," but "it is a deeply imbedded, diabolic conviction prevailing among most of the white population, including all classes, that the natural place for blacks in America . . . is at a visibly lower status than that enjoyed by whites." For McClendon, the real criterion for black fulfillment is self-determination: "Blacks must have the right of self- determination here in the American nation. It must be the same as that exercised by the most privileged and fortunate sectors or settlements of the dominant population. If black people cannot have these choices and enjoy these rights then America has no merit. . . ."

The concluding essay of this section, "The Socialization of Black Youth," written in the early 1990s, is a broad survey of the problems of instructing black youth and possible solutions to them. McClendon argues that assaults by white racism since the 1960s have been so forceful and so effective that many black family and community structures have been critically weakened and many find it extremely difficult to motivate and guide black youth to perform properly in the academic setting. One of the premises of education is that the student believes in the efficacy of the process and has received the necessary preparation within the family to respect social norms and adapt to them. The alienation of black youth and their parents from the U.S. social fabric is so profound, McClendon argues, that many black students entering school are no longer adequately indoctrinated with these value systems. McClendon proposes more effective social organization that would improve socialization, behavior instruction, nutrition and health care, beginning at pre-school through college with the support of all sectors of the neighborhoods and communities.

The editorials from *The Portland Observer* and the essays on the struggle for black education in Portland may be read as an on-going chronicle of black life in Portland. In them, McClendon reveals a powerful and principled black intelligence skilled in the disciplines of sociology and political economy. For the reflective reader, the problematic of black life that McClendon records in his chronicle of Portland, provides an archetype for the sociology and political economy of black life as it developed in the urban centers of the United States over the past fifty years.

V.
THE FOUNDATIONS OF BLACK CULTURE

THE MAJOR ESSAYS IN THE FINAL SECTION, The Foundations of Black Culture, focus upon the strengths, complexities and continuing development of black culture in America. In McClendon's definition black culture is born in resistance, as noted in this passage from "The Foundations of Black Culture":

Culture, then, is the major force in the resistance of black people to domination by others. Such culture is the collective base product of the black historical experience and political perspectives committed to achieving liberation. From culture, positive intragroup ideas motivate blacks to struggle and exert themselves for a better life. This is why the dance, the music, the poetry and the philosophy emanating from blacks in the United States and throughout the Western Hemisphere survived and flourished.

For McClendon, "black culture and black struggle are linked," and "those who suffer the absence of black cultural consciousness are most often observed to feel inferior to whites." In addition, McClendon argues, "Black culture, among other things, managed to expose the problems created by white America for the peoples of the world. And black resistance is not unrelated to the struggle for liberation and independence world-wide." In McClendon's analysis, it is the combination of struggle and critique that gives black culture its special leverage and creates a black humanism:

Suffering, despair, defeat and tragedy are met by blacks with an indomitable determination to survive. Black culture affirms that black humanity has as its cause a commitment of resistance to all human oppression. Thus black culture informs the world that black people are models of humanity and that humanistic concerns are foremost among our priorities.

MCCLENDON'S ESSAY, "The Black Perspective of Frederick Douglass," is among the finest essays yet written on Douglass. McClendon's essay is first and foremost an analysis of Douglass's political mind and imagination. In this respect it provides a refreshing contrast to current theory, which tends to discuss Douglass primarily in literary and psychological terms. McClendon finds that the cornerstone of Douglass's thought is his insistence on the necessity for blacks to practice self- determination. In Douglass's political methodology, this meant the employment of a black perspective for the analysis, solution and action upon particular problems.

Unlike other scholars who have written of Douglass in dichotomous terms, McClendon perceives the interrelationship between Douglass's strategic principle of black self-determination on the one hand and his ability to maintain a tactical ambiguity toward, and even re-define, all matters of white American custom and polity that affected blacks in America. Citing Douglass, "He who does not think himself worth saving from poverty and ignorance, by his own efforts, will hardly be thought worth the efforts of anybody else," McClendon asserts that "Douglass thus placed clearly before the blacks and the whites of this nation the perspective from which the black struggle for freedom would be launched."

In establishing this position, Douglass rebutted white abolitionist efforts early in his career to confine his addresses to plantation experiences. In McClendon's words:

Douglass in response asserted that the North could not be committed to abolitionist purposes unless the fullest expressions of black manhood were in evidence and this included the intellectual and the learned. . . . He raised the question that has convulsed deceitful white liberals ever since, 'Do you think of black men as causes and as sentient, intelligent beings, or as the raw material of crusading righteousness?'

Douglass's combination of an unwavering commitment to black self-determination and his insistence that blacks employ all their experience and wisdom to fully engage in the struggle for their own liberation empowered Douglass to develop a political abolitionism far in advance of the Garrisonians' line of non-violence, passive resistance and moral suasion.

The result was a revolution in black consciousness in America. In discussing the vast, far-ranging critique of America that Douglass was conducting in his lectures and periodicals, McClendon observes:

He expressed in philosophical terms the morality underlying all of man's struggles to achieve liberty. Black people were now being taught by a black man that they had to be activists for their own liberation and the messages of Douglass were being carried to all black people, including those who existed under the most horrendous circumstances.

But such liberty was not defined in simple binary term of inclusion versus exclusion, as McClendon points out:

He advocated and fought unequivocally for complete inclusion of blacks in the public life but when the white racist political manipulations and legal evasions prohibited this, he would immediately demand special institutions.

These were in many respects the initial steps towards local control.

Aware that many of the problems that trouble contemporary black men and women have their origins in slavery. McClendon's assessment of Douglass's masculinity is particularly germane today:

Douglass was a man in the most real and concise meaning of the word. . . . Frederick Douglass knew and taught that manhood is founded on self-respect and self-esteem.

As in his other works, McClendon's essay on Douglass emphasizes the moral issues involved in racism. Commenting on Douglass's opinion of Calhoun's 1850 speech to the Congress, McClendon observes,

. . . the speech revealed that the power attributed for so long to Calhoun had ended, as the language of his discourse was actually shallow and should be viewed as lacking in moral substance. (This is true of most of the rhetoric of the oppressors whether it is uttered by the whites or blacks.) Such rhetoric is never a force for or a source of morality, strength and liberation; it is always modified, ambivalent, or assaultive and spoken by those who are servile and obedient to the forces of repression.

Douglass's legacies of black self-determination, of cultural institutions born of struggle, of manhood based upon self-respect and regard for women, of the black perspective as the instrument of critique, are reflected in two other notable essays by McClendon, "Black Studies: Education for Liberation" and "Black Music: Sound and Feeling for Black Liberation."

His commentary on black studies, written during his tenure as Director of Black Studies at Reed College, remains a wise and prescriptive commentary on the problems and prospects of black studies today. His cautions, that blacks should not passively rely upon white definitions of black life, however informed and engaging those authors and scholars might be, are particularly cogent today. In commenting upon the work of a Daniel Patrick Moynihan, with its theses of black pathology and "benign neglect" which opened the door for the demolition of entitlement programs created during the 1960s, he observes, "A great deal of the social searching that is done about black people by whites, even if it is glaringly faulty, is permitted to be used to serve social science as a beginning to leverage even more deficient social information and social policy. Moynihan may be the criterion of what white sociologists are, but to most black scholars and students he is just another of the intellectual mercenaries."

For, the main goal of any black intellectual project undertaken today must be the improvement of the black condition, not the enhancement or mollification of an oppressive status quo. One need only look at the serious intellectual and moral crises of the so-called "black conservative" movement today to reaffirm this goal. McClendon's cogent essay on the Clarence Thomas nomination, "Dismal to Abysmal," points out the perils of the alienated and opportunistic black careerist.

For McClendon, the black perspective of an independent, self-determining black consciousness is the major tool and end product of a successful black studies curriculum. That curriculum devotes its "research and teaching proficiency toward developing Black Studies to be a major force to enable black people to take control over their own lives. White-directed and dominated education should not be lamented as having failed black people, because it never promised to do anything for them in the first place." Thus, for McClendon, "Black Studies brings into sharp focus the fact that blacks are not behavior problems, but they are unknown and unpredictable elements of human responses and reactions to the continued abuses offered up so abundantly by the racist institutions of white America."

Part of the mission of black studies professors has been to provide "certain specific insights for students in how to deal with many labels and definitions coming from white quarters which affected black life and scholarship negatively." McClendon perceptively argues that one such example was "the so-called black revolution myth (highly propagandized by the white press) which was perceived very early on as a racist attempt to deceive blacks into believing that their ego trips in manure-dipped rhetoric, plus the wearing of funky clothes, dark glasses and disarranged hair were revolutionary weapons that would intimidate less aggressive blacks and terrorize whites."

The black studies curriculum demands intellectual and moral rigor from its students, McClendon asserts: "The black community does not profit if Black Studies returns to the community students who have not oriented themselves to understanding the meaning of academic excellence with a commitment to achieve it." Instead, McClendon argues:

Black Studies will insist that students examine and comprehend a multitude of theories and teachings. The relevance of each body of knowledge to black liberation can be determined only through obtaining an understanding of the substantive content. . . There is no guarantee that a unity of thought will be found among the various scholars. This does not mean that black scholars will not continue to be able to provide scholarly direction and intellectual leadership for their students.

BLACK STUDIES IS A MAJOR NEW DEVELOPMENT in the tradition of the liberal education. The black humanism it envisions is essential for the achievement of economic, political and cultural democracy in the United States.

Black music, too, functions in "the spirit of resistance and struggle," and "reveals in its rhythms and harmonies that it is not a music of grief and despair." Citing Lena McLin's distinction, "Black people sing spirituals when they tell their troubles to God; they sing Gospel when they tell their troubles to each other," McClendon adds that in the Blues, "blacks talk to themselves (individually or collectively) and then give notice to all others of what they are concerned about." Black music is, inevitably, a vehicle for black liberation, and it anticipates at times social and political expression for black empowerment. It has become a global music, a music essential and necessary to the world's populations. Its power, elegance and transcendence demonstrate the full potential and achievement of blacks in America and are an eloquent refutation of racist theory.

VI.
CONCLUSION

WILLIAM H. MCCLENDON'S ESSAYS IN THIS VOLUME embody all the-virtues of the black experience and the black culture born out of the struggle for liberation and self determination. McClendon writes from a stance of engaged objectivity and his prose is supple in its ability to register nuance, in its persuasion, in its reasoned and thoughtful assurance. While maintaining fidelity to his views, he continues to grow, change and enlarge the spheres of his thought. His first essay, "Which College," contains within it a value system, a methodology, a style, a black perspective, that he continues to develop in his later works. His energy, his wit, his intellectual power, are relentless.

Like the nineteenth century black activist intellectuals whose traditions he inherited and advances, McClendon perceives the necessity for black leadership to be rooted in the black community and culture. The entire body of his work emphasizes the reciprocating relationship between social activism and intellectual activity. In McClendon's thought, the struggle for self- determination becomes the social means for the resolution of alienation and struggle becomes a moral imperative for blacks in America. There is only one direction: straight ahead.

Robert Chrisman
Ann Arbor, Michigan
August, 1995

A Note on the Text

The editorials from *The Portland Obsever, The People's Observer* and *The Observer* were taken from microfilmed copies of these periodicals on file at Northwestern University. Other collections are available at Multnomah County Library, Portland, Oregon and the Oregon History Center, Portland. In some instances, newspapers were missing or portions of editorials were damaged, but the author has restored the sense of the original. Terminology for blacks in America has varied over the years and we have retained whatever was current usage at the time. Notes on terms, organizations, events and persons mentioned in the text are usually explained briefly in brackets and signed, Editor's Note. William H. McClendon's notes are signed, W.H.M.

With several minor exceptions, Mr. McClendon's essays are arranged in chronological order and prefaced with notes on their dates of composition and place of publication.

I

Prefatory Essay

Which College – White or Negro?

This is the prize-winning essay in the Joel E. Spingarn Award contest conducted for college students by the National Association for the Advancement of Colored People last spring [1934]. The prize-winning essay in the high school group will be published in an early issue of THE CRISIS. Mr. McClendon is a student of Morehouse, Atlanta, Georgia. *[THE CRISIS, August 1934. Editor's Note.]*

In this changing period of social conditions, in which the fate of the Negro fluctuates with every rising or ebbing tide of economic prosperity, this question is one of vast and profound significance: Is the white college educating the Negro to the end that he will look at life more intelligently and cope with its bewildering problems more confidently than the Negro college; or is the Negro college more far-reaching in the complicated task of fitting the Negro youth for the proper social adjustment to an environment that is both discouraging and challenging to his most ambitious efforts? Without hesitation and apology, I answer that I believe the Negro college will be the saving grace of the Negro race until the fundamental attitude of the white man toward the Negro makes a radical change. The white college, until that time, can never prepare the young Negro for life.

At the present time, the Negro's economic survival depends, with the exception of a very few rare cases, upon the patronage of his own people; at the present time, the Negro's social happiness certainly is limited to the circle of his own people. Perhaps in art, the Negro is able to escape beyond the boundaries of America's color-prejudiced world. Even this assertion I make with my tongue in cheek, for daily I can read of the insults cast at Roland Hayes, Countee Cullen, and others. If, then, the Negro's means of livelihood depends upon his race; and if the Negro's associates and companions are to be Negroes, is it not a necessity that he be trained with these people and taught how to serve them, not specifically, of course, but with the idea in mind of working with them and for them? Let us look into the life of a Negro student in a "white" college. Let us see for what life he is being prepared, if for any. Then, let us consider the college life of an average Negro student in a "race" institution of higher learning.

The Lone Athlete

John Green is a very brilliant student, a junior in the undergraduate school of let us say, Ohio State university. John is a tall, handsome youth, with the features and hair of a caucasian, but with the dark brown skin that marks him indelibly as a Negro. He has maintained an average of B for the three years of his college career. In his sophomore year he "made" the varsity football team and would have been made captain had he not been a Negro. Was this preparing John for any kind of life to make him embittered, knowing that he was not allowed a small honor because he was a Negro? When John travels with the football team, he is always a problem. Special arrangements must be made for him on the trip, and frequently the problem of finding a hotel or a roommate who will accept the lone Negro football player confronts the coach, and if John is a sensitive youth he will soon feel that he is a constant source of trouble to the team and to the school; if he is of the more deplorable, belligerent type, such treatment may make him look for prejudices where there are none and make unnecessary bids on the coach's and school's liberality for his special comfort and convenience. Is this training John Green to use tact and diplomacy when he is out in the world, or is this making the Negro an egotistic ass, forever thinking of his own importance; or does it crush him with an inferiority complex that is nearly as bad and far more detrimental to his material and social success?

In this college, let us say, there are about one thousand white students and about fifty Negroes. With whom is John going to associate? If he is as brilliant, as I have presupposed, then, you may say that his mere brilliance will find him excellent company among white and black. But this hypothesis too often has been disproved. When a Negro is brilliant in the classroom, the white student always finds time to talk with him, but when they meet on the street there is a polite greeting, an embarrassed pause, and a pathetically polite, but hasty farewell. And if he is an average student, chances of John's shining in the social spotlight will indeed be slim.

Well, what is the mythical John to do for social contact of which so much is said when one speaks of college life? Is he to bury himself in a book in his dormitory room (if he is allowed to live in the dormitory), or associate entirely with members of his own race? John attempts to analyze the situation and says to himself that he will not willingly segregate himself when he does not have to. So, when he enters the library, he seats himself as far from his race as possible, not from any feeling of superiority, but because he does not believe that they should huddle together just because they are Negroes. When John enters a new course, he makes it a rule never to sit by another Negro. Why should he, unless it is a friend? And in the cafeteria, it becomes a habit for him to take a table in an inconspicuous corner where no Negro will be likely to sit. I believe that John, as many students in white colleges, is trying to look at the situation intelligently. But the white students will not let him. They are polite, too polite, but they never thaw. And the Negro students say that John wants to be white and shun him when he attempts to make himself agreeable.

No Dramatic Club

What are those extra-curricular activities of a college that give a student a wider outlook on life, some channel for the development of his latent talent, or some distinction in recognition of merit or ability? Well, there is the dramatic club. John enjoys dramatics. Is he eligible for membership? Ostensibly yes. But what part could John play in a sea of white faces? The plays would all have to be chosen with him in mind. Must he always be a Negro servant or an Arab or an Indian? And would it not disturb the delicate feelings of the audience if romance were injected into John's part? No, the dramatic club is out. How does he give in enough to his principles to join a Negro fraternity which has just about as much influence and activity on a white campus as a dead man in the catacombs of Rome. Maybe John is talented in writing. The Literary Guild? He makes his application and is accepted. "It will be wonderful for the club to hear some Negro dialect stories." John retreats into his shell in discouragement. "Why must I write dialect stories? I have never been south of Cincinnati."

With the exception of the college choir and certain athletics the Negro's chance for demonstrating or developing personal initiative or talent is very poor. Go to any campus where the Negro is in the minority and observe how in his own group he is disintegrated by a thousand and one petty cliques and jealousies. If a white college succeeds in doing anything at all, it is highly successful in tearing down the attitude of friendliness among the Negro students. All of them vie for recognition by their white brothers and sisters; and when one in the crowd gets it, like a pack of wolves, the others pounce upon him for trying to "betray the race."

Job as Red Cap?

After John has been graduated from college, where is he to teach and what race of people? Nine times out of ten he finds himself instructing black boys and girls in the delta of Louisiana or the foothills of some sunbaked Georgia town. And how does this Negro who has been taught with white students conduct himself? Does he come to the South with the feeling that it is not so bad after all; or does he still cling to the view that his education is something so greatly superior to his fellow teachers, graduates of Negro schools, that he is forever casting aspersions on these, his co-workers? Does he accept conditions as he finds them or is he constantly referring to the Negro's advantages in Columbus, Ohio? Does he make a pretense of liking his environment or does he delight in saying that "he just isn't accustomed to dealing with so many Negroes?" Nine times out of ten, these things he does. He cannot work with his people, because all his college years have been spent in trying to get away from them gracefully or in trying to approach them awkwardly and artificially. He is not prepared for life among his people or among any people, because he is unsympathetic with their aims and shortcomings, never having experienced the same group ambitions or despair. He cannot lead the people, because he has not the initiative, and he cannot follow a leader because he feels he is too superior. There is only one thing he can do successfully, and that is to deride and criticize his associates who have been "victims" of a segregated school system. He is a tragic, haunted, incapable misfit, and usually finds his way back across the Mason-Dixon line in search of a position commensurate with his opinion of his abilities, and finally consoles himself with a red cap and a blue uniform in the station of some metropolitan railroad terminus.

Normal College Life

Let us look at the other side of the picture. Life in the Negro college is wholesome and normal, not artificial and bloated with a false sense of values for the Negro student. It is a place where race relations are not tabooed; it is a place where assertion, responsibility, and initiative are easily responded to and easily developed. One is here no longer ashamed of his race, his heritage, or the future. In the Negro college there is every opportunity for the stimulation of thought without fear or without prejudice. The petty jealousies and minor envies will be cases for the intelligent Negro youth to study in order to judge human character after he will have left the college halls; for there is no better place to study and evaluate Negro community life than in a Negro college. There is snobbery, yes; there is unwholesome rivalry, I'll admit; there are ostracism and unfairness, I'll agree; but that there is a wall of indifference, neglect, and subtle ignoring which crushes the spirit of a student and which burns into his soul I will deny until the high heavens fall in ashes about me.

If any college prepares the Negro youth at all for service and dignified work, it is the Negro college. It matters not how one argues, the fact remains that we are Negroes first, and then Americans. Would that we could truthfully say that we are Americans first and Negroes next! The fact flames furiously in our faces, making us burn with a bitterness that has made Countee Cullen, the eminent poet, say in "Caroling Dusk" that he wished that a part of his education had been received in a Negro institution. Cullen is an artist; he may be a world artist; but withal, he cannot escape the fact that he is first a Negro artist.

I think that the time has come when the Negro should be shown that his plight lies with his people, until he comes into closer harmony with the other race. Furthermore, he should realize that the type of training that he needs to sharpen his innate faculties, to increase his self-respect, and to make him more companionable with his own people is not to be found in the so-called "white" schools of the country, but in the colleges designed for the training of Negro youth.

II

Editorials

The Portland Observer

THE PORTLAND OBSERVER, DEC. 16, 1938

Welcome to The Portland Observer

by Father L.O.Stone

[Father Stone was an Afro-American Episcopal priest to St. Philip's congregation, Portland. Editor's Note.]

Every community needs a newspaper to stir up interest in local problems. For it is the only medium through which knowledge can be given on subjects of interest to the community at large. A community without a newspaper is stagnant, which ultimately leads to social confusion.

A newspaper should not, in my personal opinion, be biased in its articles. But it should be neutral in all public issues and give to the best of its ability both sides of any subjects in question. A paper that is biased can cause hatred of every description. One that is neutral can build up cooperation in the community, causing its readers to work for the common good of all. There are, no doubt, many local problems that should be discussed in the manner mentioned.

The Editor has my best wishes for success in this most worthwhile undertaking. However, success cannot be achieved unless we, as interested citizens of the community, give him the kind of support that is worthy of his efforts.

THE PORTLAND OBSERVER, DEC. 16, 1938

Social Acceptance

AFTER A HARD AND VALIANT FIGHT against a stone wall of denial, the Oregon Negro has found it impossible to make the Oregon white man do anything he does not wish to do. For instance, a difficult and discouraging fight has been waged prior to this time for the purpose of having a Civil Rights bill enacted in the state of Oregon. Literally, there has been a war to make the white man associate with and welcome the Negro as an equal, although he hates and deplores such equality most assiduously.

It seems that the white man considers the Negro his inferior, morally, culturally, intellectually and economically, and refuses to be hoodwinked by sentimentality, or bulldozed by threats into this significant social acceptance. In short, this program to secure for the Negro social rights in Oregon unqualified and unreserved has met with failure. Why?

It is not because the Negro is considered a menace to America; it is not because the Negro has proven himself unworthy of confidence, but rather because he is considered an enemy to the concepts of democracy. The docility of the Negro population as a whole is detrimental to mass progress. White people respect ambition and aggressiveness, if for no reason other than the fact that the United States of America is a result of the white man's aggressiveness. The white citizen realizes and understands the privileges that are his in so far as these privileges are set forth in the constitution of the United States. It is imperative that all citizens, regardless of color, realize what these privileges are before any true evaluation be given relative to the merits of our so-called democracy. This is especially true where the Negro is concerned. Because until the Negro insists on equality before the law as provided in the Constitution of the United States; until he becomes conscious of a human brotherhood, he will not be in sight of his goal.

PORTLAND OBSERVER, DEC. 23, 1938 EDITORIAL

A Necessity

PLANS ARE NOW BEING LAID by the local branch of the NAACP to fight oppression, discrimination, and a denial of privileges as they affect minority groups in Oregon. Efforts are being concentrated toward having a Civil Rights Bill enacted. The program underway is very timely and commendable and will without a doubt prove to be very beneficial. However, it is necessary for all Negroes to realize and understand the true nature of the work the NAACP is attempting to do. If success is to be realized, the entire Negro population must give its utmost support to this program.

Some people harbor the idea that Civil Rights Bills are unnecessary, because there are certain privileges guaranteed citizens in the Constitution of the United States. This same group further believes that all citizens should be taught an appreciation of citizenship rights, and then encouraged to employ forceful aggressiveness for the purpose of elevating their social status.

The NAACP shares this opinion also, but with a few reservations.

In the event a Negro is publicly discriminated against by a Caucasian, he stands little or no chance of getting consideration in any court. This is due to many reasons. Some of them are pigmentation, ignorance, a lack of friends, and his economic position. The last seems to be the most important at this time.

At present, as in the past, the Negro is economically dependent upon the white man for his every existence — especially in Oregon. For the most part, Negroes find it very difficult to eke out an existence with their limited incomes and earning power. If the occasion were to present itself whereby a Negro could make a court test of the provisions made for him in the Constitution of the United States, his utter lack of finance would render his case a miserable failure. This is applicable to the entire Negro population of Oregon.

It is small wonder, then, that the Negro has to accept injustices mutely, receive cruelties without complaint, and suffer wrongs without redress. No wonder he cannot break through the walls of prejudice. His music, his literature, his education are not enough.

It is now an economic battle. If the Negroes of Oregon do not awaken soon to their helpless plight, and face the fact courageously and not sentimentally, the little ground the NAACP has gained for them will surely be lost.

THE PORTLAND OBSERVER, JAN. 6, 1939

Political Reverses

On December 18, 1938, the Portland Branch of the NAACP met in order to discuss methods and mediums whereby it might effectively make known its demands for a Civil Rights bill before the next session of the state legislature convenes. It was brought out at this meeting that on December 38, the Multnomah delegation would hold a meeting in the city hall for the purpose of lending its attention to matters of municipal and county interests only.

Because of this restriction, it was believed there would be little chance of bringing this issue of a Civil Rights bill before the delegation, as it is state-wide in its scope.

A discussion then ensued, which was dominated by a well-known, local minister, who apparently carried a mouthful of panaceas, but not one iota of action. After considerable tongue-lashing, verbal berating and ego-flaunting on the part of this pretentious person, another member of the executive board attempted to convince the persons who attended the NAACP meeting that it was absolutely necessary for them to be present at the meeting of the Multnomah delegation. The reason for this was based on the fact that if an opportunity presented itself for any issues of statewide importance to be considered, the NAACP would have a representative number on hand.

The erstwhile leader (the minister) then offered numerous proposals under the guise of beneficial criticisms, but which were actually well designed ruses to deter the members of the NAACP from welcoming and taking advantage of the opportunity to attend this meeting. In spite of this, the President of the NAACP and some white friends of the organization who did attend found it possible to put their pleas before the Multnomah delegation. However, it is doubtful if any advantages were gained. Why?

First, there were only five Negroes present, but more than two dozen had promised to attend. It should be readily realized that the white people of Oregon are not going to bother themselves to become interested in an issue that concerns Negroes, if the Negroes themselves do not put forth considerable effort and show more than an equal amount of interest.

Secondly, Oregon's Negro populace is full of leaders, but there are not many followers. The would-be followers sit around envying the leaders, who stand around denouncing the followers, and no one gets any place. This is typical of the sudden flame and long dark side of which the Negro is so capable.

Aside from this, it is difficult for the progressive and serious minded supporters of the NAACP to get to the heart of Oregon's Negro citizenry. It is amazing to know just how few Negroes know or have heard anything about the workings and accomplishments of this body. However, the ministers of the various churches could render valuable assistance toward relieving this situation.

Almost every church has within it many clubs and guilds, or similar organizations. Instead of these placid local bodies meeting now and then to pass resolutions and sip tea, there could be supporters in every church in every community to educate the masses as to the benefits to be derived from the program the NAACP now has underway.

There are at least four Negro churches in the city of Portland. However, the ministers of these churches cannot, or do not, inspire their members to lend moral and financial assistance to the NAACP to serve as defenders and as leaders of their people.

One may quickly grasp the idea that the Negro is not doing a fraction of what he could do to better his condition in Oregon— the Negro leaders are doing even less. Because many people wonder why the NAACP cannot rise above amateur politics, attention has been given this all-too-long oversight.

THE PORTLAND OBSERVER, JAN. 13, 1939

Political Wisdom

ON JANUARY 9, 1939, Charles Sprague was inducted into the Governorship of Oregon. This occasion should be of great significance to Negro citizens of this state, because an examination of Mr. Sprague's political activities in the past shows him to be vitriolic in demanding equal rights under the law for every citizen, regardless of color or creed.

For example, when Mr. Sprague was editor of *The Statesman,* numerous editorials were written by him for the purpose of fighting segregation and discrimination. One editorial in particular demands attention. It appeared in *The Statesman* on February 10, 1937, under the subject "Against Discrimination." This editorial was written in sympathy with the plea of Senator Angell, who had prior to that time introduced the Civil Rights Bill SB32.

Here are some of the things to which Mr. Sprague gave his attention: "Although Negroes, for example, are given equal rights under the law, they are not given equal consideration in life. They are excluded from many places of public resort, from theaters, from hotels, from restaurants. Negroes of intelligence and good character are often barred from better class hotels, though Negroes are there as servitors.

"Racial and religious prejudices die hard. One thing to the everlasting credit of Russia has been its removal of discrimination against persons of different races, though from reports, there is a revival of race consciousness even there. It was this fact of tolerance which caused Paul Robeson, famous Negro singer, to leave his young son in Russia to be educated, where he would escape the slurs and ignominy heaped on the Negro child in this country. Even though civil rights are guaranteed equally to all races and creeds in this country, it is a notorious fact that there is widespread discrimination, even in the fields where the law is supposed to function for freedom, in schools, in juries, and in the courts."

It is easy to perceive that your new governor has concentrated his efforts toward winning non-discriminatory treatment for minority groups in Oregon. This alone should do much to quell the feeling of antagonism toward the governor on the part of some Negroes.

It is quite satisfactory to know that there is at the helm of our state government an intelligent, fair-minded person who believes in the essential worth and inherent rights of the human being, and in the fundamentals of democracy. Instead of enmity, contempt, and unjust neglect on the part of your chief executive, it seems that friendship, respect, and justice will be ever-evident. It would be wise for the Negro population of Oregon to welcome the administration of Governor Sprague with hearty enthusiasm.

THE PORTLAND OBSERVER, JAN. 20, 1939

Equality and Justice

FOR THIRTY YEARS the National Association for the Advancement of Colored People has played a distinct and distinguished role in the social life of the American people. Centuries from now, the noble names of Arthur Spingarn, Moorfield Storey, Oswald Garrison Villard, Walter White, Mary White Ovington, and W.E.B. Du Bois will send a ringing challenge down through the ages for other lovers of human justice to fight valiantly for equality and freedom.

In reviewing the various battles waged by the NAACP, the following cases loom large in American minds as typical of its programs and principles: various investigations of lynchings and maltreatment of the Negro before the law; cases of disfranchisement in democratic primaries; testing the legality of segregation laws and residential zoning statutes; prosecuting breakers of equal rights laws in states where these laws exist; fighting resolutely to stir up public opinion to enact a federal anti-lynching bill; waging frequently successful battles against the appointment of prejudiced public officers. In fact, it has been the Negroes' only shield of defense against the tumultuous floods of the white man's streams of jealousy and hatred.

Since the stock debacle of 1929, this has been a world that has turned solely on the axis of economic laws. Previous to this time, the Negro, as an economic participant, was so insignificant that many of his advances were gained while his white brothers were in a state of economic hypnosis.

When prosperity disappeared, the white man awoke to find the Negro holding jobs, building houses and becoming educated. Then!—the tide turned. It was a matter of the law of survival and self-preservation, and the erstwhile plutocrat, impoverished and confused, began to see red, and unfortunately that red has too often been the blood of the struggling Negro.

Contrary to many beliefs, the bars of racial prejudice have been raised much higher in the past five years.

Since the advent of the New Deal, new problems have risen, new jealousies have sprung forth, and the tide of racial prejudice and discrimination, instead of receding, has rushed forth over America, leaving in its wake a baffled and a bewildered people.

If the Negro is to be led out of this bewilderment, it will be because the NAACP intelligently diagnosed the situation and transformed its platform to show that whites need the Negroes' society and association on the basis of equality and justice.

THE PORTLAND OBSERVER, JAN. 27, 1939

The American Serf

PEOPLES THE WORLD OVER LOOK with disdain upon the purges and pogroms directed at the Jews in Germany—particularly the people of United States. The chief executive of this nation has taken it upon himself to call attention to and denounce the treatment the Jews are receiving, and to offer refuge by suggesting they make their homes in America.

The astonishing thing about this gesture is, can any nation that mistreats and exploits its own citizens effectively shelter and safely provide for the outcasts of another? And if such were possible, does it not seem that a rectification of atrocious conditions at home would be more in order, before offering this nation as a haven for others who are distressed and oppressed?

There are many conditions existing in America that need to be assuaged. Of national interest at this time is the plight of the tenant farmers, commonly known as sharecroppers. Each day, it is more forcibly realized by liberal-thinking Americans that the Civil War by no means destroyed the plantation system. It has continued to exist through the development of farm tenancy.

From Eastern Virginia to Western Texas are found the richest farm lands in America. It is in this district that the largest number of America's poorest and most dependent tenants and their families are found.

The vast majority of farm tenants and their families have a low plane of living. This is shown by the houses they live in, the clothes they wear, the food they eat, the dietary diseases they suffer from, the midwives and patent medicines they rely upon, the crude equipment they farm with, their low incomes, and the high rates of interest they are required to pay.

A typical tenant house has not more than three rooms and is built of a single thickness of rough boards with no inside finish. They are really just barren cabins put there to keep the wind out. Many of these cabins have no window sash, no window panes, no screens, and the roofs are full of leaks.

The sharecroppers diet is just as inadequate as his house. It consists mainly of fatback meat, cornbread, sorghum molasses and sweet potatoes. Fewer than one-half of the tenant families have a cow. Some of them have some sort of garden, but this usually amounts to little. More than one-fourth of them do not have any canned fruit and vegetables. It is safe to say that a sixth of the total number of tenant farmers have not eaten a single chicken or egg during the year. Pink salmon or a can of sardines among these people are rare delicacies.

A diet of this caliber would naturally result in low vitality, rickets, pellagra and unnecessary sickness. Indirectly, it is responsible for a large number of orphans and a high death rate. The death rate among the children is much higher in sharecropper families than in owner families.

The aforementioned facts are set forth vehemently in a 400 page volume entitled *Preface to Peasantry* by Dr. Arthur W. Raper, eminent sociologist and director of research for the Commission on Interracial Cooperation.

Fair-minded citizens will acknowledge that a life spent under such conditions is a most unbearable atrocity. For this reason, it is necessary to call their attention to the fact that more than one thousand sharecroppers are now huddled around improvised shelters and non-warming campfires along highways 60 and 61 in Missouri. These families, for the most part, have little or no protection from the chill winds and dampness. They are there because they have been evicted by the landowners in order that the landowners may receive government pay. Any landowner who can show that he has no farmers living on the premises as sharecroppers, but instead is employing day labor at 75 cents a day, will receive government pay. The American Agricultural Association has testified as to the truth of this.

The pitiful aspect of this situation is that practically all of these families are NEGROES. So far, no refuge has been offered these suffering humans. Relief has been promised.

THE PORTLAND OBSERVER, FEB. 3, 1939

Socialized Medicine

NEGROES IN AMERICA SUFFER MORE tuberculosis and syphilis than do the white groups; however, less is done for Negroes than for any other groups. Not nearly enough has been done to control and exterminate these diseases among the Negro population. The Negro death rate from these diseases in 1937 per hundred thousand population was one hundred and fifty. Many remedial measures have been proposed in an effort to alleviate this exorbitant death rate. Among them have been programs designed to increase the Negro's purchasing power and, as far as possible, to make him self-sufficient. All of these programs have to some extent increased the health protection of the Negro, but this has not been enough. There is another program underway which many persons feel will prove more beneficial than any offered before. This program has been labeled "Socialized Medicine."

Every citizen should know by this time that good medical care for all the population is essential to the nation's well-being. However, the general accessibility to the many medical techniques and skills for the masses of Negroes has not kept pace with their development, as indicated by the differential disease and mortality rates among the different economic levels of the Negro population. The common diseases that continue to impair and kill relatively large proportions of the Negro population, particularly in the poorer classes, have been brought under control only among those able pay for the services.

Under a system of "Socialized Medicine" the cost of sickness would be distributed among all of the people. The persons who are under medical care would be adequately remunerated periodically. In this way persons ill and unable to work would be supplied with the necessary finances to meet their obligations during the period of confinement.

The quality of medical care would not be sacrificed to economy and cost, as has been true of the past. In each community, there would be clinics and hospitals with necessary scientific equipment for accurate diagnosis and adequate treatment. In many instances, tuberculosis and other diseases cannot be recognized without the aid of elaborate technical equipment.

On the other hand, the medical service of the community would provide for a systematic and intensive use of preventive measures. All profit-making agencies would be liquidated and preventive and curative measures would be correlated in policy and administration. Provisions for medical care for dependents and the sick would be obligations of society.

Some persons will object to a program of this sort on the grounds that taxes will be increased, dependency will be encouraged, pauperism will become rampant, and too often the poorer who are permitted to receive medical care free will show a marked decline in initiative, as far as providing for themselves. However, after considering the relatively high death rates among the poor, the civic- and progressive-minded citizens should quickly turn deaf ears to all who voice arguments of this sort, and place them with the dead where they belong.

THE PORTLAND OBSERVER, FEB. 10, 1939

A Civic Organization

ALL TOO OFTEN THE MASSES OF NEGROES are unaware of the significant struggles and accomplishments that are taking place among them. In view of this fact, an effort is being made now to acquaint Portland's Negro populace with the aims and principles of one of its not-too-well-known civic organizations—The Voter's Benefit Association. This organization has not concentrated its efforts toward touching the upper strata of the Negro citizens—those who are well removed from racial persecution and gross injustices, but rather it has centered its attention toward solving the problems of unfortunates, and championing the cause of individuals who are too weak politically, socially and economically to fight for their rights. It has as its main theme "to see justice done at any cost." For example, the case of John Bird offers an excellent illustration of the nature of the work being done by this organization.

John Bird, eighty-four, has been a dependent for a number of years. After the advent of Social Security with its old-age pension provisions, Bird was given a grant of $23.00 per month to take care of his immediate needs, such as food, clothing and shelter. In December, 1938, this grant was reduced to $19.00, which amount was far less than what it took to provide fairly satisfactory accommodations for this old man. Thereupon, the members of the Voter's Benefit Association took it upon themselves to try and get more monetary consideration for Bird.

After a thorough investigation, it was found that a large number of persons had their allowances cut—some justly and some unjustly. In most instances where these cuts had been made, little or no explanation was given to the cases, except that the social worker handling the case had decided that the case involved was able to have his or her grant slashed. The Association realized, in every instance, the worker was supposed to be defending the concepts of the relief organization; therefore, no harsh criticism was directed at the persons who handled the cases.

After an itemized explanation was given relative to the needs and expenses of John Bird, the officials of the relief committee promised the representatives of the Voter's Benefit Association that they would do their utmost to see that he received just consideration. The results, so far, have been satisfactory.

There are many other cases of somewhat different natures with which this worthy organization has concerned itself. Among them have been the gaining of employment for Negro boys and girls, fighting for the re-employment of any discharged Negro workers, when proof could be established that the discharge was due to prejudice or false accusations, teaching disinterested persons the value of voting and the power of the ballot, and encouraging all of its members to become civic-minded. In our present society with its petty jealousies, strife and conflict, it is difficult to teach mass appreciation for a local organization with such noble principles. Just so long as these inconsequential idiosyncrasies continue to dominate the Negro's activities, just so long will darkness continue to envelop the race.

THE PORTLAND OBSERVER, FEB. 17, 1939

An Interested Citizen

CERTAIN MEMBERS of Portland's Negro citizenry have questioned the honesty and efficiency of Edgar Williams and have made vituperative criticism of his occupying the position as president of the Portland Branch of the National Association for the Advancement of Colored People. Often, he has been falsely accused of having selfish motives, interested only in personal advancement, rather than mass progress. For a man less courageous, less steadfast in his convictions, less interested in winning consideration for his people on the basis of equality and justice, these slurs and ignominies would surely have sapped his determination and destroyed his ambition to see his true desires fulfilled. However, he has suffered many embarrassments, numerous humiliations, and more than his share of insults, but in the face of it all, he has fought valiantly to better the condition of Negroes in Oregon. His fight for the passage of the Civil Rights Bill is an excellent illustration of the splendid service he has rendered.

If attention could be given to every noble effort he has put forth for the passage of this bill for the past two years, it is doubtful if this paper would have space for them. His masterful discourse on the purpose, aims and aspirations of the NAACP before the Senate Judiciary Committee at the state capital in Salem, Oregon, on the night of February 15, demands attention.

With a calm, unassuming dignity, Mr. Williams proved without a doubt that he knew what he was undertaking to do in attempting to convince the Judiciary Committee that Civil Rights are democratic necessities to the Negro. He was questioned from every angle, but each time, he had a factual reply.

Many arguments came from the members of the opposition. Among them were the following: (1) Apartment house white tenants could not be educated to accept an interracial infiltration. (2) Negroes are not disliked, as their being employed in the various hotels is an indication of the truth of this statement. (3) Business would suffer as a result of hotels admitting Negroes, and residential property would lose its value if Negroes were permitted to buy in certain districts. (4) The Civil Rights Bill has no practical value, as the act is not nation-wide in its scope.

To counteract these absurd arguments, Mr. Williams pointed out that Democracy is concerned with equality and justice, and the stressing of property rights over human rights is by no means democratic. He further stated that this bill applies to human beings—citizens of the United States. If the bill does not pass, it is likely that Fascism will dominate where Democracy has not even been tried. In addition to this, he explained that there really was no such thing as a "class"—and that such a concept could only exist in the prejudiced mind. To show that this program for Civil Rights is nation-wide, he informed his listeners that in twelve states, Civil Rights Bills had already been passed—starting with New York and coming across the continent to California and Washington.

At present, the Civil Rights Bill is hanging in the balance. To prevent its passage, there is Fascism with its accompanying prejudice and class hatred, and to effect its passage, there is Democracy with its noble aspects of equality and justice. Edgar Williams has striven to bring about a victory for Democracy. May his efforts reap a rich reward.

THE PORTLAND OBSERVER, MAY 5, 1939

Is This a Reason?

IN A LETTER ADDRESSED to Mr. Harlow F. Lenon, written by Donald M. Erb, president of the University of Oregon, relative to the atrocious practice of prohibiting Negro women students from residing in the women's dormitories at the University, the following quotation is contained:

"In spite of the fact that, as an institution, we welcome students of ability and character regardless of race, color, sex or economic conditions, we are not as yet able to break down the prejudice which individual students may have. The usual practice has been for the girls in our dormitories to group together in threes and fours voluntarily and sign up for suites. Until groups of white girls are willing to include colored girls in their number, we are up against a problem for which there is no solution."

A man who occupies a position as leader of an education institution that practices segregation and discrimination toward one sex of one particular group of people, and who gives his support to these practices, because he feels that prejudice on the part of a limited number of students cannot be overcome, is indeed a mere shell of an educator. In due time, his inadequacies will result in his removal. It is not expedient to believe that the white people of Oregon will permit an administration that shares the beliefs of Mr. Erb to handle the training and higher education of their children. Not another school in the state of Oregon adheres to a program of this sort.

In Mr. Erb's attempt to offer a reason for this discrimination, he merely submitted an excuse. How long are the Negro taxpayers of Oregon going to permit this excuse to bar them from receiving the benefits of what is justly theirs under the law? How long will the white people of Oregon continue to let their children be educated at the hands of people who believe that prejudice is a necessary evil?

THE PORTLAND OBSERVER, MAY 5, 1939

Mortal Wound – *[Guest Editorial. Editor's Note.]*

THE RAMPARTS OF RACE PREJUDICE are so securely built in this country that there are few persons who would dare open an assault. But it remained for a woman to step out and inflict a mortal wound on the monster within. Mrs. Franklin D. Roosevelt took the dare.

In discreetly resigning from the Daughters of the American Revolution, because it so flagrantly insulted all decent-minded people in its brutal refusal to allow Marian Anderson to sing in Constitution Hall, Washington, D.C., many of those who have been smugly complacent in their prejudiced views will stop and consider, now, before risking public censure or public rebuke for their attitude. Even the hidebound members of the D.A.R. must be, if they have any self-respect left—a little sick of their position, now that the spotlight of world publicity has been focused on them.

To Mrs. Roosevelt, who has on more than one occasion shown that she is truly a great woman, we offer our weak words of thanks and praise. For an act so magnanimous she can hardly be thanked; and for an act so distinctly symbolic of the spirit that we so devoutly wish to be that of America, praise is futile. Either a person is great, or he or she is not great. Not for approbation could one take such a stand. Only because one wants to do it, and because one believes it the right thing to do, could such an action be taken.

Apart from this being a mortal wound to the monster that is race prejudice, it is an example of tolerance and good will which will live in the memory of this generation, causing it to pause when intolerance and bigotry are rising to prominence in our national thinking. If for no other reason that she took this stand, the First Lady of the land is truly the First Lady of the land now. She is first by tradition, because she is the President's wife; but she is also first, because out of the welter of possible bitterness that might follow the cruel and unreasonable banning of Miss Anderson in the National Capital, Mrs. Roosevelt took prompt and direct action that at once upheld the principles of Americanism, rebuked bigotry, and showed that the White House is still representative of the best that America affords. (Reprinted from *Calvin's Digest.* W.H.M.)

"Fighting Today for Tomorrow's Victory"

THE PEOPLE'S OBSERVER

DECLARATION of POLICY

THE PEOPLE'S OBSERVER is convinced that during these turbulent times the Negro People have been afforded ample opportunity to learn and understand the curse of faint-heartedness and submissiveness. We have, as all minority groups must, come to honor and appreciate courage, militancy, and aggressiveness.

THE PEOPLE'S OBSERVER supports to the utmost those fighters who will go to all possible lengths in the defense of oppressed peoples, who will fight valiantly all types of discrimination, whether it be easily discernible or sophisticated; who are not to be hoodwinked by sentimentality or bulldozed by threats into surrendering concessions detrimental to the establishing of complete equality for the maltreated and exploited portions of America's population; who are unwavering and unrelenting in their opposition and attacks upon restrictions, legislation, and statutes that threaten to curtail the progress of labor and the Negro People.

THE PEOPLE'S OBSERVER is a firm advocate of the philosophy that "Each man is his brother's keeper."

A philosophical declaration of this nature compels **THE PEOPLE'S OBSERVER** to be a valiant defender against segregation and its related evils; a vigilant champion for freedom, liberty, equality and justice; an alert guard against all social atrocities; a vitriolic analyst and severe critic of discriminatory practices; a sentinel to warn of all impending retrogressive social trends and tendencies.

This is unquestionably a **PEOPLE'S POLICY—**

THIS IS THE POLICY OF THE PEOPLE'S OBSERVER.

THE PEOPLE'S OBSERVER, JUNE 29, 1943

Background for Riots

PRIOR TO THIS WAR OF GUNS AND TERRORISM, and more so since the involvement of the United States as a participating belligerent, we have all been aware that our democracy had many glaring shortages.

Due to long years of spirit-crushing abuse, intimidation, persecution and torture, Negroes are dubious when American whites speak of the liberty and equality of all men in the United States. Special privileges and opportunities for the fortunate few, limitations upon the rights of suffrage, segregation and discrimination on the basis of race and financial potency, exploitation of the weak and defenseless, aggrandizement for the strong without restraint, have caused Negroes to suffer social deprivations incessantly.

In the administration of justice, *Denial* has been the keynote when concerned with the Negro. In courts, at the polls, in all walks of social participation and conduct, injustices are constantly heaped upon American citizens whose means of redress are stultified. Court procedures throughout the nation are notoriously unfair to Negroes. Investigations show that Negroes are convicted with less hesitation than any other racial group; most times they are repeatedly convicted on evidence which for whites would be inadequate.

In many areas, labor shortages affecting some of the most critical war plants are now apparent. Yet, in many of these localities, there are American Negroes who could be employed on most war jobs. Discrimination and prejudice against these potential workers are sabotaging the victory effort of this all-out war program. In many instances, this vile and insipid practice of closing the doors of economic opportunity and social participation to persons because of color can be attributed to plant owners and officials. In even more instances the blame for this atrocious denial of equality can be placed positively in the laps of union leadership. Here in Portland, Tom Ray, of the Boilermakers union, HAS UNCOMPROMISINGLY REFUSED ADMISSION TO NEGROES in the Portland local No. 72. He has made every effort to read the "riot act" to progressive Negroes for refusing to accept his vocal denial of work privileges to them as the last and final word. In defying the slanderous remarks of Ray and other iniquities he feels prone to visit upon them, these courageous workers have seen a struggle begin that, as it gains momentum, clearly shows the disruptive forces of this reactionary clique to be pro-fascist as well as anti-Negro. Regardless of whether the "Victory Effort" is disrupted or not, these forces stop at nothing to close doors of economic liberation to the Negro people.

The currently existent conglomeration of ignominies, proscriptions and discriminations to which the Negro people are subjected in all quarters of our civilization are not conducive to the development of morale. There are at present a multitude of fascist whites who would rather risk defeat than grant freedom to the Negro people. This is manifested ever so forcibly by the reaction of white supremacists to the most elemental requests that Negroes propose in an attempt to bring about a level of equality. These people feel that they have nothing to fear from a Hitler victory. They believe that a victory for Hitler would create a situation whereby they will be in position to force the Negro back into shackles and chains. The victory they will fight for best would force the Negro to seek slavery as an escape from the more vile and vicious forms of cruelty and brutality that are already identified as the spearhead and the dominating theme of their medieval culture and development.

No line of demarcation can be drawn to separate the philosophies of the "white supremacists" who foster poll-tax, lynching and Jim Crowism, from those of Hitler and his followers in Europe who are intent on enslaving the free people of the world and establishing "Aryan superiority" over the face of the globe.

Despite tremendous handicaps and overwhelming obstacles, the Negro people are gradually realizing some advancements in industry and in government. These advantages are not being gained merely because the ideologies of prominent leaders of our government have dictated such measures. They have been realized because military necessity and productive expediency have compelled a relaxation of tense prohibitive barriers in certain areas. They have been realized because the Negro people are now awakening to the clarion call of Frederick Douglass, Negro leader of immense mental stature, who taught his people eighty-three years ago that men "Who would be free, themselves must strike the first blow."

THE PEOPLE'S OBSERVER, JULY 16, 1943

The Auxiliary Evil

THE PEOPLE ARE ACQUAINTED WITH THE CONTROVERSY which has arisen between Tom Ray, financial secretary of the Boilermakers' Union, and Negro shipyard workers residing and working in the Vancouver-Portland area.

Many social struggles have ensued as a result of Ray's acrimonious attacks upon the Negro people and his determined attitude to refuse Negro shipyard workers admission and membership into Local No. 72 of the Boilermakers' Union. The magnificent stand taken by the Negro shipyard workers in their attempts to combat the ravages and implications arising from segregation and bitter discrimination has attracted noteworthy attention from progressive and liberty-loving peoples throughout the United States.

As a result of a conference held Nov. 10, 1942, between government representatives and union officials to determine whether or not the Portland Metal Trades Council and the Boilermakers would have to abolish their discriminatory practices, Ray conceived the idea of establishing an auxiliary union for Negroes. Auxiliary unions, in brief, are labor union officials' prized devices to render Negro workers helpless in the face of the discriminations that will be practiced against them in the future. Negro workers have no method under this arrangement for reporting grievances, or to negotiate agreements, relative to wages, hours and working conditions, for all such business must pass through white committees who will act only *if they wish to do so*. It is prejudice plus trickery, and will defeat whatever plans may be made for the betterment of working conditions among Negroes. It is the most rotten form of white paternalism now in existence, in that the power and privilege of determining the status and longevity of the auxiliary rest upon the whims and egoism of one person.

The more significant and detrimental social implications to spring forth with intensified vigor as a result of auxiliary unions being established solely for Negroes are: the flagrant practicing of segregation of the Negro people and other minorities; the heaping of various slurs, insults and abuses upon these people, whose means of retaliation are feeble; the creating of vast amounts of dissension in the labor movement; the developing of strong and bitter antipathies of race against race, group against group, person against person. In addition to this, auxiliaries compel the most ruthless policing and dictatorial aspects to assure their effective operation; they prevent the emergence and

NEGRO WORKERS, BEWARE ! ! !

by Frederick Perry

rise of a militant rank and file Negro labor leadership, which is now far more necessary for the advancement of the Negro people than the leadership which has been developed within the professional and middle class groups; they tend to subjugate completely Negro women and deny them adequate participation in the social, economic and political programs which are vital to the welfare of the whole group; they provide the poll-taxers, Jim Crowers, pro-lynchers and race baiters in the top legislative and judicial brackets with arguments to further their vicious attack upon the Negro people. All of these things and many more are the inevitable products of any such arrangement as an auxiliary union.

Negroes, on the whole, have taken an adamant stand in opposing membership into auxiliaries. However, it must be remembered that many Negroes have been migrating into this vicinity from communities where they previously had practically no experiences in trade union deceitfulness and chicanery. These workers, unfortunately, have either been duped into accepting memberships into the auxiliaries or they have been compelled to sign up under duress.

Such unscrupulous exploitation and abuse will not furnish our enemies, the *white supremacists,* any truly noticeable advantages, because they have underestimated this time the resourcefulness to be found in this organized effort of Negroes to throw off the yoke of oppression. The Portland branch of the National Association for the Advancement of Colored People and the Negro Shipyard Organization for Victory are fighting as one to show the decent, freedom-loving people throughout this hemisphere that such conditions cannot persist forever when diligent, intensive and intelligent attacks are made to alleviate such atrocities.

THE PEOPLE'S OBSERVER, JULY 31, 1943

Crystallized Collaborations (No. 1 of Series)

THE BULK OF NEGRO LEADERSHIP that has come from among the professional and white-collar element in this area has succeeded from time to time through its actions and activities in bringing about serious social reverses for the whole group. Often controversial issues have been developed to a point that progress was completely stultified.

Some of the issues that have been promulgated and propelled through conceit, selfishness, avarice, greed, egotism, faulty prognostication and false premises have been extremely detrimental to the Negro people's advancement. Also, a division has been created between Negro and white workers through thoughtless and unplanned action. Occasionally, evidence reveals that the actions of certain individuals are designed solely to ingratiate the mass of Negro workers to these persons who label themselves "panacea bringers." Moreover, these same individuals, while proclaiming in a most bombastic manner their convictions of the equality of all mankind, have positively been guilty of promoting class-consciousness and attempting to develop divisive and defined strata within this minority's ranks.

Such deceit is a serious blow to unity. Without unity, the cohesiveness essential for victory over both foreign and American Hitlerism is an utter impossibility.

Since the appearance of just, sincere, labor organizers and representatives on the local industrial scene, a diligent fight has been waged to educate the Negro rank and file as to the benefits to be derived from organization. Every effort and energy has been concentrated toward providing clarity for these workers who, through no fault of their own, are politically undeveloped to transcend the vast social and economic chasms that have served to increase the discrimination that is constantly practiced against them.

The results of this intensive program have been exceedingly gratifying. However, there is a larger and more significant problem. The white and the Negro workers must both be clarified as to the true natures of their respective leaders. If the leadership is faulty, it must be replaced with a leadership that is humane, understanding and sincerely interested in the welfare and uplift of all workers. There must be inaugurated at once a program, backed up by policy and philosophy, to align *the masses of workers regardless of race, national origin or political beliefs for complete economic and social emancipation.*

The advent of the Negro upon the American industrial scene is in itself a significant economic and social development. The fact that the officials of certain trade unions and industrialists have conspired to keep these workers in sub-standard occupations and pay them sub-marginal wages is a challenge to the integrity of the progressive groups of both white and Negro workers in every quarter of our industrial and economic existence, because these workers have a materialistic understanding of the unconditional necessity for unity and equality in the American trade union movement.

The even greater test of ability for the rank and file of white and

Negro workers lies in the issue concerned with the acceptance of all workers into trade unions whose officials and policy-makers have decreed that Negroes would be barred from membership.

This is indeed a major problem and a difficult one to solve. For in keeping alive the agitation and persistent fight for unreserved admission to these organizations, many sacrifices are to be made by the participants. In addition to this, the educational program necessary to insure the success of this undertaking calls for unwavering determination, unusual mental resourcefulness and the establishing of mediums of clarity heretofore unseen in this community.

For those citizens among the white and Negro people who understand that racial prejudice and discrimination are disastrous indulgences, there must be formed immediately a broad citizen's committee whose functions will be directed toward giving the lie to false fascist doctrines, weakening and eventually removing offenses against labor and the Negro people by industrial employers and giving publicity to the fact that auxiliary unions are rackets designed solely for collecting tribute. A committee of this type will be indispensable in the crystallizing of public opinion and the developing of fraternal relationships between white and Negro workers.

This collaboration will undoubtedly furnish one of the most damaging blows to domestic Hitlerism ever conceived and put into operation.

THE PEOPLE'S OBSERVER, AUG. 18, 1943

Crystallized Collaborations (No. 2 of Series)

IN BUILDING A FIRM FOUNDATION for the cooperative efforts of our progressive working class population to achieve faultless operation in the fight against discrimination and for establishing unity, attention must be concentrated upon certain mediums that definitely serve to publicize the true nature of the Negro people's battle for equal rights and participation.

Consideration has been given to the forming of a broad citizens' committee, which will use its influence and power to carry basic social concepts before the mass of people for the purpose of wiping out fascism at home. In this life and death struggle for freedom and equality many methods of procedure have to be utilized in order that the enemies of labor, race-baiters and Jim-Crowers, will be unable to deal knockout blows to any distinct program that may appear as an end in itself.

As a whole, many people in this area are sadly lacking in political development and social consciousness. In order to overcome this vast degree of mental lethargy, a special appeal must be made to the Negro and white workers, their sympathizers, allies and friends to give the utmost support to organizing a mass meeting featuring a nationally prominent, progressive Negro as the principle speaker. This would serve as a magnet to arouse the interest of people of all stratas over the necessity for citizens taking action against the horrible conditions that are natural outgrowths of unchecked and unhalted manifestations of prejudice on the part of local Hitler elements. After weighing carefully the valuable assistance that has been given to the progressive Negro shipyard-workers' determined stand against Jim-Crow unions by the officials of the national office of NAACP, it seems that a man of Walter White's mental stature and experience in fighting Negro battles should prove an ideal candidate as the principle speaker.

Many persons who heretofore have not taken any noticeable action to assist or participate in these worthy attempts to break down the anti-Negro barriers of Locals No. 72 and No. 401 of the Boilermakers and the Kaiser Company will recognize the true significance of these efforts merely because the name of a nationally known champion of human rights is linked with the downtrodden faction. Moreover, the progressive whites who obviously are not sure what attitudes the Negro people in other parts of the country share will perceive readily the fact that the issues involved here are typical of what the fight for democracy on the home front really is.

Fair-minded persons, regardless of race, who wish to assist the Negro shipyard workers in this magnificent program to strengthen the ranks of labor and unite to produce more of the essentials for victory, will begin to collaborate more effectively, once they are convinced the Negro population in every quarter of American life is concerned over the anti-Negro labor and industrial policies now rampant in this community. The presence of Walter White, or some other Negro of equal stature, at a mass assembly or rally here will serve to crystallize and solidify the straight-forward and progressive programs that are to be inevitable products of an alliance of democratic forces.

THE PEOPLE'S OBSERVER, AUG. 31, 1943

Crystallized Collaborations (No. 3 of Series)

THE BUILDING SERVICE EMPLOYEES' INTERNATIONAL UNION OF AMERICA has included within its initiatory obligation the following paragraph: "I promise never to discriminate against a fellow worker on account of creed, color or nationality, nor will I knowingly wrong a brother or see him wronged if in my power to prevent it."

Negro workers are at this very moment pondering over how union policies can be shaped to include such vitally necessary stipulations as this. We are all aware of the tacit refusals and rituals of certain unions which bar Negro workers from gaining admission.

There are in this vicinity two defense plants whose service employees are not working under union jurisdiction and protection. They are Commercial Iron Works Shipbuilders and Albina Iron and Engine Works. Of particular concern to the Negro people is the peculiar position occupied by the Negro janitors at Commercial Iron Works. At this plant the workers are working union hours with union conditions at a rate of pay that is higher than the prevailing rate for janitor work in this area. Overtures are being made by the Building Service Employees' Union to organize these Negro employees. Apparently the Negro workers can see no immediate advantage in becoming members of this union, because the union does not promise a higher hourly rate of pay than they now receive. For this reason, a brief review of some of the obviously tangible benefits to result from organization will be cited.

The janitors at Commercial Iron Works do not receive premiums, as do other workers, in accordance with shifts that are worked. The Building Service Employees' Union will be sure to see that this arrangement does not persist. Aside from this, the Negro workers in supervisory positions will not have to put forth any especial efforts to hold the good-will of any particular personality of management in order to hold a job. Work conditions will be protected by the union. If the Negro janitors of Commercial Iron Works will come forward and unite with the trade-union movement, this will be a decisive step toward breaking down the sub-marginal wage rates now being paid to the employees of the same category in the Kaiser yards in this area. In the Kaiser yards in California, janitors receive 88 and 89 cents per hour and premiums for swing and graveyard shifts. In the Portland-Vancouver area, the prevailing wage for this work is 74 cents per hour. The fact that the wage standards of the Negro workers in plants where there is no union jurisdiction are higher will furnish the union with a sound basis for wage increases and adjustments for all concerned. Due credit will be given to the fact that Negro workers were instrumental in making possible this necessary correction in the local economic scheme.

The Building Service Employees' Union does not subscribe to the theory that women should receive lower rates of pay than male workers when working at the same craft or trade. Consequently, an immediate result from Negro workers of the Commercial plant aligning themselves with democratic white workers, and becoming a functioning force in trade union circles, will be the equalizing of wages for men and women. The removal of discrimination on the basis of sex, as well as race, is a positive policy of this organization.

Everyone knows by now that the labor union demagogues in this community who continue to deny Negroes membership in certain unions have used as their main theme for this refusal the refrain, "Negroes are not union material." White workers have long been taught to believe that Negro workers are the "boss' pets", "company lovers," "stooges," "scabs," and sub-marginal labor. The fact that Negro employees may be enjoying a temporary work advantage, because of the financial enticement given them by their employers and are not enthusiastic about joining a labor organization that has taken a definite stand against discrimination, both in its own ranks and in the A.F. of L. as a whole, will serve to portray the Negro workers as uncooperative and undeserving of the collaboration of white workers on issues that may arise of even greater significance.

THE PEOPLE'S OBSERVER, SEPT. 30, 1943

Remove the Trojan Horse

FOR SOME TIME NOW, progressive Negroes in this community have waged an intensive struggle on all fronts to stifle brazen manifestations of the white man's prejudice, discriminatory practices and cruelty. In reviewing the accounts of each struggle in which the progressive element has lent its support, we find there have been no victorious decisions or disposals made of any given issue or incident. This, to some people, may appear discouraging and arouse complexes of futility among the masses. Quite to the contrary, the victory which has been realized is all the more significant. In spite of having

Negro traitors, sycophants and "Uncle Toms" conniving with the powerful white factions of the opposition, progressive Negroes have organized and rallied their forces time and time again to meet courageously the vicious onslaughts of their enemies.

If each fight of the past twelve months involving Negro rights were placed under examination for a study of flaws in policy and mistakes in procedure, it would be found that those persons who have undermined and sabotaged every effort to obtain equality were successful in their endeavors solely because of the assistance lent them by deceitful Negro people.

The value of all Negro traitors to scheming white demagogues is measured in terms of how well they can deceive and mislead the mass of Negro people.

For instance, there would be no possibility for the officials of Boilermakers Local No. 72 ever establishing an auxiliary union for Negroes, unless some Negro becomes despicable and degenerate enough to head this vice. There will never be any danger of the Negro war workers in this area being victimized with a segregated recreational program, unless selfish Negro cat's paws are cheap and unprincipled to the point that they will cater to the whims of prejudiced white political aspirants just to receive a meager monetary hand-out. Separate educational facilities will never be possible unless some Negro first collaborates with prejudiced whites in creating such an arrangement.

Thus, we perceive, the main battle of the progressive forces must be centered around exposing and condemning the Negro who sacrifices principle for personal aggrandizement. The Negro who measures his own progress in terms of his ability to sell other Negroes down the river must be exposed and discarded.

Negroes who day after day are committing unforgivable atrocities against their people, and who are violating every standard of ethics in relationships with their fellowmen, are doing so by cloaking themselves with the blanket of security that comes from belonging to progressive Negro organizations. These individuals must be expelled from the company of freedom-loving people!

Arise, Negro leaders, thrust these snakes into the camp of the enemy, at least categorically. Better still, cast them into eternity.

THE PEOPLE'S OBSERVER, OCT. 20, 1943

Remove the Trojan Horse – Negro Apostate

IT IS DISGUSTING BUT INDISPUTABLE that Wyatt Williams, the local boy who never does any good, is again playing his customary roles as protector of prejudiced whites and vicious enemy of the Negro people.

When Rev. J.J. Clow was elected to the presidency of the Portland branch of the National Association for the Advancement of Colored People, this editor made an analysis of the progressive developments that would accompany the selection of Rev. Clow as head of this organization. In this election, renegade Williams was the defeated candidate.

In expressing his indignation at not being reelected, Williams promised his vengeance upon the progressive element for daring to remove him from his position, which he cherished. To what extent renegade Williams has found it possible to get revenge is difficult to say. How far he can go in his efforts to check the progressives depends upon what degree of success he will have in his attempts to get a Negro Auxiliary union organized for those bigoted reactionaries of Boilermakers Local No. 72, who feel that Negro workers should remain as sub-marginal factors in all phases of American life and activity.

The Portland branch of the NAACP (also the National Office) has gone on record as being opposed to the flagrant discriminatory practices against minorities in this area—especially those ignominies which are aimed at the Negro people. To clarify its position in these matters, this organization assumed the responsibility of carrying through to a bitter finish the case of Lee Anderson vs. Boilermakers Union No. 72 and the Oregon Shipbuilding Corporation that were sued for having conspired to keep Anderson, a Negro worker, from following his craft as a welder and firing him from his job because he refused to join an auxiliary union. Every sound-thinking Negro and all liberal whites, workers and professionals, have recognized the legitimacy of Anderson's charges. Moreover, an even broader fight carried on by the Shipyard Negro Organization for Victory against the Boilermakers local No. 72 and the Kaiser Company of Vancouver, Washington, for the same reason is pending at this time. In fact, the results of this struggle will determine largely the place of the Negro worker in the American industrial scheme for many years to come. The President's Fair Employment Committee will hold hearings in Portland on November 15th and 16th, 1943, to determine what disposition can be made of the charges which the Negro workers and their militant organizations have proferred against these two powerful reactionary bodies. The claims of the Boilermakers will get sympathetic attention at the hearings, providing they can prove that there is a tangible, workable Auxiliary Union serving Negro workers. At present they do not have such machinery in operation. The Auxiliary which they speak of is a mere paper charter around which they may place Negro stooges, if they can find them available.

In replying to charges leading to his expulsion from the National Association for the Advancement of Colored People, and which he was too cowardly to face, renegade Williams used "the daily press" to call Negroes "hoodlums." This is just one of the many abominations that this misguided and unprincipled individual has made against Negro people who have enemies among whites. These intolerant persons are at all times ready and willing to permit the use of their publicity mediums to slur minorities. Williams claims that leading Negroes and whites are behind him in his organizing efforts. It is needless to say that there are no persons of character, integrity and self-respect who would dare associate themselves with an apostate. Before the conclusion of this struggle, instead of heading an Auxiliary Union, the renegade will find himself a fleeing leader of the Amalgamated Negro Traitors, Sycophants and Uncle Tom's league or some similar organization.

THE PEOPLE'S OBSERVER, DEC. 12, 1943

Race Identity Closes Union Door

HARRY MILLS, NEGRO LONGSHOREMAN who has worked on a permit basis as a longshoreman on the Port of Portland for over 12 months, is the most recent victim of flagrant discriminatory practices and race-baiting, which has become extremely deep seated in this community since the beginning of this war for freedom. For more than a year, Mills has worked out of the hiring hall of Local No. 8 of the International Longshoreman and Warehouseman's Union, CIO. Twice in this period, Mills has been passed upon for membership in this union by the local's executive board. In two membership meetings held to decide his fitness for admission to the union, he has been unable to attain this objective.

In the first meeting, the matter could not be taken up because of poor attendance on the part of the union members. In the second meeting it was just the opposite. It is significant to mention at this time that all work on the waterfront by longshoremen ceased completely in order that these workers might convene and enjoy the festivities resulting from practicing racial persecution. In this meeting, all business other than that dealing with the Negro question was dispensed with and ruled out of order.

One longshoreman who brazenly boasted of his prejudices and resentment to the acceptance of Mills into this local had this to say: "Harry Mills' character is impeccable; he is a good worker; we would accept this man any day; we are not opposed to Harry Mills! We are fighting the Negro race. We cannot open our doors to any of the Negro people after having kept them closed all of this time."

This is indeed contrary to the win-the-war philosophy of the International. It must be remembered that not one ship was loaded, nor were any supplies moved through this port in the direction of our fighting forces, while these venomous personalities assembled to do what they termed as "fight the Negro."

THE PEOPLE'S OBSERVER, DEC. 21, 1943

Another Complication

So far we can safely say that there are few white writers, analysts and thinkers available who are currently putting forth any definite effort to provide clarity for the masses on the real struggles of the Negro people of the United States during this episodic war. Whatever has been done in this direction surely has not always been done for the benefits that would accrue to the Negro. It has become clear to all Negro students of social problems that the role of the Negro people in the whole life of the United States, both in this war and after, is destined to be sub-marginal and inferior – that is, if nothing happens to change the basic philosophy of superiority now revelled in by some American Caucasians.

Farsighted and intelligent Negro thinkers were quick to recognize that the vast extension of Jim Crow policies, throughout the armed services; flagrant discrimination by lily-white trade unions and industrial management in the matter of employing and upgrading available Negro workers; the renewed efforts of the white press to slur Negroes whenever possible; the persistency of so-called white progressives to seek to subordinate the legitimate, heart-felt griev-

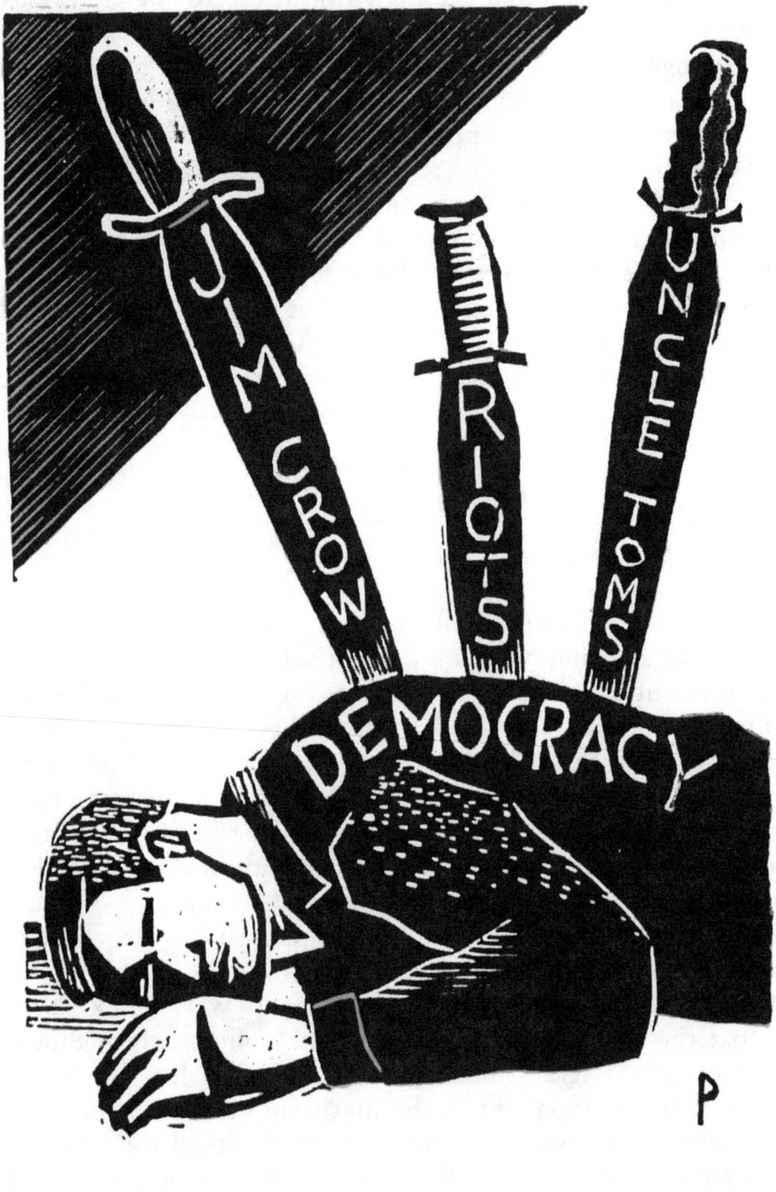

by Frederick Perry

ances of the Negro people against oppression and brutality at a time when the people of the world are avowed to remove these evils, would serve as conditioning instruments to maintain a system of outrageous subjugation for this portion of America's population. Some white persons who have proceeded to give even lip service to this magnitudinous problem are quick to supplement their progressive contentions with "everything must wait until the war is finished." This is a most absurd paradox, when applied to the Negro's struggle. The Negro people in their efforts to acquire freedom and equality in America serve as the vanguard of all liberty-inspired movements. The success or failure of their attempts will determine whether or not there will ever be any practical application of democracy.

Today, as in days gone by, prejudiced Southerners and reactionary Northerners are utilizing their vast resources and collectively concentrating their energies toward depressing the standards of existence to even lower levels than that now endured by the Negro people. Moreover, certain factions pretending to be part of the liberal element are also collaborating and assisting vigorously to bring the full current of white opposition to bear upon the Negroes. Every avenue of progress is being obstructed, and the obstacles placed in the way of this down-trodden people in their march for freedom are becoming more difficult to surmount. White persons who are able to deceive Negroes by professing friendship and sympathy for their predicament, have been able to get certain intelligent Negroes to explain in detail the true, real attitudes and opinions which the Negro people harbor relative to their expectations, aspirations, aims and demands during this current holocaust. The honest disclosures on these matters have not always brought gratifying results.

Daily we read magazine, newspaper and even book accounts of the intransigence of Negro people, which for the most part are always written by white authors. Such factual, undeniable and obvious discourses serve a two-fold purpose. First and foremost, the controlling and leadership factions of America's reactionary white population is kept on the alert to waylay and side-track any unusual ambition that might be manifested from within the Negro people as a whole. Secondly, the poor Negro, who by the way is still not politically astute, will be deceived to the point of believing and accepting these assorted discourses as spearheads in the battle for their advancement. "What fools these mortals be!"

All over the land now there are movements underway dedicated solely to circumscribing the Negro people and holding them in their place – whatever this may mean. For every incident that may signify one advantage for the Negroes, there are ten to indicate the overwhelming strength of these vicious suppressionist movements. My people, this does not happen accidentally. It is the intention of those who control, and yes! those whom you trust, to always keep you in a mendicant's position and forever treat you as a serf, if you are content to expect freedom merely by asking for it. A request for anything so important must be backed by the desire to sacrifice and the will to act in political unison.

THE PEOPLE'S OBSERVER, APRIL, 15, 1944

Workers Efforts May Compel Restraining Order Here

PROGRESSIVE AND MILITANT MEMBERS of the Portland branch NAACP have finally beat back the opposition of pseudo-liberals and reactionaries to carry through on the Lee Anderson court case. For more than a year now, this case has been awaiting action on the part of the Portland branch.

Many readers of the *Observer* will recall also the *Anderson vs. the Boilermakers' Lodge No. 72 and the Oregon Shipbuilding Corporation* case as a significant and momentous labor struggle involving the rights of a citizen to work in government-controlled defense plants, even though management and prejudiced labor demagogues might carry out strenuous programs of discrimination based upon color, etc.

Several months ago, members of the NAACP voted for the Portland branch to assume the responsibility of fighting this case and carrying it, if possible, to its logical conclusions. In the event Anderson should win his case, a court decision would be rendered restraining the Boilermakers from forcing Negroes to join auxiliary unions and compelling the discharge of workers from their jobs, because they may refuse to pay dues to an auxiliary.

Many veiled and disguised attempts have been made by both Negroes and white members of the NAACP to prevent this case from receiving attention and getting financial backing. Insidious political insinuations have been cast at the legal staff handling this case by portions of the branch leadership. Self-centered, glory-mongering individuals have made innumerable attempts to inject other programs and fights of far lesser scope in order to becloud the main struggle of the times – the Lee Anderson case. These deviationists, while proclaiming in a bombastic and ostentatious manner their

UNITY FOR VICTORY

by Frederick Perry

belief in this struggle, have been conspicuously inactive in preparing strategy and tactics to further the effectiveness of this fight.

On April 14th, the NAACP is sponsoring a Four Freedoms Dance for the purpose of raising some of the funds needed to carry this case to court.* Citizens' groups, organizations and businesses in every community are lending their support to making this occasion a huge success. Captain H.S. Peyton of the Veterans' Guard and Patrol ably assisted by two subordinate patrolmen will contribute their services to this event. Joe Crane has assembled a rhythmic six-piece band to furnish the music.

Negro workers from Portland, Guild's Lake, Vanport, Vancouver, McLoughlin Heights, Columbia House, Swan Island, East Vanport and Bagley Downs communities will participate in order to make this affair a success. Churches of the city are being asked to send contributions to assist in this fight. The Albina Victory Club on N.E. Russell St. has made a contribution. Many volunteer solicitors are working diligently, canvassing businesses, organizations and individuals for donations to win.

---

*In a message to Congress, January 6, 1941, President Franklin D. Roosevelt stated that Four Freedoms should prevail throughout the world: freedom of speech and expression; freedom of worship; freedom from want; and freedom from fear. These were substantially incorporated into the Atlantic Charter and subsequently became the cornerstone of the United Nations Charter. Editor's Note.

THE PEOPLE'S OBSERVER, APRIL 15, 1944

Today! Tomorrow Will Be Too Late

SERIOUS DISCREPANCIES on the part of Negro leadership in certain quarters of our community life again compel intimate evaluation of these channels for deliberately false guidance they carry to Negro people. Today, on every front, in every sphere of activity, programs are being conceived and put into operation which offer some measure of equality and justice to downtrodden groups, providing enough support can be mustered to carry them through to a stated or given objective. The more advanced social programs have as a requisite the cooperative fusion and integration of all national and minority groups. This is very necessary if there are to be any concerted beneficial social advantages extended to the peoples of America who are customarily neglected and abused.

Honest, sincere trade union leaders—rank and file members

also— have recognized that definite steps toward full inclusion and integration where minority workers are involved must be taken and achieved before any tangible solutions to complex racial problems and tensions will be discernible. This is very evident when consideration is given to the difficulties encountered in the attempts of Negro groups to alleviate pressing problems peculiar to this people without the assistance and collaboration of other national groups.

In preparing and directing criticisms at individuals for daring to ignore the incontestable and indisputable soundness of the aforementioned assertions, it should be borne in mind that personalities do not play an important role relative to influencing our decisions. In this period of incomparable hysteria and magnified psychoses, many persons endeavoring to arrive at a program or method of struggle to remove some of the horrors of oppression will inevitably blunder and fumble. Since all errors are costly in this battle for freedom and basic human rights, a positive effort is made to level criticisms at the mediums and tactics attached to the stated program. There is one exception: If it becomes obvious or definitely proven that a Negro is exploiting position, prestige or circumstances to poison the minds of white people against the Negro people and other minority groups, or if a Negro knowingly affiliates himself or herself to movements, personalities or organizations whose objectives are to preserve segregation, poll-tax, lynching and related forms of persecution, then this publication will definitely adhere to its policy which states clearly that "*The People's Observer* will be a valiant defender against segregation and its related evils."

Accentuated by a firm desire and unwavering determination to pursue this policy through to its fullest development, it is mandatory and imperative that we observe with careful scrutiny the methods which the committee of management of the Williams Avenue department of the YWCA will employ to remove the complications that have developed as a result of a socially undeveloped executive formulating policies for this group.

At present the national aim of the YWCA is to bring about full integration of all national groups into the YWCA program. In this community, many concrete illustrations exist to prove that the Negro staff member of the Portland YWCA does not favor integration for Negro women and has gone to great extremes to further segregation in order that the program of integration will be unsuccessful here.

On other occasions the advice has been extolled freely that when individuals charged with leadership responsibilities find it impossible to work in a positive manner for the elimination of all forms of segregation, then the people of the community must work in a positive manner for the elimination of the misleader.

Favorable response to this utterance is not anticipated. However, those members of the committee of management who refuse to act now to avert a rapidly-shaping social calamity facing the Negro women in this area will surely be strong enough to face the wave of criticism and wrathful condemnation that will eventually emanate from the awakening progressive Negro youth who will suffer for the committee's mistake.

THE PEOPLE'S OBSERVER, JUNE 8, 1944

Deception In The FEPC

ON MAY 12TH, 1944, the Boilermakers Local No. 72 again demanded the beginning of mass lay-offs of Negro workers in the Kaiser Vancouver, Oregon and Swan Island shipyards. The reason given for this order was non-payment of dues to Auxiliary Lodge No. 32 of Vancouver, Washington.

When these mass lay-offs were first begun, Negro workers sent a telegram to Malcolm Ross of the FEPC (Fair Employment Practices Committee) notifying him of this move. By return wire, he advised these workers to prepare a detailed report giving names, numbers and dates of the discharges. According to his wire, after this information is received, the FEPC would be in a more favorable position to investigate these matters.

At the last regular meeting of the Portland branch of the NAACP, a detailed discussion on the *Lee Anderson case vs. the Boilermakers Local No. 72 and the Oregon Shipbuilding Corporation* revealed that the aforementioned discharges have been imminent for more than three months. It was disclosed at this same time by a Kaiser Company agent that the Kaiser corporation had notified the FEPC of the demands being made upon the company by the Boilermakers. It was further brought out that the Kaiser company requested a second hearing of the FEPC in order that it might be able to state its position on these discharges, but the hearing was denied. However, the Kaiser company was advised to refrain from issuing all of the stop work orders to the Negro workers at one time. They were told to pass out these orders intermittently.

The previous summary clearly indicates that the methods of handling cases of clear-cut discrimination by the President's Committee is well steeped in the technique of evasion.

It is difficult to comprehend the reason for Malcolm Ross, chairman of the FEPC, demanding the Negro workers to furnish him with details which he could obviously acquire from the Kaiser company if he so desired. Moreover, these Negro workers were in no position to furnish this information. If they had undertaken to perform this task, it is reasonable to believe that their time would have been so pointlessly occupied that all corrective or remedial objectives could never be achieved.

Kaiser company is exploiting the fact that it has signed an agreement with a prejudiced group of labor demagogues for the purpose of ousting Negro workers from their jobs. This company is further utilizing to the fullest advantage the refusal of the FEPC to grant a second hearing as an excuse for complying with demands of the Hitlerites in local No. 72.

In the meantime, no mention is made of these salient points: Auxiliary lodges are ridiculous appendages attached to bona fide unions only when there are Negro or minority group workers available from which to suck blood money. In the case of Auxiliary lodge No. A32, Negroes have successfully demonstrated their resentment to accepting membership. Those who have been compelled to join in order to exist do not function because they have no enthusiasm for "Jim Crow" arrangements.

Surprising though it may be, Auxiliary 32 is not a union but a person by the name of Homer Parrish, business agent of Boilermakers Local No. 401 Vancouver, Washington. This individual takes time out from his various duties to write Negro workers residing in Oregon and employed in Oregon industries receipts to a non-existent fraternal racket. It is hoped that the Negro people of this area will become conscious of their responsibility to assist in the prosecution of the Lee Anderson case. If this case is fought successfully, Negro workers who have been financially enslaved by these detrimental conspiracies on the part of the Kaiser company and officials of Local No. 72 will eventually reap some degree of emancipation.

THE SAME TODAY AS A YEAR AGO

THE PEOPLE'S OBSERVER, JUNE 30, 1944

One Reason Why!

ONE OF THE MOST THOUGHT-PROVOKING COMMUNICATIONS ever received by this paper since its publication one year ago is found in another column of this page. The question which has been posed here is and has been a subject for many heated and extensive discussions. The writers are deeply concerned about whether or not they should support the fifth war loan drive because discrimination based upon color is no longer theory with them. Some of their close friends have been victimized by prejudices which are alive and flaming here in the very community in which they have lived for many years.

The issue first and foremost in the minds of American Negroes today is simply this: In the light of all the brutalities, tortures, persecutions, economic and social discriminations that are heaped upon the Negro people and other minorities (and which are increasing in geometrical proportions), am I obligated to continue to serve my country faithfully during this present world crisis? If so, why?

The role of minority peoples in the American social structure during this episodic war is incomprehensible to a vast proportion of the population – especially the part of the American Negro. For many decades the Negro people of the United States have pleaded for just the elementary privileges of freedom. Primary requests for liberty and justice have invariably been denied. In every crevice of American life ,both sophisticated and brutal discrimination are practiced against these people. There is no corner of the United States today which is devoid of prejudice and hatred against Negroes. Despite these irrefutable facts, it is the conscious responsibility of every Negro citizen to support, in every way possible, the prosecution of this war. The very fact that nations and groups which profess to be democratic and desirous of democracy are involved in this life and death struggle is ample reason for Negroes to cooperate fully. The realization of democracy is also the ultimate aim of the Negro people. It is true that many of the persons of international prominence who today are fashioning the future political and social destiny of the world are not sincere in their overtures to minority and colonial peoples. However, a prerequisite for all under-privileged groups to acquire equality and freedom in the post-war world will be determined largely on the basis of how effectively they participated in this colossal effort to destroy the strongholds of Fascist ideologies and principles.

This matter of local officials denying to a local citizen the right

PERRY
UNITY
JIM-CROW

to enter a public golf tournament because of his color is merely a petty-Fascist expression. It is the logical by-product of an infinitesimal and weaseled mind. Many such acts are springing forth now with renewed ferocity.

With all this and hell too, continue to buy your bonds. This is a first obligation to the men in the armed services who are not even afforded the opportunity to question the vicious prejudices that surround them. Your bonds will help bring these valiant and courageous fighters back home again. Undoubtedly, the sufferings they have endured, the sacrifices you have both made, will develop a natural unity of purpose. The home front believers in true democracy and war front fighters for freedom can and will assemble themselves for vigorous political and social action. This ultimately will prevent the emergence of any such ridiculous prejudicial tendencies as this one centered around a public golf tournament.

THE PEOPLE'S OBSERVER, JULY 31, 1944

Part 2 — Presidential Candidates

OF GREAT CONCERN TO THE NEGRO PEOPLE is the matter of the coming presidential election. Significance is attached to this event by minority and colonial peoples everywhere, mainly because the current pace being set by the mighty Russian army and the notable successes of the British and American armed forces since D-DAY indicate the next president of the United states will also be seated at the world peace table. This realization compels the American Negroes to take a more than usual interest in the political theater today. The destiny of these people on the economic and social fronts of post-war life is directly linked with how decisively, as voters of America, they will select a representative that may voice effectively their aspirations for liberation.

The basis of judgment for all nationwide political decision is customarily laid at the national conventions of major political parties. The first convention of this campaign was held by the Republican Party. Consequently, the first approach would be to weigh carefully the proposals set forth in this convention that will have both negative and positive implications for minority peoples in the post-war world. The Negro people have come a long way toward understanding the intricacies of machine politics. As an exploited and maltreated portion of American life, this group has learned that under no conditions can they expect an equitable apportionment of political consideration. They understand fully that where anti-Negro personages are candidates for election their chances for even a status-quo arrangement are slimmer. It is almost a certainty that a desperation of standards under which Negroes are now forced to live will result.

This brings us to another matter which is all important: What is the record of the candidates seeking office on matters pertinent to the welfare of labor, the Negro people and other minority groups? In only a few instances will there be found persons who can explain and interpret the past activities of political candidates as an index to what may be expected of these figures in the future. In this respect the following considerations should be borne in mind.

At the world peace table, the fate of the underprivileged people of the world will be one to receive serious attention from internationally recognized diplomats who will be on hand from every corner of the globe. Some of these persons will not have the best interests of the broad masses of people at heart when they voice their proposals for a new world of peace. If the American Negro voters wish to make a concrete contribution to a world peace conference, their efforts will be redoubled toward installing the strongest and most astute political mind available in the presidential chair. This is imperative if the darker peoples of the world are to be afforded any degree of the four freedoms for which this war is being fought. Remember this, poll-tax sympathizers, escapists on matters pertaining to anti-lynch legislation, labor haters and red-baiters are not the best agents for the establishing of FOUR FREEDOMS.

THE PEOPLE'S OBSERVER, AUGUST 20, 1944

Critique On Leadership

Ever so often, Negro reactionaries and Uncle Toms are summoned to the forefront of public life by some conniving and demagogic whites who have ulterior political or social motives which are intended to victimize the broad mass of Negro people. The appearance of George Streator at a meeting held Friday, August 11, in the Federal building is an excellent illustration of how this technique is utilized. Rev. Thomas J. Tobin presided.

George Streator is infamously known from coast to coast as a Negro apostate. As would be expected, this knowledge is a dishonor among Negroes, but it is likewise his stock in trade where prejudiced whites are concerned. Streator's true nature became obvious to Negro workers here many months ago when he appeared on the local scene as a government agent investigating Negro shipyard workers' problems. He emerged from his role of investigator as the great promoter of the Boilermakers' Auxiliary. *Need we say more!*

This individual attempted to show at the meeting that Negroes are in a turmoil because of the distrust and confusion existing between the many factions of Negroes and their Negro leaders. The fact that he would dare place himself in a role of an authority on such problems is a matter of utmost ridiculousness. In the first place *he* was here at the request of those local white disciples of the great cult of Jim Crowism. No Negroes in this community are desirous of his presence. The whites wanted "Little George" to salve their consciences for them before they took the final step toward setting up a segregated Negro recreation center in the Albina district. Although much care was taken to restrict any forward thinking Negroes from attending this meeting, a few progressives found their way to this chamber of racial abuse and persecution. The fact that there was one unwelcomed minister courageous enough to come forth and criticize this fourflusher for his useless attacks on the Negro people residing in this area is supposed to indicate that George was correct in his charges that dissension exists among Negroes.

This is refutable. Streator is not a Negro representative or leader by choice of the Negro people. No Negro can be considered a representative of his people unless he reflects both in actions and in words their organizational aims and aspirations. To be perfectly frank, only one Negro was present at this meeting who can by the most elastic stretch of the imagination be considered a true representative of the Negro people, and that was Rev. J.J. Clow, president of the Portland branch of the NAACP All other Negroes making utterances at this assembly merely reflected their own personal attitudes, which, according to reports in the local daily papers, were disgusting.

It is high time that the Negro people begin to realize that individual Negroes are not their leaders because the individual claims such a position. Neither do Negroes become leaders because white people designate them as such. Recognition as a true leader comes as the result of diligent participation in crusading welfare organizations. Amazing, but positively true, is the fact that Rev. Clow was the only

Negro present who possessed any of these credentials.

White leaders attempted to portray the purpose of the meeting as something aesthetic and idealistic when it became apparent that the Negroes who were invited to represent the Negro people were incapable of a logical defense in the face of Rev. Clow's burning tirade. This was to no avail.

There were many lessons to be learned from this meeting. Chief among them is this one: Negroes who have resided in this community for many years were among those who were invited to this meeting to listen to an elementary discourse on the necessity for segregating the Negro people. These individuals sat tight-lipped, and voiced not one word of objection to the fascist theme of this gathering. In addition to this, not one of them notified any militant member of their national group that such a meeting was scheduled. Not only are these persons not courageous enough to defend their people in the face of white prejudicial attacks, but by their passive presence they give impetus to the undemocratic practices within our community.

THE PEOPLE'S OBSERVER, AUGUST 31, 1944

Index To The Future

PARTISAN POLITICAL LOYALTIES and attachments are not customary identifying characteristics of this publication. However, a positive effort has been exerted on previous occasions to serve as a medium of political clarity for the people of this community who rely upon progressive analysis and criticisms for understanding. This policy has been followed diligently and relentlessly because we have come to realize that our readers are largely persecuted and oppressed citizens. These citizens must know the truth regardless of the mental anguish it may create.

The coming election has certain necessary and inevitable implications for minority peoples residing in the United States. For example, the proclaimed national policy of equality and opportunity irrespective of color is seriously involved. This issue looms directly as the most significant and deserving of serious attention from Negro voters. At present the role of Negro people in American life is unquestionably that of serfs. Consequently, first and uppermost in the minds of freedom-loving Negroes is what methods of struggle are suited to changing and improving the current position of the Negro people.

The many conflicts, overwhelming confusion, hysteria and painful sacrifices that have sprung out of this war, and the perplexing national and international arrangements that will come after it, are all products of political thinking and decisions. This realization demands that Negroes put forth every effort to become politically astute, for their own destinies are centrally linked with their future political actions.

For the first time in history, the Negro voters of America are in the position of being able to determine the outcome of the impending election in communities where they have never before experienced such a privilege. This is due to the fact that among white voters, registrations for both the Democratic and Republican parties are nearly equal.

In order that this distinct advantage will not be lost, it is mandatory for every Negro voter here to register who can satisfy the state requirements for voting. If the task of registering to vote is taken lightly, or indulged in only to the extent of the monetary compensations awarded selfish political functionaries for their false promises, then disaster is the ultimate result. Already there are indications of petty bickering and indecisive action on the part of Negro politicians who fancy themselves as being members of the "inner circle" of certain segments of the American political scheme. These victims of grandiose delusions must prepare to revise their tactics and develop a sincerity of purpose, or cause themselves and their people agonizing grief on the social and economic fronts.

THE PEOPLE'S OBSERVER, SEPT. 20, 1944

Index To The Future – Part 2

As the date for the national election draws nearer, it becomes imperative that a few remarks be made concerning an issue of considerable magnitude. It has to do with the evaluation of the worth of the Negro people by the white politicians of this community. Not being subsidized or even partially supported by any political group, this publication is in a position to give an impartial judgement on any matter of significance which may arise relative to the role of local Negroes in politics.

From the beginning of the campaign to elect candidates in the Oregon primaries up to this current political fight between the two major parties, many overtures for the services of this publication have been made by representatives and agents of varied political groups. In the course of our business maneuvers with some of these individuals, we have been able to make many valuable, informative and logical deductions. Some of these findings, while being typical of political bosses and small-minded campaigners, come as a surprise. It would seem that the importance of the Negro vote in this area would result in some of these persons viewing the Negro people with something more than thinly veiled contempt.

It has been noticed that most of these white politicians refer to the Negro functionaries of their respective political groups and the Negro voters as "boys". This manifestation of paternalism has been from time immemorial resented and contested by clear-thinking Negroes.

The fact that any white man will refer to his Negro associates in this manner bespeaks an ignorance of the struggle of the Negro people for equality. Any politician unacquainted with the role of the Negro people in the American class struggle is definitely not in position to offer panaceas to any minority or oppressed group.

More ridiculous, however, is the attitude of the Negro functionaries who do not question this disrespect, but assist in its gaining momentum and expression even in the most insignificant quarters of political activity.

Prominent Negroes in this community can attest to the fact that consideration of the true aims and aspirations of the Negro people in local political circles is practically non-existent. Negroes who have interested themselves in politics have found that every effort is being exerted by the demagogic leaders of political outfits to confine the participation of Negroes solely to minor vote-gathering procedures. For this function, the Negro receives a paltry hand-out unbecoming even to a mendicant.

It is true that the Negro people as a whole are politically naive. However, brazen efforts to keep alive atrocious social patterns are readily perceived by most Negroes. The fact that politicians are the practitioners of such policies is denounced to the extreme by this publication and all progressive Negro people. Tremendous sums of money may be spent in some spheres of Negro life to have local Negro votes delivered to a specific political group. This will be to no avail. Already, information concerning the characters of some Negro political stooges have preceded the activities of these persons in communities populated largely by Negroes. The voters are on their guard. Ministers are also concerning themselves to see, regardless of the declaration made at the registration booths, that Negro voters will cast their ballots for the candidates who have previously demonstrated their sincerity in struggling for the complete freedom of minority peoples in the United States.

THE PEOPLE'S OBSERVER, SEPT. 30, 1944

Not In The Swim

MANY APPROACHES HAVE BEEN MADE here of late to have this publication take up political alliances which are unanimously recognized as inimical to the best interest of the Negro people. Both Negroes and whites have insisted that such attachments would be financially lucrative as well as a significant boost to our prestige in quarters that heretofore have regarded this paper with enmity.

Already an adamant refusal has been made to all such offers and proposals. Under no condition will the *Observer* prostitute its position as a reliable source of information to the Negro people and other minorities in order that race-baiting, poll-taxing, labor-hating, defeatists and state's rights political aspirants can gain a foothold. They may win their political contests anyway, but never will they be able to claim this paper as an accessory to the crime.

Seen And Heard

One of the most exasperating pieces of small time political campaigning ever witnessed in this part of the country was carried on at McElroy's dance gardens Monday night, September 18.

The ever paternal and patronizing "Pops" McElroy was on the alert to exploit an entertainment gathering of the Negroes (which they were required to pay for) to solicit Negro votes for two of his political friends. Scene of this contemptible act was the "Tiny Bradshaw" dance.

Bradshaw, in attempting to gain the attention of the dancers for the speakers, clearly indicated his disgust for such an interference. Before the vast majority of the persons present had realized what was taking place, the orchestra resumed its playing. Consequently, the political effectiveness was completely lost. For this, we are grateful. Such attempts to indoctrinate the Negroes with fallacious political propaganda by any person or group will not go unnoticed or unmentioned.

Reply To Students

In another column there is a letter submitted by Negro students from Jefferson High School. *(The letter follows this reply. Editor's Note.)* The purpose of the letter is clear as it stands. This is a brief reply to the question that was posed. "Are our boys fighting to come back to a world of segregation, a world under the rule of the white man's whims?"

No, the Negro soldier is positively not fighting for the preservation of white supremacy. All over this land now, Negro crusading organizations and the Negro press are laying plans and formulating programs to resist to the bitter end every attempt the white man may make to bring complete subjugation upon the Negro people. Already, our people are being told by their writers and their speakers that they may expect "A peace more terrible than the war."

The only method whereby this can be averted is for every Negro – young and old, students and workers, soldiers and scholars – to resist the southern fascist pattern of segregation and discrimination wherever it appears.

A great deal of sacrificing will be made in an effort to dispel these practices from our national existence. "Uncle Toms" and "sell-outs" among the Negro people will make these difficult tasks even harder. But even so, you must never lose sight of your objectives, which are freedom, justice and equality, and opportunity.

To many people here – even a few Negro people – your letter will appear ridiculous. Be not discouraged, however. You are now coming face to face with a condition that southern-born Negroes meet before they are out of the cradle. It is the eventual lot of every Negro born in the American social order. Your continuing to resent and resist the growth of this monster will be another ally to the varied forces now fighting for Negro liberation.

Letter to Editor from "A Few Disgusted Negro Students" September 30, 1944

Letter to Editor:

Things have come to a pretty state of affairs when you can't even speak of your school with pride; when you consider school just a place that you have to spend six hours a day in an ever-lasting struggle for everything you get. You don't enter into any of the school's social activities, you don't go to any of the dances, and why don't you? They practically tell you that they would rather not have you on the floor. You no doubt wonder about this, for this is supposed (and we say, supposed) to be the most democratic of times; our schools, if no other place, should be a place where democracy prevails despite race, color, or creed. If you cannot find it there, where can you expect to find it? Our parents pay their taxes, and, therefore, we should be entitled to the same rights as others, but are we? The answer, you know as we do, is NO.

At Jefferson High School (we know for we are students there) on Friday, September 28, 1944, there was held a school dance. The entire school was invited, but when we Negro students arrived and had danced a few dances, we were told by our student body president acting under the authorization of the Dean, that NO Jitterbugging was allowed.

We explained that we were not Jitterbugging. (A white couple was doing the same steps we were doing, but they only shook their heads at them). They also told us that they would like for us to learn to dance as they do. They further explained that perhaps at some special time or to some special record, we could dance as we pleased. Perhaps, said they, if we dance in a place designated for us, they could arrange for us to jitterbug.

Tell us, isn't that segregation with a capital "S?" Is that what our boys are giving their lives for; fighting to come back to a world of segregation, a world under the rule of the white man's whims?

Sincerely,
A Few Disgusted Negro Students

THE PEOPLE'S OBSERVER, NOV. 22, 1944

Discourse On The Super-Phonies, No. 2

NOW THAT THE ELECTIONS ARE IN THE BACKGROUND of everyday activity, other matters of human interest will come to the attention of the people. Some issues that heretofore have never been foisted upon the minds of Negroes will stimulate a noticeable degree of mental consideration.

Persons, cliques, organizations will all have their respective "fish to fry" for the post-war era, and no time is being lost by some insidious operators to get in on the ground floor. For example, the fact that the elections have favored, on the whole, the mass progress and improvement of status for minority groups should not be construed to indicate that any of this will occur without a most bitter battle for complete liberation being waged by the Negro people and other affected minorities on all fronts.

Already, in our fair city the southern wing of immigrants, the northern reactionaries, western Ku-Klux-Klanners, silvershirts et al. are busily engaged in preparing their anti-Semitic, anti-Japanese, anti-Negro strategy. Organizations of every conceivable nature are springing up over night as part of this monstrous program for the "assured continuity of unconditional white supremacy."

Many of these super-schemes have appearances, which if unexamined, will deceive numerous persons into accepting them as bonafide welfare organizations. Often they propose to do everything from acquiring complete justice for Negro victims in prejudiced, biased courtrooms to establishing in this lifetime complete social equality.

Close scrutiny of these organizations reveals some startling information. For instance, let us look at the mythical but illustrative "International Amalgamated League for the Expression of Intangible Benefits to Colored Peoples."

Now this organization has no known officers. It is not incorporated. It is fronted by Negroes of dwarfed mentalities or questionable reputations. Its membership fee is exorbitant. The originators of this outfit are white persons who have no desire whatsoever to let other white people know of their deep concern over the plight of Negroes and other minorities. Only their inner circle friends will share this knowledge – those who will participate in acts of subtle persecution and programs of economic and social denial.

The programs of this organization are in all probability similar to the programs of the NAACP. It is the activities of its founders and members that are definitely inimical to the welfare of all minority groups. In this respect the organization is diametrically opposed to everything bespeaking actual progress for the Negro people.

Uppermost in the minds of these tacticians for suppression of minority group militancy is the pressing need for helping and forcing the Negro to find his place in the American structure. That place, of course, must be submarginal in every respect. No deviations are acceptable or considered.

Another theme of such organizations is the sponsoring of meetings whereby the Negroes are given an opportunity to voice their opinions on matters of justice, freedom, equality, etc. Usually enough conflicting ideas are introduced to create a furor among those attending. This eliminates any possibility of establishing a unified organizational program for social benefits and uplift.

Frequently, you will notice that the applications for memberships in such organizations are filled with leading questions concerning the life of the applicant. These questions, if answered correctly, will enable prejudiced white pressure groups to harass and coerce employers to remove Negro employees from their plants and industries. This point should not be forgotten as the era which may bring a shortage of jobs draws nearer. This method has been utilized over and over again in the southern and northeastern regions of this country. Sometimes, phony welfare organizations gather this type of information for the sole purpose of selling it to prejudiced pressure outfits.

It is high time that the Negro people begin to take a serious interest in all groups working and operating supposedly for their welfare. Many of these machines have nothing to offer but a difficult time for the efforts that freedom-conscious, oppressed people may exert for complete liberation. By close and skillful evaluation it will be possible for alert Negroes to determine the sincerity of purpose governing many of these arrangements. However, all of the people should become acquainted with the nature of these dastardly instruments of social deprivation. Once the indignation of the Negro people can be aroused to the point of complete resistance to their overtures, the crisis in the eternal struggle for their destruction will have been passed.

THE PEOPLE'S OBSERVER, NOV. 22, 1944

Letters To The Editor:

THIS IS JUST A NOTE TO EXPRESS, as far as feeble words can, my appreciation for your good work in my behalf during the campaign. You went to town in a big way and I shall be forever grateful to you.

I appreciate your friendship and help. If it were not for friends like you, I would not have been elected. You can rest assured that I will work to the utmost of my ability to prove worthy of the confidence that you and your friends have in me. From the bottom of my heart I thank you.

With warmest personal regards, I am

Sincerely yours
James R. Bain

THE PEOPLE'S OBSERVER, DEC. 16, 1944

The Season's Greetings

IN THIS EDITION ONLY TWO ITEMS WILL BE REVIEWED for the readers to ponder during the Christmas holidays. It is believed that the unrationed abuses and surplus sophisticated atrocities of this type are indicative of the many things to come as the war draws nearer to a close.

1. Fifty Negro seamen are to serve 15-20 years in prison as a result of a naval court-martial where they were found guilty of mutiny because they refused to load ammunition and high explosives. Many of these sailors were survivors of the Port Chicago disaster. Moreover, the majority of them are trained and qualified specialists capable of performing far more responsible tasks than stevedoring. They are also 25 years of age or under. Such militancy as they displayed in the face of an obvious and complete defeat is deemed dangerous in the post-war world, where white supremacy theories are sure to be contested. *Twenty years imprisonment will knock a lot of fight out of the most courageous crusader!*

2. Negro shipyard workers are beginning to feel the economic pressure of the combined forces of fascist-minded industrialists and reactionary trade union leaders. Already, electricians in this area are being eased out of their jobs in certain yards. Many of them have been union members for long periods, too. The reason given at the time of the discharge is "reduction of forces." When these same workers go to the union hiring headquarters to apply for other available positions in other yards, they are informed that there are no openings. If they loiter around for a few minutes, a white worker may come in and, upon applying for work, be immediately dispatched to another job. Many incidents of this nature have transpired during the first two weeks of this month. Does this make for a happy holiday season for the Negro worker?

As long as the Negro people have to concentrate their attention and energies toward the correction of subjective and immediate ills such as those previously itemized, they will find that the fullest joys to be reaped from any special season of the year are impossible for them to experience.

THE PEOPLE'S OBSERVER, JAN. 18, 1945

"It's Easier To Convict A Negro" – Folkes

THE FORCES IN THIS VICINITY OF THE UNITED STATES that had prior to the war been able to keep Portland a big city operating on small town ideas were rocked from their narrow seats of provincial complacency, when it became obvious that Portland was to be a war production center. These same factions suffered increased mental anguish when the economic and political signposts began to indicate that the Negro population would, of necessity, emerge twelve times greater than in pre-war years. Being both prejudiced and provincial, these persons and their organizations were confronted with a dilemma: how to thwart the influx of Negroes and at the same time make sure that the migrant whites, who were also compelled to come into this pseudo-sacred province, would find only a temporary economic existence. In neither endeavor have they been successful, but they overlooked no opportunities to continue to inflict hardships on the Negro people.

Moreover, in this area during the earlier portion of 1943, the Negro citizens who held many years of passive residence here as employees in submarginal capacities, gave impressive expression to the class lines of demarcation that were being drawn at this time. Peculiar though it may appear, the royal order of Portland's original Negro population was quite willing to regard the in-migrant Negro worker as a strange and unusual animal. Extension of a bond of fellowship to many of their blood comrades was never forthcoming. Only a few isolated cases exist wherein the struggles and hardships encountered by incoming Negroes were given assistance and support by the established local population. In many instances, Negro renegades and "white folk lovers" launched programs, functioned in organizations and made perfect fools of themselves in an effort to put into motion political and social machinery that might tend to drive away the incoming Negro workers.

These actions, though disgusting to the Negro progressives, were pace setters and examples for the white reactionaries to mimic and emulate whenever matters of vital importance to the broad mass of Negro people were brought before them.

The case of Robert E. Lee Folkes is an excellent example in every detail of the complaints that are being listed herein. The publicity and the infamous notoriety of this case, coupled with vicious whispering campaigns defaming all of the Negro people, incensed the majority of the white population to a point bordering on mob hysteria. A most shocking aspect of this case is that even today many Negroes are not conscious of their personal obligation to resist and protest the taking of this youth's life without his guilt being clearly established. The indifferent and impersonal attitudes taken by many Negro citizens toward this case led many white persons, who could have been effective in gaining clemency for him, into assuming that he was believed guilty by his own people, so why should they be concerned?

No one stopped to think at the time this case first broke that it was Folkes' misfortune to be the principal figure in a vicious scheme that would engender hatred in the hearts of all people against Negroes. That this hatred, if aggravated, would lead to anti-Negro expressions of such intensity as to halt completely the westward migration of the Negro people. If this could have been accomplished, the wrath of the "powers that be" would have been appeased, the ruffled furs of the "prejudiced" would have been rubbed the right way, and the role of the Negro as an inferior individual in this community would have been guaranteed for all time.

Long, drawn-out legal maneuvers concluded with Folkes' having to die anyway. Now that he is dead, it is mandatory that an even clearer picture of what is happening to the Negro here be presented.

The human elements possessing the power to comply with meager requests for justice had no intention of jeopardizing their political futures by giving the full benefits of American legal consideration to a Negro. These persons realized that any expression of fairness to Folkes and the Negro people would be construed to mean that they were incapable of protecting white supremacy concepts. This would be equivalent to political suicide. The issue concerning the return to the west coast of gallant Japanese-American citizens has already been greeted in this state by the formation of anti-Japanese organizations. Many of the persons who constitute the roster of race-hating outfits of this sort are instrumental in the winning of important political contests. They immediately view any displays of favoritism toward one minority as indicative of the way another minority shall be dealt with.

Many people view this portion of America as a locality where legal guarantees to minorities are strong and durable. Folkes' death is Oregon's refutation of this.

THE PEOPLE'S OBSERVER, FEB. 28, 1945

Reaction vs. Progress

FOR THE SAKE OF CLARITY a few remarks will be made here concerning an incident of vast community import. It has to do with the current practice of a grocery merchant refusing to sell foodstuffs to Negro war workers who live in the vicinity where he operates his business. Many Negroes who do not comprehend the varied methods involved in reactionary responses have already branded the atrocity as an excellent example of the current belief that things are getting worse for the Negro people.

In the first place, Maxwell is a feeble old man who probably has hated someone constantly all of his life. It is likely that his heritage, as far as associates and acquaintances are to be considered, consisted mainly of persons who shared fascist beliefs. In recent years, with the abundance of literature, meetings, whispering campaigns and other mediums supplied by pro-nazis and bundists, it was comparatively easy for a warped mind such as Maxwell possesses to become diseased with the germ of racial hate.

This particular discrimination that Maxwell is directing at American Negro war workers is no new thing, although it may be the first time such a program has received the marked attention that is being given to this one. American Japanese are encountering the same discriminations daily as they return to their homes on the West Coast.

Such abominable actions on the part of persons steeped on philosophies of supremacy for whites and ostracism for minorities are direct retaliations of reactionaries to the greater liberties that are inevitably coming to the minority groups here. The more pronounced the indications of justice, equality and democratic respect for American minorities, just that much sharper will be the measures employed by anti-democratic forces to prevent these social and political revisions.

The main struggle of the Negro people and their friends here is to fight first, last and always for the passage of an effective civil rights bill. This matter should get the fullest support of all groups interested in overall liberation. It is practically impossible to counteract seriously any prejudicial moves on the part of race-baiting individuals and groups unless the legal means for resistance and attack are decisively established.

Incidentally!

It is interesting to note that President Roosevelt, after having conferred with Stalin and Churchill at Yalta, Crimea, met with Ibn Suad of Arabia, Farouk of Egypt and Haile Selassie of Ethiopia. Selassie, who was allowed to visit for a short period one afternoon, is the man who predicted all of this current warfare and horror before one of the League of Nations conferences. This visit had one good purpose, however. Roosevelt was able to inform him that the grazing lands of Ogaden province, which the British are now occupying without formal consent, will be returned to Ethiopia after the British-owned cattle have been fattened.

Selassie, it will be remembered, submitted claims to the war guilt commission for millions of dollars against the Italian government for damages suffered when the Mussolini hordes invaded and laid waste his country.

According to the opinions being expressed by Dr. W.E.B. Du Bois, "the gate has been left open for another war." He based this assertion on the fact that China's resolution on racial equality for the Security Council was kicked out in the recent Dumbarton Oaks Conference. Maybe Selassie will have some more momentous predictions to make!

THE PEOPLE'S OBSERVER, MARCH 19, 1945

Glitters, But Not Gold –

IN A RECENT EDITION OF THE OREGON JOURNAL, there appeared an editorial written by a former Lieutenant Commander in the United States Navy, which was concerned with the provocative complications of the GI loan bill.

The GI loan bill is supposed to provide for a loan up to $2,000, guaranteed by the government, to service men separated from the service. These loans are to assist the ex-service man in buying real property or establishing a business of some kind.

In discussing the procedure to be followed in getting one of these loans, the writer says that "a GI is first sent to the RFC in this city. After a rigid questioning about the purpose of the loan the hopeful applicant is advised of the following things:

1. The RFC does not lend money, only approves loans made.

2. No loan can be made unless and until a bank refuses the loan.
3. No consideration can be given one's professional reputation or record of success.
4. No loan can be made without good collateral.
5. Any loan must be applied for within two years after separation from the service.
6. The RFC cannot even consider an application for a loan until the veteran has completed a series of forms that go from the RFC to the Veteran's Administration in Portland to the Veteran's Administration in Seattle and from there to the office in New York and then either back over the same route or somewhere else."

It was further shown that if a man had good collateral he would not need any special type of loan; he could go to a bank and get whatever money he needed within his credit limit. Few if any returning Negro service men will have the collateral adequate to satisfy the demands of a really beneficial loan. If property is purchased, it is required that it must not surpass by far its normal price in cost. There is no such property available for a Negro to buy. If the ex-soldier waits more than two years to use his right to apply for a loan, he automatically forfeits his right to receive any benefit from the GI bill.

This should be of interest to returning Negro soldiers, in that there are a number of them in this community who look forward to purchasing homes and making business investments with the money they expect to get by applying for a GI loan.

The insidious methods that have been effected in this area to herd Negroes into a ghetto – to force them to live in houses that are priced far beyond their actual worth – is certain to remove the possibilities of any loans being approved for the purchase of homes. Since the economic life of the Negro here is largely, almost entirely, centered around holding jobs for other employers, it is unlikely that any impressive changes will be noticed in the types of businesses that are now controlled by Negroes. The limitations previously outlined will thwart the plans many service men may have toward embarking upon a business venture.

We Must Never Forget

The Filipino community of Portland under the leadership of Jorgi Dumlao, president, has raised and sent to the Philippines War Relief,

Inc., Washington, D.C., the sum of $400 to purchase medicine, food and clothing. The need for these articles is urgent.

Interested Negro citizens have remarked that history will record the noble deeds and acts of courage displayed by these friendly peoples living in the islands of the Pacific, in frustrating the imperialistic jingoists of Japan. Their resisting enslavement has been a decisive help toward preserving the democratic rights of all peoples. As a minority group the Filipinos, like the Negro, have struggled for their freedom against overwhelming odds. Whenever possible, Negroes should contribute to the assistance of these magnificent people.

THE PEOPLE'S OBSERVER, MARCH 31, 1945

A Necessary Step Forward

It is now time for the Negro people of this area to take stock of the social and political efforts that have been made for improving their status here in the past five years. In viewing the present state of affairs from this angle it becomes shockingly obvious that this group of people has no representatives to date who are holding responsible and authoritative positions that would tend to develop a more serious and appreciative feeling for Negroes on the part of other groups residing in this community.

At this writing, there is no Negro holding a full-fledged policeman's job in the city of Portland. Many explanations have been offered for this appalling laxity. Some are plausible, and others entirely unsatisfactory to a people that in peace and in war have demonstrated that they are capable of assuming obligations of every conceivable nature and discharging any and all duties efficiently.

In some quarters the thought has been advanced that there are prejudiced and racially biased individuals dominating the operation of the local police department here. These persons are alleged to be bitterly opposed to the extension of full police authority to any Negro regardless of his qualifications. Many attempts to circumvent any such possibility have been forthcoming. The use of temporary Negro police officers lacking in training and ability in communities tenanted largely by Negroes is an excellent illustration of this.

These functionaries are not empowered to carry out assignments on a basis comparable to that of men who have full police authority. Consequently, it is impossible for them to have self-respect, respect from the people, or the respect of white policemen who know the limited extent of the Negro functionaries' authority, preparation and training.

On the other hand, it is claimed that Negro men of good moral character, with fair educational backgrounds and within the age limits prescribed under the civil service regulations, have never made application for appointment on the Portland police force. The truth of this utterance may be more far-reaching than can be imagined. Anyway, there are many Negro men who have established residence in this community while working in defense plants and war industries. A number of these workers are qualified in every way for police positions, that is, if the civil service requirements hold no specific briefs for color.

As the war work in this area gradually diminishes in quantity, it would be wise for as many Negroes as possible to investigate and study the possibilities of becoming police officers. Negro welfare organizations and liberal elements from among the white population will champion the right of this acceptance. No longer can the Negro wait for these opportunities to be presented. Initiative and determination must be applied to create them.

THE PEOPLE'S OBSERVER, MAY 15, 1945

Another Suggested Plan

ONE GLARING TRUTH blandly exposing itself for the benefit of those who care to observe is the indisputable fact that the Negro community of Portland is gradually disintegrating. Accentuating this program of decay are the base and lackadaisical attitudes of the Negro people relative to all pertinent social issues. In practically every quarter of Negro activity, the prominently functioning individuals are continuing to four-flush, daydream and carry on a foolish practice of glory-mongering. The fact that there is little courage and aggressiveness among this people is becoming more noticeable daily. The lack of unity on the part of those who feel they are fit to lead and their persisting in keeping alive personal antagonisms and time-worn grievances portends stultification completely of all progress that may be made by the members of this minority group.

Here of late, the Negroes have shown a strong tendency to revel in delusions of grandeur which center around a few mad ideas about their nonexistent but pretended self-sufficiency. On the other hand, these same persons are infamously known to bow and scrape in the presence of petty white politicians and law enforcement authorities. The damage to result from such folly is obvious even to the mentally deranged. Many evils gain momentum while the main body of the Negro people and its leadership sit idly by. For instance, it is doubtful if there has been one case recorded in the past fifteen months where a Negro was charged with a crime and had a trial by jury that he was not convicted and sentenced. It is doubtful if a checkup of the records in the county clerk's office would even show any marked extensions of leniency to any Negro. The same can be said of cases that have to be tried before most of the judges here. In this matter, conditions have reached a point where a Negro must accept a criminal conviction if he is charged with a crime, even if he is not proven guilty. One reason for this is that it is practically impossible to find an impartial and unprejudiced jury. When lawyers defending Negro clients conduct the usual inquisitions to determine if jurors harbor racial prejudices, they are unable to get admissions on this score from those whom they question. Moreover, the division which now exists throughout the ranks of the Negro community prevents the concentration of an effective group program to alter such situations.

These same factors, however, are having tremendous influence upon the employment of Negroes in the postwar period. For example, it will not be long before character references will be far more necessary to gain job privileges than they have been during the war era.

At the present time, more than ten petty organizations embodying Negro functionaries who express only subjective and inconsequential intentions and futile ambitions are in existence. This does not include the many similar groups that are to be found in the war housing projects in this area. All of them claim to have programs designed to resist discrimination and segregation. It is needless to say that all of this overlapping on the same theme is disgusting and superfluous. Not one of these groups will ever be effective in a single endeavor, because the persons whom they must influence know before hand that these groups have only factional backing and do not offer overall representation.

There are only two organizations with offices here that have the machinery to promote any basic changes in the race relations structure of this country and community, as far as Negroes are concerned and involved. These are the National Association for the Advancement of Colored People and the National Urban League. National organizations are undoubtedly far more effective in the struggles to better the conditions of oppressed peoples, because they are capable of taking an objective position based upon a nationwide abusive situation. In recent weeks many incidents have occurred to show the Negro people how determined the "Professional Negro Lovers" are to increase the division that already exists within the ranks of this minority. They have imported skillful Negro informers into this community many times to explain in detail the various limitations that surround Negro activity in every field. These figures serve well the white persons who seek to capitalize upon the current efforts of minorities to gain recognition and opportunity by using these attempts as mediums to catapult themselves into dominant and authoritative community posts. They find it very valuable and profitable to know what significance Negroes attach to petty meetings, tea sippings, conferences and other gatherings that carry a flimsy social import. With this knowledge at their disposal, these persons frequently make arrangements for affairs of this sort, where an interesting practice of acceptance and exclusion of various Negro personages is carried out. This is usually done in a veiled, subtle manner. It would be the height of redundancy to say that such tactics create a condition of total disruption throughout the ranks of the Negro population.

This column has no chosen or picked Negro figures to endorse as the panacea bringers for the Negro people residing in this area. And by the same token, it does not accept all overtures of deep concern and interest that many whites appear to evoke over this long-labeled Negro problem.

There is an acid test for all of these professed well-wishers and self-appointed saviors. Firstly, the Negroes must dissolve all of their personal antagonisms and grievances. The ministers, professional persons, interested workers, labor representatives and social-work functionaries must assemble to determine how they can collectively assist the programs of the two national Negro organizations that have representation in this community. They must then resolve themselves to carry forth, in every respect, a program that will develop an impenetrable united front to the white supremacists and the economic and political reactionary groups. If this is done, the Negro will witness the flight and evacuation of many pseudo-liberals from the scene of the Negro struggle. Only the honest and sincere individuals will remain to contribute to what, in all probability, will be a successful attempt to gain a greater measure of respect and justice for the Negro living in this area.

THE PEOPLE'S OBSERVER, MAY 31, 1945

A Valuable Service

AN INTERESTING STUDY OF THE ARMY'S METHODS to promote better race relations was offered Thursday, May 31, at the Paramount theater, when the Musical Variety Show, "Kapers in Khaki," was presented by the special services division from Ft. Lewis, Wash. This show was staged primarily to encourage buying of war bonds during this seventh War Loan. As a result of its having been staged here, $1,600,000 worth of bonds were sold.

The most surprising feature about the show was a Negro, Sgt. Lloyd Pinckney. He was the director of this production. Moreover, much of the very fine music that was used for this event was arranged by him. Through the most intricate phases of the orchestral instrumentation, his baton directed a 32-piece aggregation composed of the white musicians in 359th MTS band, and the Negro musicians of the 448th ASF dance band. This feature alone developed a new recognition for the Negro on the part of the many white persons present.

There were three Negro tap dancers who were unusually proficient and adept at their routine. Rounds of applause were received by them for a marvelous performance. The Ft. Lewis Choral group consisting of both Negro and white vocalists under the direction of Sgt. Pinckney were excellent.

The show was interspersed with a riotous amount of slapstick comedy. Most gratifying to the few Negroes present, however, was the fact that it was not of the "Rochester" type, nor did any of the Negroes participate in it. In no way and by no stretch of the imagination could a Negro be charged with playing an "Uncle Tom" role in this show.

One disturbing factor, however, is that Sgt. Pinckney does not hold a commission in the army. Whites with the same ability as he possesses usually are Captains or Majors. Pinckney was educated at the New England Conservatory of Music and studied advanced educational administration at New York University. He spent more than five years touring pre-war Europe as a musician. During this time, he studied as well as performed. He has also been a school teacher and has produced creditable musicals and shows. In every respect, it seems that he qualifies for any commission that can be bestowed upon him.

There is a strong possibility that if he were granted a commission commensurate with his ability he would probably be buried in some outpost where his talents would be lost completely. This has happened many times over during this episodic war to Negroes who may have made contributions on the home front that would have improved the lot of their people in American life noticeably.

The work of Sgt. Lloyd Pinckney means far more to Negro people, as long as it rocks the portals of white supremacy and conservatism, than if he were signally honored with a distinguished commission and a viciously circumscribed talent.

THE PEOPLE'S OBSERVER, JUNE 30, 1945

Another Year Passes

THIS ISSUE MARKS THE COMPLETION of another year's operation for the *Observer.* As would be expected, during this past twelve-month period, attention has been constantly focused upon those issues of vital importance to the Negro people living in the Portland-Vancouver area. Repeatedly, analysis has been made of intricate problems affecting this group. Recommendations have been proposed from time to time which were intended to minimize the agony and suffering that comes from vicious persecution that is often leveled at this people by the forces of reaction.

In the same period, the *Observer* has centered much of its attention to evaluating the marked provincial attitudes and prejudices alive in this community. In so doing, the adherence to its stated policy was always complied with. The militant and sound position of the Observer on all issues directly related to minority people's progress has led to this publication becoming recognized and accepted as a valuable journalistic instrument by individuals and organizations interested in social progress and advancement. Commendable acknowledgements and praise for the editorial stands and news features contained in this publication for the past two years have been received from every section of the United States.

The *Observer* can proudly offer itself as one medium championing the rights of minority groups (especially the Negro people) that has consistently presented its series of protests in a strategical and socially compatible manner that often had some measure of political effectiveness. Early in its development, the guiding hands of this paper recognized that in all struggles to be waged separately from the battles to gain improvements in the work status of minority workers, caution and principle must be rigidly followed. Libelous charges, false accusations, gross exaggerations of minor social breaches and the over-emphasizing of purely subjective grievances have never been positions that could be labeled as typical of this publication. A diligent effort has been constantly put forth to give attention to all news that reflects creditably on the Negro people and other minorities. Only in instances where it appeared absolutely necessary and expedient has a purely nationalist philosophy been expounded in this paper.

Not once has the *Observer* failed to step forth and offer its assistance to all community programs and projects centered around uplift and welfare. At all times, a positive effort is exerted to prevent the development of controversies that will create conflicts and misunderstanding with other racial, religious and progressive political groups. It is without any trace of emotion or regret that the publisher of this paper adamantly refuses to assist individual Negro glory-mongers and self-sustaining egotists in their vile schemes to dupe the masses of Negroes into believing they alone are capable of devising methods for the removal of all problems that beset this oppressed people. With vigor and determination, the support of the *Observer* is consistently cast with bonafide, established protective and welfare organizations where plans for resisting the persecution of the Negro people are always well steeped in democratic and honorable procedure. It is the aim also of this paper to be in the vanguard to attack all evidences and indications of bigotry and deceit in social agencies that normally should be devoid of such chicanery.

The publisher of this paper is well aware that the role of minority peoples, Negroes in particular, in the American social structure is incomprehensible to a vast proportion of the population. For many decades, the Negro people of the United States have pleaded for just the elementary privileges of freedom. Primary requests for liberty and justice have invariably been denied. In every crevice of American life, both sophisticated and brutal discrimination are practiced against this people. There is no corner of the United States today which is devoid of prejudice and hatred toward Negroes. Consequently, the aim of this paper is to lend an interpretation of the position of the Negro in this community that may assist in the alleviation of many hardships and uncalled for humiliations.

To do this is not an easy task. In the more recent issues, there has been an unusual amount of discussion trained upon the necessity for the complete unity among the Negro welfare groups having more or less the same programs and ideologies. This phase of our work is by far the most difficult to handle. Every attempt to unify the Negro people on any matter is immediately accompanied by a corresponding development of antipathies and antagonisms, which in many instances create irreconcilable differences. It is the aim of this publication to show that people who are socially submerged, economically subjugated, oppressed, harassed and intimidated cannot expect any basic changes in their political and social status as long as silly conflicts and sharp personal distinctions are kept alive in their ranks.

In the coming year, the reactionary groups will take steps to add to the confusion that already exists among the Negro people. Many race-baiting factions will carry out plans designed to force the Negro's standard of existence to even lower levels. Discriminations will be more marked in every quarter of our local life. Discouraging as it may appear, not one Negro should permit himself to believe that any of these conditions will be remedied by emotional ravings and petty sensationalism. Careful study and diligent planning by qualified and experienced specialists, who have the staunch support and confidence of the people they are selected to serve, will offer the most promising avenues for improvement.

It is the renewed pledge of the *Observer* today to remain on the alert to guard against further social atrocities and to offer if possible sound suggestions as to how the Negro people can cooperatively assist in the many programs that will be carried out to improve their lot in America.

With this purpose in mind, your *Observer* begins another year with courage and determination in the service of the people.

THE PEOPLE'S OBSERVER, JULY 20, 1945

"Fighting For The Right To Live"

WHITE SUPREMACY RECEIVED A SENSATIONAL JOLT in a California court room last week when Benny Carter, internationally famous orchestra leader, stated while testifying July 3rd in a restricted covenant case that he considered himself a Caucasian because his ancestry beyond a certain point was mixed. This case is typical of many that have arisen in Los Angeles due to the rigid restrictive covenants that apply to minority groups in various residential sections of that city. In the past year, an unusual number of cases have been aired in the California courts to determine the legality of such restrictions.

The assertion made by Carter that he is also Caucasian and substantiated by his reference to his ancestral heritage is a valid argument that the Negro people have overlooked employing in their defense against this type of discrimination for a long time. Conservative sociologists have estimated that approximately two-thirds of the total Negro population of the United States are the products of mixed ancestry. Moreover, it is a widely accepted fact that more than 10,000 Negroes pass themselves off as whites each year, because they possess the features and physical characteristics that permit them to do so undetected. These facts serve to illustrate that the spirit of restrictive covenants is not only unconstitutional but also predicated upon a fallacy. Carter's attorney pointedly told the attorney for the plaintiff that his pink skin and white hair was proof of his racial identity. He further emphasized that blood strains are now so confused that there is a question whether positive racial identities can be established for anyone.

Often cases of this sort receive scant attention from the Negro people who are removed from the immediate scene of action. It is of prime importance that the weight of the arguments being advanced by the Negro defendants in this case be carefully scrutinized and considered. There is no Negro in America who will not eventually feel the weight of heavy oppression if such conditions are permitted to continue. Likewise, Negroes in every section of the country will be permitted a more pleasant participation in the life of the country if such restrictions are removed.

The Local Scene

In Portland the Negro people are passively witnessing the development of a first-rate ghetto with all the potentials for squalor, poverty, juvenile delinquency and crime. This project has been under construction for quite some time by the white overlords and city fathers who love to enforce ostracism and segregation upon the Negro people and other minorities. It is obvious to the most unconcerned individuals that the herding of Negroes into the district extending from the river front to Union Avenue and from Russell street to the Steel Bridge portends economic and social problems of far-reaching significance for this city.

Portland is a city where restrictive covenants are existent in practically every desirable residential district. In areas where restrictions no longer exist, the realty board and its members effect the necessary barriers to prevent Negroes from purchasing desirable property.

It has long been a widely accepted opinion among dwarf-minded whites that the presence of a minority residing in a community predominantly settled by whites results in a diminishing of property value for the nordics. This strange economic illusion, of course, is created by the whites themselves and for this reason should not cause any alarm in minority groups' thinking on this matter. If all residential districts were open for bona fide American citizens to live in, it would be impossible for minority baiters to present discriminatory economic arguments against Negroes holding residence in any particular section.

The same arguments, reasons and logistics that will win the right of Negroes to live where they are able to buy in Los Angeles will serve as basic and irrefutable contentions to bring the same privileges in Portland and elsewhere. The problem of furnishing adequate housing on the west coast for the vast population that has developed since the beginning of the war looms large in the minds of many postwar planners. The struggle to get a more equitable housing arrangement for all minorities will require the undivided attention of all socially conscious minority group leaders. Plans must be made now to prepare an effective strategy for tackling the primary phases of this issue. The case of Benny Carter offers many valuable guide posts.

THE PEOPLE'S OBSERVER, JULY 31, 1945

A Necessary Step Forward

[On March 31, 1945, *The People's Observer* wrote the following editorial:]

"IT IS NOW TIME FOR THE NEGRO PEOPLE of this area to take stock of the social and political efforts that have been made for improving their status here in the past five years. In viewing the present state of affairs from this angle, it becomes shockingly obvious that this group of people has no representatives to date who are holding responsible and authoritative positions that would tend to develop a more serious and appreciative feeling for Negroes on the part of other groups residing in this community.

At this writing, there is not one Negro holding a full-fledged policeman's job in the city of Portland. Many explanation have been offered for this appalling laxity. Some are plausible, and others entirely unsatisfactory to a people that in peace and in war have demonstrated that they are capable of assuming obligations of every conceivable nature and discharging any and all duties efficiently.

In some quarters the thought has been advanced that there are prejudiced and racially biased individuals dominating the operation of the local police department here. The persons are alleged to be bitterly opposed to the extensions of full police authority to any Negro regardless of his qualifications. Many attempts to circumvent any such possibility have been forthcoming. The use of temporary Negro police officers lacking in training and ability in communities tenanted largely by Negroes is an excellent illustration of this.

These functionaries are not empowered to carry out assignments on a basis comparable to that of men who have full police authority. Consequently, it is impossible for them to have self-respect, respect from the people, or the respect of white policemen who know the limited extent of the Negro functionaries' authority, preparation and training.

On the other hand, it is claimed that Negro men of good moral character, with fair educational background and within the age limits prescribed under the civil service regulations, have never made application for appointment on the Portland police force. The truth of the utterance may be more far-reaching than can be imagined. Anyway, there are many Negro men who have established residence in this community while working in defense plants and war industries. A number of these workers are qualified in every way to fill police positions, that is, if the civil service requirements hold no specific briefs for color.

As the war in this area gradually diminishes in quantity, it would be wise for as many Negroes as possible to investigate and study the possibilities of becoming police officers. Negro welfare organizations and liberal elements from among the white population will champion the right of this acceptance. No longer can the Negro wait for these opportunities to be presented. Initiative and determination must be applied to create them."

THIS EDITORIAL WAS STUDIED AND CONSIDERED SERIOUSLY by both Negro and white citizens of this community who were in a position to do something about the issue involved. Consequently, out of their combined efforts comes a most encouraging announcement.

According to information received by the staff of this publication from authoritative sources, special police officer, Captain Harry S. Payton, has been notified that his recommendations for six Negro men to assume the duties of regular policemen on the Portland police force will be honored. The men approved by Officer Payton will be given the regular prescribed training required for all full-fledged officers serving with the Portland Police department and will be vested with the same authority. In the election held November 7, 1944, Commissioner Bowes stated to the publisher of this paper that he favored the integration of qualified Negro personnel into all brackets of civil service employment and functions in Portland municipal life. He expressed his belief that Negro policemen could perform a valuable service to the citizens of Portland. He promised that if he were re-elected he would encourage the inclusion of Negroes in this important capacity. Commissioner Bowes kept this promise and The Observer takes pride in the fact that its political judgement has brought social benefits to the Negro people here.

Officials of the Portland Police department have been pleased over the many valuable services that Captain Payton and his veteran guard and patrol auxiliary police unit have rendered during these critical war years. The performances of Officer Anderson Alexander and others have demonstrated conclusively that the Negro can carry out police assignments with dignity and efficiency.

The *Observer* is proud that it is the first to make public this fact to the Negro people of Portland. It is the intention of the staff of this paper to assist in every way possible the full integration of the Negro into every field of endeavor wherein an opportunity is offered to create a greater degree of recognition and appreciation for all minority groups residing in America.

THE PEOPLE'S OBSERVER, AUG. 17, 1945

For Better Understanding

THE NEGRO COMMUNITY in the Williams Avenue area is slowly regaining some of its equilibrium after having witnessed a near riot, which resulted in the severe beating of a Negro police officer and the shooting of one Negro soldier and arrest of three others who were in Portland to celebrate the war's ending. This incident, while being just a by-product of larger social ills in this city, has caused great concern among Negro citizens. This was the only outburst of emotion displayed so far by Negroes here since notice was given of Japanese capitulation. Many Negro people are fearful that the ending of this global war will mark the beginning of a new series of atrocities to be heaped upon them.

At this time, interest is to be concentrated on a significant matter that has been expressed in a limited sense in this column before. It is absolutely necessary that qualified, well-trained and equipped Negro policemen be placed on the Portland Police force. Likewise, the white officers in this police department should be rigidly schooled in the science and techniques of dealing with minority groups – especially Negroes. This incident, which occurred last Wednesday, is just one of the many that is liable to happen here unless a conscientious effort is put forth by those in authority to alleviate the causes for repetition.

Few white people actually understand the psychic twists and ofttimes spontaneous transitions that take place in the minds of Negroes. Rarely do police officers ever have an opportunity or the personal interest to learn what racial restrictions, prejudice, ridicule, persecution, wholesale oppression, flagrant brutality, consistent court room injustices, exploitation, poverty, squalor and abject contempt can do to the everyday thinking of Negroes. Unless there is a program inaugurated to bring about this type of understanding, no improvements will be noticed in the settling of problems affecting Negroes during this new era.

Negro men in the armed services, particularly those who have been exposed to the tyrannical supervision of southern reared officers and commanders, are in all probability suffering from varying degrees of hysteria. These soldiers regard the war's end as a blessing and as a refuge from the hatred and venom to which they have been subjected while offering their lives and efforts for the defense of their fatherland. The abuses to which most Negro soldiers are subjected in battle areas and in the United States is resented more than death is feared. Every Negro that has worn a U.S. uniform in World War II is determined that his return to a civilian existence will not be dotted with the same persecution as when he entered the service. These outlooks and attitudes lead to the development of pronounced and extremely magnified revolutionary and rebellious tendencies. As a result, Negro servicemen will quickly show their resentment to many things the average citizen will overlook. Moreover, every opportunity to show their disrespect for white supremacy and their hatred for a lack of equal opportunities in all spheres of American life is readily utilized. It is pathetic, but true, that in most instances, what they assume is a logical retaliation for injustices is in reality a misdirected insult without any reasonable premise. Many times over, the stream of their assaults has found another Negro for the target. This is what happened Wednesday when the Negro soldiers found themselves at odds with a Negro police officer who was summoned to quell a disturbance which it had been reported the soldiers were creating.

This brings us to the more deplorable part of the incident. The Negro officer had called for further police assistance to quiet a condition that was swiftly reaching a riot stage. When the white officers arrived on the scene, they found the Negro officer using his gun to stall off an attack by his soldier adversaries. The white officers proceeded to disarm the Negro policeman, but they did not give him protection from the group of men attacking him. In fact, the white officers are alleged to have walked away, whereupon the mob-minded soldiers closed in and beat the Negro officer severely. His escaping from their clutches was due to his agility and presence of mind. Much to the disgust of onlookers, after the badly bruised and bleeding officer made his way to the squad car of the white officers, they delayed more than twenty minutes (clocked time) before they carried him to the hospital. It is generally believed that these officers deliberately delayed taking the Negro officer away from the scene of action for ulterior reasons known only to themselves. This is the first time an incident has ever been brought to our attention where officers of the law outright refused to give protection and coverage to a brother officer.

Not more than twenty days past, Captain Keegan told this writer that this Negro officer had distinguished himself as a policeman and had rendered valuable service to the city of Portland. If this is true, surely an investigation will be conducted to learn why the Negro officer was not protected by his white allies. It is hard for us to conceive of a companion Negro officer walking away under the same conditions. It would have been quite a blemish on the Negro soldiers and the Negro community if the negligence of these white policemen had resulted in a mob murder involving only Negro participants. Much rejoicing would have taken place in that circle of whites who wish to see Portland's police department kept clear of Negro functionaries.

Whether it is ever recognized or not, it behooves the Negro citizens of Portland to remember that certain elements in this city have labored long and contemplated deeply on making this community a ghetto. The militant and positive manner in which Harry Payton has fought criminal elements in this locality has kept this community a livable place for its workers, their families and children.

THE PEOPLE'S OBSERVER, AUGUST 31, 1945

Letters to the Editor: Demand For An Investigation

(Following is a letter written by a local attorney in which logical reasons are advanced for all decent, law-abiding citizens to demand an investigation by the district attorney's office of the murder of Ervin Jones, Negro resident of Guilds Lake. Jones was killed in his home by mistake by white detectives who claimed they were looking for another Negro guilty of murder. The officers later found the man they were searching for. W.H.M.)

To the Editor: May I call attention to the apparent absence of official investigation into the recent killing of Ervin Jones, an innocent Negro, in his Guilds Lake home by members of the Portland police department. Newspaper accounts state that about 2 A.M. three detectives went to Jones' residence in search of a person allegedly there who was wanted for a murder. Two detectives covered the front of the home, one the rear. Refused admittance, the detectives in the front broke open the door, the one in the rear a window. At this point, Jones, believing the police were robbers, although they claim they said they were officers, allegedly fired shots at the detectives in the front while the detective in the rear shot Jones in the back and killed him. Search of the premises then disclosed that the person sought by the officers was not in Jones' home. A few hours later, the detective who shot Jones was summarily exonerated by his superior officer.

Oregon laws, section 23-416, specifically enumerate four conditions under which police officers are justified in taking life. From the published accounts of the incident, there seems to be at least reasonable grounds for suspecting that none of these conditions obtained. Section 26-1530 permits breaking into a person's home to execute a warrant for arrest if refused admittance, but I have no information that the police had any such warrant in this case. Section 26-1532 and 26-1533 permit forcible entry without such warrant only if Jones had been the guilty person or the person actually sought for arrest.

I do not believe the public should be satisfied with such summary dismissal of this case by the detectives' superior officer. Jones had as much legal right to protection in his home as any other person in this community. Certainly the least that should be done when an admittedly innocent man is killed is that a thorough investigation be conducted by the district attorney's office. If the officers were legally justified in taking life, they should be exonerated. If not, they should be indicted and prosecuted.

Irvin Goodman
Spalding Building, Portland, Oregon

THE PEOPLE'S OBSERVER, SEPT. 20, 1945

Oregon's "Justifiable Homicide"

PLANS ARE RAPIDLY TAKING SHAPE to have the wife and family of Ervin Jones, Negro, who was killed in his house approximately a month ago at Guilds Lake by Portland detectives, allegedly seeking another criminal suspect, return to Portland for a District Attorney's investigation.

Welfare groups and citizens interested in a just and impartial settlement of the circumstances surrounding the Jones killing believe that the testimony of Mrs. Jones will play an important part in clarifying for the public the methods employed by local police when they are dispatched to apprehend a Negro suspected of crime.

Jones was the father of five dependent children. He was partially insured, but his family cannot collect this insurance, because Detective Captain Fleming declared this killing a justifiable homicide and exonerated the officers responsible for this shooting. The insurance carried by Jones is not payable under this condition. The facts in the case have shown so far:

1. The detectives did not reveal to Jones that they were Portland police.
2. They attempted to force entrance into his home.
3. They were not armed with a warrant for his arrest.
4. They were seeking in reality another person who did not know Jones and who did not resemble him in the slightest degree.
5. Jones never fired into the door as charged – he fired one shot

above the door near the ceiling. Jones was shot in the back.

6. Jones never knew until he was taking his dying breath that the men he was resisting within the confines of his house were policemen.
7. The taking of Jones' life was ruthless in the most elementary sense. The detective who fired the death dealing bullet had to shoot directly across a bed where two babies were lying, frightened and screaming. The lives of these children, being endangered, did not deter this officer from his murderous impulse.
8. The officers later found the criminal for whom they were searching. He admitted his guilt and denied ever having known Jones.
9. Officers' reason for going to Jones' house is alleged to be that another Negro told them they could find the criminal they were seeking there. Obviously, no further investigation was made or believed necessary.
10. The life of a Negro is obviously as cheap here as in the hinterlands below the Mason-Dixon line. Instead of viewing an officer of the law as a protector and a friend, Negroes will soon begin to feel that they are human carriers of brutality and death.

The killing of Jones shows what can happen to a Negro as a result of Portland Police not being given courses in racial tolerance and understanding, as was suggested by the City Club Committee, when the committee members interviewed Chief of Police Harry M. Niles. The committee reported, however, that Chief Niles showed a lack of enthusiasm for such a program.

THE PEOPLE'S OBSERVER, OCT. 10, 1945

Learn a New Lesson

NOT MUCH ATTENTION HAS BEEN GIVEN to those factors that are directly responsible for many problems that now beset the Negro people here relative to employment and housing. The time is getting nearer when many persons will begin to realize that these two matters should have received serious study and positive actions long before the war moved into its final stages. Many Negroes have become unemployed in recent weeks due to war plant cutbacks and closings. Because of gross neglect on the part of the Negro people generally on such issues, problems of a most perplexing nature have been created for the panacea bringers and masterminds to solve.

For those who feel that they have the experience and ability to deal with these issues successfully, there are certain lessons of the past that may well be kept in mind.

It is worthwhile to recall the stupidity which the long-time Negro residents of this area displayed in matters concerned with improving the general status of Negro workers. The records will show that only an infinitesimal percent of the pre-war Negro population expended any efforts toward collaborating with aggressive and militant migrant Negro war workers in their many struggles to bring about better working conditions, job opportunities and promotion privileges. Frequently, persons will be discovered parading themselves before the unknowing as great benefactors of their people. Truthfully, the contributions most of these individuals made during the entire war was to keep the enmity-filled whites and others of the opposition informed on the next intended move of frenzied Negroes seeking an immediate release from oppression.

This sort of activity was carried on for many reasons. The chief ones were, first, that the established Negro Portlanders attempted to be sophisticated and astute by echoing without question the vile utterances of prejudiced whites who resented and resisted the influx of Negro war workers. Second, the older residents felt no loyalty or allegiance to the newcomers, even though their positions in American life were similar. In fact, an enormous amount of the unfavorable propaganda that was circulated in white quarters against the incoming Negroes was done because the self-styled good Negroes of Portland had voiced their distaste over having more of their people move into the community. This ridiculous attitude was revelled in, since it appeared that the "old timers" were safe from any of the economic mishaps that might suddenly confront the newer arrivals.

Believe it or not, at one time Negro residents actually assembled in meetings and discussion groups to decry the infiltration of more Negro citizens into the same community. In the meantime, the new Negroes were already compelled to wrestle with reactionary white trade union bosses and a hostile local white population for the right to help win the war. As a result, now that unity among the Negro people is exceedingly necessary, many members of this group will find themselves unable to become reconciled to accepting the overtures and adjustment that must be made between conflicting factions.

Thus we perceive the crux of the major problem now existent on the local scene: Will it be possible to have the many cliques of a disintegrated and confused Negro population reach the point that they can dissolve differences that have all the symptoms of being flaming antagonisms?

The basic program to be launched now to offset further accentuation of these previously discussed ills is one that will be designed to teach Negroes in every walk of life that their real struggles are not against one another.

THE OBSERVER, OCT. 31, 1945

Preparation for Abnormalcy

IN SOME QUARTERS where this paper logically looks for favoritism and approval, there have come burning criticisms due to an opinion advanced in the last editorial. It will be recalled that the said editorial was based upon the inevitable confusion and mental disruption that overwhelms Negroes, because they are so often the victims of social misfortunes such as the one which befell the family of Erwin Jones. Herewith quoted is the paragraph which has disturbed some sincere friends of the Negro people.

"These ridiculous and despicable techniques of dealing with the unfortunates in our national confines have caused catastrophic social convulsions in the thinking of the Negro people. It has left them in the depths of depravity. Basically, but not admittedly, there are only two consuming mental dispositions shared by the majority of Negroes toward white America. One is hatred—the other is fear. Both of these are seats of terrific psychic affectations. The minds of Negroes, like warped wheels on a bent axle, revolve on a continuous axis of hate and grave apprehension. This leaves them without the ability to make decisions of a social import strong enough to offset the extreme racism of a numerical majority that is crazed, too, by its fanatical adherence to philosophies of racial supremacy and purity."

Instead of apologizing for these electrifying remarks, this is an honest intention to qualify them. The long time existent conglomeration of ignominies, proscriptions, prejudices and discriminations to which the Negro people have been subjected in every quarter of our civilization are not conducive to the development of a philosophy of "brotherly love."

Due to long years of spirit-crushing abuse, intimidation, persecution and torture, Negroes find it impossible to have mental compatibility with American whites who speak of liberty and equality for all men. Special privileges and opportunities for the fortunate, exploitation of the weak and defenseless, aggrandizement for the strong without restraint, have caused Negroes to suffer psychological and social atrocities incessantly.

In the administration of justice, denial has been the keynote when concerned with the Negro. Court procedures throughout the nation are notoriously unfair to Negroes.

In fact, this is an abnormal nation that has contributed greatly to the abnormalcy of the world. White people thinking as they do about the relative inferiority of other racial groups and professing to be the vanguard of democratic thought and ideals, offer one of the most splendid examples of mass schizophrenics. It is impossible for a Negro to develop into a normal person in this world of overwhelming social contradictions and under a system of government that is filled to the brim with political contraries. What's more, there are no changes in sight.

THE OBSERVER, DEC. 10, 1945

Preparation for Abnormalcy (#3 of 6)

MORE AND MORE NEGROES are expressing their true resentment to this system under which many of them perish. A few Negroes have taken uncompromising positions in their efforts to surmount the wall of prejudice that encompasses them. Some of the stands that have been taken on issues concerned with liberty and opportunity will send a ringing challenge that may emanate from within minority groups down through the years to all fighters for freedom. To be truthful and straightforward, the tangible gains Negroes have made in their battles against American persecution are not many. Most of those individuals who have fought courageously and valiantly for changes in the social order have seen their programs repeatedly suppressed to a point of despair.

Daily, Negro servicemen are returning to their homes in this country. Daily, these men are learning there have been no basic changes in the pattern of life they have customarily been relegated to throughout the existence of America. As a result, they are prone to show a type of indignation that defies description. Their psychological reactions and physical relations to this grave injustice may be understood by many persons in similar categories, but in all probability there will be few, if any, realistic interpretations lent to the resultant human eruptions that are sure to spread over this land like a deadly plague.

The most regrettable feature is that in their moments of greatest disillusionment, circumstances will provoke these men to show vicious resentment. Most often this will be done in Negro quarters. Because they live and move in a limited and circumscribed society, the persons closest to their activities will be the first to suffer from their social irregularities. Already many incidents have occurred to indicate that the Negro war veterans are not satisfied with what they are finding to be their role in American democracy. At the same time, no one can deny that many of these demonstrations were carried out in a manner that developed even more contempt and disrespect for Negroes on the part of whites.

Meanwhile, the fact cannot be ignored that white people do not actually comprehend the acute psychic twists and spontaneous transitions which take place in the minds of Negroes. Rarely do they ever have an opportunity, or the interest, to learn what racial restrictions, prejudice, ridicule, persecution, wholesale oppression, flagrant brutality, consistent court room injustices, exploitation, poverty, squalor and a submarginal citizenship rating can do to the thinking and attitudes of Negroes. Unless there are programs inaugurated to bring about this type of understanding, no improvements will be forthcoming in the settling of problems affecting the Negro in this community or in national life.

THE OBSERVER, MARCH-APRIL 1946

Editorial

IT HAS BECOME OBVIOUS that the activities of some local welfare organizations are not intended to benefit the Negro people. Yet, in most instances, it is this minority which organizational spokesmen proclaim to be the focal point of their concern and attention. During the past year, the Negro people here have been passive about the malpractices of most of these self-styled panacea bringers. Now that many evils of their social maneuvers are beginning to loom large in the eyes of the public, and their efforts are beginning to show in terms of a general wave of retrogression, it seems this is an appropriate time to call the attention of our readers to the dangers that lurk behind the professed intentions of insincere welfare functionaries.

The bulk of the Negro leadership that has come from the professional and white collar element in this area has been instrumental at various times, through its selfish motives, in bringing about serious social reverses for the whole group. Often, controversies are developed to a point that progress is completely stultified. Expressions of conceit, envy and greed by a few stellar personages have definitely arrested Negro advancement. Moreover, these same individuals, while expounding in a most bombastic manner their pretended beliefs in the equality of all mankind, have positively been guilty of resorting to RED BAITING, promoting class consciousness and attempting to create divisive and defined stratas within the ranks of the Negro people.

Such deceit is a fatal blow to unity!

Thus it is perceived: the main battle of the progressive Negro group must be centered upon exposing and condemning the Negro who measures his own progress in terms of his ability to thwart the social and economic growth of the masses of his people. In fact, it would be far better if all such turncoats were liquidated. Negroes who day after day are committing unforgivable atrocities against their people, and who are violating every standard of ethics in their relationships with their fellowmen, are doing so by cloaking themselves with the blanket of camouflage acquired by participating in and belonging to progressive Negro organizations. In the meantime, these persons are giving atomic energy to the flagrant practices of segregating the Negro people and other minorities; promoting the heaping of various slurs, insults and abuses upon people whose means of resistance and retaliation are feeble; stimulating vast amounts of dissension, and developing strong and bitter antipathies between groups that should be closest in the struggle for minority group uplift.

In addition to this, it is now almost impossible for a Negro RANK AND FILE leadership to emerge here. Yet no one can deny that this is definitely more necessary from a standpoint of Negro welfare than the WINDOW-DRESSING LEADERSHIP now being furnished by CAUCASIAN-LOVING Negro agents.

Lest it be forgotten, the Negro community is now populated largely by Negroes who have migrated into Portland since the sailing of the first "Kaiser Caravan." Many of these persons are from localities where it did not require excessive preparation in universities to detect the chicanery that Negro representatives use in dealing for whites with other Negroes. Many of these persons are already commenting that it is NOW extremely difficult to bridge the vast social and economic chasms that have been created because one Negro has attempted to establish himself as an "Ultimate Authority" on all matters pertaining to the Negro people.

This individual has proceeded to show in meetings and writings that the Negro people are in a turmoil because of the distrust and confusion existing between factions and cliques. His comments on such matters are not backed with experience. Such remarks are ridiculous and provocative of further disruption. This is what his white supporters accept and evidently desire. By the way, the presence of this type of Negro in any community is always at the request of the white disciples for the sophisticated promotion of the system of Jim Crow.

It is mandatory that Negroes be taught to realize that an individual Negro is not their leader merely because the individual claims such a position. Nor is a prestige-crazed Negro the leader of the Negro people, here or anywhere else, solely because white people designated him as such. This is the way all "QUISLINGS" get their start.

Respect for Negroes claiming leadership status should be determined by their diligent participation in actual drives and crusades to compel a halt to the ruthless maltreatment of the Negro people in all phases of American life. Tea sippings, cocktails and honey-coated words in stereotyped closed circles do not bring any new opportunities except in the boudoir. Then it's just animalism!

Another thing to notice is the respect and support the white sup-

The Observer cover, April-May 1946,
"Spring Spirit," by Ruby Wright

porters and board members of organizations allegedly serving Negro interests give to actual protests which may be voiced unintentionally by their Negro stooge. Methodically, these persons sit tight-lipped, not objecting to any atrocity. Never is a position taken that requires a resolution committing these fine white persons to any given stand or action.

To face the facts presented herewith, and those that will follow with more details, will exact a terrible emotional toll from a large number of persons. However, it is impossible for the Negro people and other minorities to gain the freedom they desperately seek unless it is demonstrated that four-flushers and renegades run the risk of EXPOSURE and OSTRACISM immediately upon detection.

THE OBSERVER, APRIL-MAY 1946

Editorials

MENTION HAS BEEN MADE BY THIS PUBLICATION many times over of the vicious suppressionist mechanisms utilized by the white city fathers under the guise of benevolence for the poor, bewildered Negro. Often it has been stated that the unfortunate role to which Negroes are relegated here is no mere accident – it is deliberate and well planned by those who chart economic destinies in this area. Chief concern of this discourse, however, is to explain further the functions of NEGRO agents who make the ulterior intentions of white reactionaries a living reality.

At one time, this publication went on record supporting a contention that national welfare organizations might be more effective in carrying forth the struggles to better the conditions of groups living submarginally in this community. Frankly, it was believed that such outfits would be able to set up concrete objectives. Incidents and events of the past few months have caused sharp reversals in this attitude.

Slowly, but definitely, it is being realized that skillful Negro informers have been imported into this community to study and reveal in detail the various limitations that surround Negro activity in every field. This is done so that the "Professional Negro Lovers" may be able to discredit with finesse and polish all efforts of a few progressive Negroes to raise the social and economic standards of their people. These services are valuable to white persons who aim to capitalize upon the current efforts of minorities to gain recognition and new opportunities. They use these attempts as mediums to catapult themselves into dominant and authoritative community posts. They find it profitable to know what significance Negroes attach to cocktail lappings and petty interracial conferences that carry a flimsy social import. Frequently, we find these whites through their man "Friday" arranging affairs of this sort where interesting practices of acceptance and exclusion of various other Negro personages are carried out. This is done in a veiled and super-sophisticated manner. To say that such tactics create a condition of total disruption throughout the ranks of the Negro population is just putting it mildly, for sure.

It is the height of folly to watch these Negro stooges "bow and scrape" before even the humblest white person. At the same time, these multipersonality figures will bleat long and loud to Negroes of their self-sufficiency and independence of thought and action.

These perforated emissaries for Caucasian supremacy are gifted with the techniques for instigating the utilization of weak personages in important tasks of struggle. This is one sure method whereby they can create a general impression in this community and even in national circles that there is crying need for their personal services here. Often there are subtle alignments made between some agency fronters and other bureaus who claim an interest in the problems besetting minorities. This usually amounts to nothing more than stimulating undue publicity for *sagacious bureaucrats.* Sometimes it may also give rise to a wide display of mutual admiration between the aligned groups whose major functions amount to nothing more than glorified, domestic service outlets.

It has been reliably reported that an organizational representative had the executive board of the organization he fronts for the "Great White Father" pass a resolution restricting the business of any board meeting from being discussed with the general membership. As a result, many strong and militant Negro personages have turned a cold shoulder to the work of this organization. *They are distrustful of its motives and its leadership.*

Experienced political functionaries and even ordinary social thinkers are well aware that veiled, sly and apologetic references to the political affiliations of progressive thinkers are always uttered with malice aforethought. Yet, this insidious practice is part and parcel of one individual's daily routine. Regrettable is the fact that not one of the persons who has been smeared with these vicious rumors has ever been guilty of exploiting minority peoples for personal advancement. *Is it possible that the propagandist can make the same assertion?*

In this life and death struggle for freedom and equality, many methods of procedure are employed by the reactionary elements to deal the KNOCK-OUT BLOW to any distinct program for the uplift of Negroes that may appear as an end in itself. Since the powers-that-be in this community are not sure what attitudes the Negro people share toward the atrocious limitations affecting them, it is imperative that a *Negro quisling* be provided for this community. This is done so that strong and durable demonstrations against the horrible conditions here will not be able to gather momentum and go unchecked. Remember the shipyard organization?

Many serious repercussions and implications can result from this. As long as Negro functionaries are identified with the forces that control and keep minorities in mendicant positions, it will be impossible for the Negro people to lay plans and formulate programs to resist the variety of social, economic and political approaches that will be used to subjugate them completely. *This makes the new peace perilous.*

Not once has this publication failed to step forth and offer its assistance to all community programs and projects centered around uplift and welfare. At all times a positive effort is exerted to prevent the development of controversies which bring about conflicts and misunderstandings with other racial, religious and progressive groups. Consistent with this position has been the adoption of an adamant stand insofar as refusing to assist self-sustaining egotists in their attempts to have the masses of Negroes believe they alone are capable of devising the methods for the removal of problems that beset this oppressed people. With vigor and determination, support is lent to protective groups of all types, regardless of personality composition, whose plans are well steeped in democratic and honorable procedure. Whenever bigotry, evasion and deceit are evident, it is our desire to be listed in the vanguard of the counter forces that seek to *resist, attack, and destroy.*

THE OBSERVER, MAY-JUNE 1946

For Posterity

IN ALL UTTERANCES OF THE TYPE TO FOLLOW, it is to be understood that there will be drawn sharp controversial lines. These opinions are not expressed in order to create marked divisions in personal attitudes. It is with a sincere sense of duty and loyalty to one's friend that these logical and unembellished evaluations of the community worth of a deceased individual are now being mentioned.

Charlie Garrett was a good fellow.

Charlie believed in his ability to master the situation at hand. As one of his close friends has put it, "Little Charlie never came face to face with any circumstances that he couldn't control." His mind could conceive of no problem too difficult to solve, especially if to find the solution was the means of making progress.

There has never been a welfare program that Charlie failed to support or give contributions if he was approached for assistance. More often his generosity in this respect was voluntary. There are no persons of any group to contradict this.

In the normal friction of living, the inconsistencies of human nature rendered it well nigh to impossible for any individual to move along life's way without making some enemies. All Charlie ever sought out of life from friend or foe was an even chance.

From the very depths of a business depression and near poverty, Charlie labored diligently and untiringly toward the realization of his cherished goal, which was to establish a business in Portland that would be, in every sense, comparable to any similar establishments, regardless of ownership, in this area. In this respect, Charlie's efforts have reflected creditably upon the business acumen of the Negro residing in the Northwest.

Charlie was increasingly subjected to all of the hardships that are customarily encountered by Negroes in business. The opening of the Madrona Radio & Record Shop at North Williams and Broadway was his triumph over these obstacles. Charlie was already giving serious consideration to exploring some of the more intricate phases of this business. He was to produce, if possible, some of the merchandise offered for sale in his record shop. We are inclined to believe that these plans were nearing maturity at the time of his death.

The Portland Observer, a militant weekly newspaper first appearing in Portland in December, 1938, included Charlie as a silent partner. It was Charlie's firm conviction that this organ was

Cover, The Observer, June-July 1946, "McClendon & Son" by Ruby Wright.

necessary if the people at large were to know of the problems besetting minorities in this area. Unlike many individuals who merely said they felt a paper was needed, Charlie stepped forth and helped to create one. Action and deeds have always been the methods by which Charlie indicated his belief in any program or venture.

Among his acquaintances, Charlie had many loyal friends. These persons are found in every walk of life. Many of them will suffer an irreparable loss now that he is no longer active among them.

The Observer takes pride in the fact that it is one of the progressive news mediums in this state. In relating a few of the noble aspects of "Little Charlie's" progressive life, we are conscious of the fact we offer to the world the only lasting and enduring public record of his ambitions and activities. We would rather, much rather to be honest, that the circumstance had never arisen wherein a loyal supporter need be eulogized. However, we are honored that this publication is the instrument in which memories of the worthy attributes of a valiant and courageous friend may be recounted. Long after critical voices are stilled and their echoes are inaudible, the previously inscribed passages guarantee that the honorable features of "Little Charlie's" life will be preserved.

THE OBSERVER, JULY-AUGUST 1946

Un-American

INCESSANT RIDICULE AND CONDEMNATION is being leveled by progressive forces at the wide assortment of brutalities which are part and parcel of life for non-white groups residing in the United States. In the main, it seems there is a distinct effort put forth to label every incident of discrimination, every act of torture and persecution within the confines of this country as un-American. Apologetically, one can understand that a mind inspired with a strong concept of justice and a firm belief in bourgeois democratic ideals may falsely interpret this to be traditionally American.

This idea is advanced by misleading publicity of all types. Any historical review will reveal that these concepts were accepted and practiced by hordes of humanity and were also part of the national life of countries whose heritage and history date back to ancient ages.

The American nation is a nation of political contradictions and social inequities. Consequently, the broad mass of its people are social misfits and psychologically unbalanced. This affliction cuts through every racial, cultural, religious, political and social barrier that has been erected.

For example, a horrible war that was allegedly fought for the erstwhile FOUR FREEDOMS took a severe toll in American life and limb. The sacrifices made by the people of the nation to carry this war from a state of violent destruction to the present stage of temporary passitivity has not taught them any noticeable lessons of tolerance and consideration for minority peoples.

Throughout the shooting war years, Negroes in this United States have been the victims of the most gruesome brutalities ever to be conjured by the human mind. Negro servicemen who have returned to this country have learned that there are no basic changes in the deplorable pattern of life to which they have customarily been relegated throughout this nation's existence. As a result, many of them are meeting grim deaths, because they are furiously indignant. In retaliating against the awesome power of subjugation and virtual slavery that is demanded of them in many quarters of the nation, they become the victims of mob massacres.

Incidents such as those associated with Columbia, Tenn., Aiken, S.C., Monroe, Ga., and Athens, Ala., make the words AMERICA and HELL synonymous. Actually, it is a crime to be a Negro living in any section of the universe that comes under American or British influence.

Lynchings are again on the incline. Court room injustices have remained notoriously high. The time-worn adage of White America that "No Negro has any rights which a White man is bound to respect," has not been repudiated as yet. Every law passed in this land supposedly to afford protection and security to Negroes is flaunted with contempt by arrogant whites upon the slightest provocation. However, these things are pictured as un-American! Don't Believe It.

Here in Portland, there are political functionaries who acknowledge now that these things can happen here. Are they kidding? Don't ever forget the Ervin Jones case and the white-washed coroner's inquest. This will forever be a farce insofar as legal lynchings and investigations are concerned. Negroes who have lived in the North and the South feel that by comparison, the Gestapo of this municipality runs that of any southern city a close second.

There are innumerable groups in this area professing an interest in the plight of unfortunates. Many of them claim to foresee the possibilities of serious racial clashes if the mayor continues to ignore all of the warning signals as he has done in the past. Many civic and politically conscious individuals are hopeful that the police department will become an instrument of friendliness and protection to Negro citizens now that the direction of this bureau is again under the leadership of Chief L. V. Jenkins. Suggestions from many groups and agencies encouraging emphatic race-relations training programs for police officers are now rapidly forthcoming. Such plans may be vigorously objected to by Ku Klux Klansmen in this vicinity. However, if these objections are brought out openly, progressive citizens may find it possible to convince the public at large that such action is necessary, if atrocities that are perpetrated against underprivileged people are to be alleviated.

(To be continued)

THE OBSERVER VOL. 5, NO. 7, JULY-AUGUST 1946

Still Waiting

FOR A LONG TIME, SORELY NEEDED SOCIAL ADJUSTMENTS and remedial measures have been overdue in minority group circles here. Most of the changes that have been previously cited as necessary have not been instituted, much less effected. Many examples can be offered to illustrate the marked inconveniences and handicaps that contribute greatly to the misery which goes hand in hand with living as a Negro.

In the latter part of 1942, the need for housing for Negroes in the Portland-Vancouver area had become desperately acute. Federal War Housing projects were in the construction stage during this period, and residential districts where Negroes could live in this community were dangerously over-crowded. At this time, a local daily paper published a full-page study of the increase in Negro population. It was shown that more than 6,000 new Negro inhabitants were being forced to try to find living quarters in a 25-block neighborhood and a few westside hotels formerly owned by Japanese.

(Around this time a special committee consisting of Negroes holding established residence in Portland met with Mayor Riley to discuss the problem of Negro housing. Some of these persons advocated the concentration of incoming Negroes in the previously stated confines. The idea carried.)

There were no recreational facilities to take care of this heavily increased Negro population. Even after the opening in 1943 of the Vanport and Guilds Lake housing projects (the only two in which Negroes could live), there was still a problem for Negroes in securing available housing as rapidly as it was needed, even though units were available.

The problem of housing for ex-servicemen and their families has taken on the semblance of a national catastrophe. The local situation is at best a dilemma. Moreover, there have been no noticeable advantages gained by the majority of persons desiring better housing and sanitation who have lived here through the bitter war years.

There are still in effect the many sophisticated restrictions that prohibit the movement and participation of Negroes and other minorities in civic life. The use of Negroes as police officers with full authority has yet to become a reality. This is very necessary if there is to be adequate police protection for crime prevention. Apprehension after crime is committed does not reflect creditably upon minority group communities. Besides, no really consistent and dependable program has been laid to incorporate derogatory acts and law violations committed by minority members into regular streams of publicity without placing emphasis upon the group to which the violator belongs. This condition should be changed, and could be, if influential whites who are interested in interracial goodwill were to protest actively to local metropolitan papers against such practices.

Contrary to opinions advanced by wishful thinkers, many Negro war workers have remained in this area to become a stable part of this community. A conservative estimate places the total number of Negroes in this area at 18,000.

Job opportunities for many of these persons are very limited. In fact, the ratio of Negroes per one thousand unemployed is in extreme disproportion to that of whites.

It takes no special social preparation for one to recognize that the Negro problem is about the most vital issue on the American scene today. This has been further accentuated because Negro and white interests became closely interwoven during the war. Separation of these interests is utterly impossible in this postwar era. To change this, however, reactionary elements are tenaciously clinging to ideas and practices that prevent further Negro gains in the direction of equality and freedom. Regrettable, but irrefutable, is the fact that to offset this, minorities will need weapons of far greater potency than those associated with mail order race relations and mutual admiration conferences. This is especially true if Negroes are ever to improve their present status.

THE OBSERVER, SEPTEMBER 1946

Gestapo Kiss-Off

MOST NEGROES ARE WELL AWARE by this time that the police department of the municipality is not supposed to function in their behalf, especially if the complaints leading to police intervention involve a white inhabitant.

For this reason, the following basic truths are appearing with the hope and intention that the obviously submerged sense of justice and fair play of a few city functionaries will be ruffled if not revived.

Recently, a Negro parent who is also a home owner and taxpayer who did not just come here on Kaiser's Caravan, reported to the police that an adult degenerate white male had made an unsuccessful attempt to attack her four-year-old son. Substantiating the complaint were white and Negro neighbors who were eyewitnesses to the incident. A full description of the criminal was furnished as well as his place of residence. The parent was told by the uniformed officers that they could do nothing in this case except advise her to swear out a warrant for the arrest of the offender. The following day the mother attempted to do this. She was prevented from having the warrant served by the city attorney.

Assistance in this matter was promised by the detective bureau. So far, nothing has been done. Now, all parents in this vicinity are apprehensive and fearful over the welfare of their offspring. If the racial composition of this incident had been reversed, the first officer to appear on the scene would have solved this problem permanently in his own inimitable manner. By the way, many, many Negroes have suffered excruciating penalties at the hands of policemen for far less than this.

Another Negro parent made three different reports to the police bureau wherein specific incidents of harmful molestations were directed at her children, ages 5 and 7, by teen-age white children who were obviously following the dictates of their parents. It was tactfully explained by police officials that this condition was one over which they had no control. After it became apparent that a more serious disturbance might result from this continued agitation, the police broke down and investigated the plaintiff. Upon his next approach to them, he was greeted with the information that the investigation revealed he was a good citizen. Phooey!

Reports to juvenile authorities have likewise proven ineffective, and not because there was some degree of controversy evident, either.

Welfare organizations are daily calling attention to the fact that the mayor and other city officials are closing their eyes to the aggravating circumstances under which Negroes are living. What seems to be the main trouble with these protestations is that they are not directed into the right quarters. If unity among the many groups working in the race relations field ever becomes a reality here, the people responsible for many atrocities will receive much adverse publicity and political attention. Their names are not well kept secrets, and that's for sure!

Negroes have had to tolerate inferior policing for a long time. During the war, untrained and unprepared special officers were given assignments that even full-fledged, well-trained, regular policemen shunned. As a result, many times over this publication has gone on record insisting that these special officers should have been thoroughly schooled in modern police methods and then given full authority, rather than the limited privilege of watching over derelicts and providing surveillance for Negroes only.

THE OBSERVER, NOVEMBER 1946

Just A Reminder . . .

(NOTE: A recent edition of the "Emerald," official newspaper of the University of Oregon, carried the following editorial, which is more or less self-explanatory. W.H.M.)

"An editorial must have a point. Our point: Bob Reynolds. An editorial must be timely. Timeliness, to do with Saturday's football game. An editorial should include facts not covered by news reports on the subject. Said facts: Reynold's attributes as student, friend and liberal.

"We know nothing of football. Sports writers tabbed Bob's Saturday efforts as perhaps his greatest game. No game is actually Reynold's greatest. His fighting heart would deny that one moment's effort surpasses another in terms of zeal, physical or mental.

"Reynolds could be categorized as the 'All-American Boy.' Like his brother, Walt, Bob has consistently studied hard, played hard and believed hard; believed that good sportsmanship has only a little bit to do with the gridiron or cinder track.

"One of the One World club's initial organizers, Reynolds has been actively engaged in furthering the causes of minority peoples for more years than most sports fans realize. His work for inter-racial understanding has been magnificent. Bob Reynolds is a realist. His thought is as taut and responsive as his muscular coordination.

"If Reynolds is being heralded as the savior of a football game, then perhaps we should add to his laurels the title of intellectual and athletic abilities combined. In Bob we are privileged to witness such a coalition.

"We should be proud that our university can send forth specimens of its manhood, in the form of men like Reynolds, astute on sporting field and in debating hall alike. Our hat is doffered respectfully to a fine citizen, Bob Reynolds."

Sports observers, writers and critics have given an unusual amount of discussion to the fact that Coach Tex Oliver used Reynolds only in the fourth quarter of the Oregon-UCLA football game. Reynolds' showing at this time was spectacular and little short of miraculous . . .

(We have omitted the "Emerald" commentary. W.H.M.).

The coach, Tex Oliver, seems to always utilize the services of his star players until they reach a point of complete exhaustion before a substitute will be used. Many persons are of the opinion that in order for the University of Oregon football team to win over such strong opposition as the UCLA eleven, it is necessary that playing time be spread equitably among players of similar abilities.

Further reports indicate that Oliver prefers that all athletes under his supervision be of the docile, passive type. Interests in life beyond the development and display of physical skill are not encouraged. Reynolds' academic, civic and social motives apparently make it rather difficult for Oliver to use him often, because he is not reconciled to the fact that persons with multiple aims and ambitions may acquit themselves honorably when an athletic crisis is imminent.

THE OBSERVER, DECEMBER 1946

The Moving Finger – A Plea For Unity

As THE YEAR COMES TO A CLOSE, review of the past twelve months should loom large in the minds of all persons interested in a more profitable and pleasant 1947. Community functionaries must begin now to focus constant attention upon those issues of vital importance to the Negro people living in the Portland-Vancouver area.

Repeatedly, analysis must be made of the intricate problems confronting these citizens. Recommendations must be forthcoming from time to time from dependable and established quarters, which will minimize the agony and suffering that comes from the vicious persecution that is often leveled at minorities by the forces of reaction.

In the coming year, attention must first be centered upon removing the marked provincial attitudes alive in this area. A militant but sound position on all issues related to minority people's progress must be steadfastly adhered to. It must be recognized that in championing the rights of minorities (especially Negroes), protests presented in a strategical and compatible manner are oftentimes effective. Caution and principle in this endeavor are essential and cannot be overemphasized. Libelous charges, false accusations, gross exaggerations of minor social breaches and the magnifying of purely subjective grievances must avoided.

Every individual, organization and business should not fail to step forth and offer assistance to all community programs and projects that are concerned with uplift and welfare. A positive effort should be exerted at all times to prevent the development of controversies which will create conflicts and misunderstandings with other racial, religious and progressive political groups. Without any trace of emotion or regret, these same forces must adamantly refuse to assist individual Negro glory-mongers and self-sustaining egotists in their varied schemes to dupe the masses of Negroes into believing they alone are capable of devising methods for the removal of all problems that beset this oppressed people. Reputable protective and welfare organizations whose plans for resisting exploitation and abuse are well steeped in democratic and honorable procedure and must be supported with vigor and determination. Evidences and indications of bigotry and deceit in organizations and groups that normally should be devoid of such chicanery must be attacked and removed.

It is common knowledge that the role of the Negro minority in the American social structure is incomprehensible to a vast proportion of the population. For many decades, the Negro people of the United States have sought just the elementary privileges of freedom. Primary requests for liberty and justice have been invariably denied. In every crevice of American life both sophisticated and brutal discriminations are practiced against this people. There is no corner of the United States today which is devoid of prejudice and hatred toward Negroes. Consequently, the aim of all progressives who feel keenly the problems of living as a Negro in this community must prepare to assist in a colossal struggle to alleviate some of the hardships and outrageous humiliations.

To do this is not an easy task.

In times past, there has been an unusual amount of discussion focused upon necessity for complete UNITY among the Negro welfare groups having more or less the same programs and ideologies. This has been and will continue to be very difficult to accomplish, until the competitive philosophy of our system of life can be separated from the intentions of such bodies. Every attempt to unify the Negro people on any matter is immediately accompanied by a corresponding development of antipathies and antagonisms, which in many instances create irreconcilable differences. It is an irrefutable fact that people who are socially submerged, economically subjugated, oppressed, harassed and intimidated cannot expect any basic changes in their political and social status as long as silly conflicts and sharp personal distinctions are kept alive in their ranks.

It is expected that reactionary groups will take steps to add to the confusion that already exists among the Negro people. Many race baiting factions will carry out plans designed to force the Negro's standard of existence to much lower levels. Discriminations will be more marked in every quarter of our local life. Discouraging as it may appear, not one Negro should permit himself to believe that any of these conditions will be remedied by emotional ravings and petty sensationalism. Careful study and diligent planning by qualified and experienced specialists who have the staunch support and confidence of the people they are selected to serve, will offer the most promising avenues for improvement.

Now is the time to become alert to guard against further social atrocities and to offer, if possible, sound suggestions as to how the Negro people can cooperatively assist in the many programs that will get under way in order to improve their lot in America.

With this purpose in mind, *The Observer* begins another year with courage and determination in the service of the people.

THE OBSERVER, JANUARY 1947

To Be Truthful

THE *OREGON JOURNAL* HAS CARRIED as a regular advertisement for the past several Sundays in the Home & Garden section one of the most contemptible and racially insulting displays to appear within this decade. This advertisement is sponsored by an Oregon flower fancier known as Roy Hennessy. The influence and prestige of this person is of such potency that one of the white board members of a borderline crusading organization offered to resign from his post of pretentious Negro-loving rather than take Hennessy to task for his brazen effrontery to the Negro people.

Even more deplorable is the gross neglect of which Negroes themselves are incessantly guilty on all such issues. For those who feel that these matters should be dealt with effectively and uncompromisingly, there are a few basic truths to be kept in mind:

1. Some long-time Negro residents of Portland have customarily displayed appalling stupidity in all operations planned for improving the status of Negroes generally.
2. At the present, more than ten organizations embodying Negro members and operatives are in existence. All of them claim to have programs designed to resist discrimination.
3. Up to the time of this writing, these usually vociferous groups have not registered any protests with the Journal publishers for having approved this type of advertisement for publication.

Some time ago it was brought to public attention by certain organizational representatives in this city that the editors of the daily papers were in favor of supporting programs of tolerance and interracial goodwill. To assist in this endeavor, the use of racial labels was even to be omitted from crime stories. The appearance of the Roy Hennessy flower advertisement is irony in the atomic sense.

The continued reprinting of this advertisement is a deliberate act that has been carefully premeditated. From all indications, one may assume that the feeble progressive campaigns which have been waged here of late to reduce the number of wanton ignominies currently being heaped upon Negroes have now aroused the wrath of ruthless and unscrupulous reactionaries. Consequently, it can no longer be assumed that powerful interests, such as those which operate the daily newspapers in this community, are too magnanimous to resort to petty retaliations toward groups who struggle in vain to achieve the privileges of democracy. The forces of oppression and hatred have been marshalled to reiterate a traditional American adage, "Negroes have no rights which whites are bound to respect."

As a result of conferences and meetings, there are some Negro functionaries who have been duped into conveying to their supporters and dependents the idea that certain difficult and remote social objectives were attainable. The Roy Hennessy advertisement removes all illusions anyone may have on this subject.

As time goes by, many more interesting and bitter lessons will be imparted to the Negro people and other minorities who may have fancied themselves escaping from the octopus-like tentacles of racial prejudice and uncurbed discriminations. Politically conscious observers have spoken ardently and written forcefully on numerous occasions, attempting to show the necessity of organization and collaboration of all factions and persons opposed to reactionary and fascist practices. Somehow it appears that the wide and varied attempts to break down certain concepts of self-sufficiency and individualism on the part of a representative number of Negroes in this area are not noticeably successful. Meanwhile, from every angle social liberties and economic opportunities for Negroes have been narrowed down to a frightfully small sphere.

The current pattern of denial and exclusion as practiced toward Negroes in all quarters of our local life will have many far-reaching implications. The Negro people in this vicinity will spend another quarter of a century suffering and enduring untold social abuses and economic hardships in their feeble attempts to bring about a few elementary democratic expressions. To further accentuate this, the Negro functionaries who should be the most articulate and organizationally effective in bringing about sharp remedial adjustments are themselves the victims of disunity and distrust. Moreover, there is an alarming gap which has not been bridged since the early days of the war between Negro leadership and the rank and file. It is redundant to mention that this gap is fast becoming a chasm.

THE OBSERVER, FEBRUARY 1947

A Place In The Sun

ALREADY THE YEAR 1947 HAS BEEN FILLED with tough lessons for minorities on the subject of white supremacy. The line-up of acting instructors in this vast educational program is as surprising as the features of a "Believe it or not" cinema review. Taxi drivers, wholesale florists, merchandisers, national magazines and metropolitan newspaper editors comprise the newest bodies and groups performing the most effective work in teaching the Negro people their place in the American scheme.

At the opening of Brotherhood week when all persons were supposedly interested in furthering the philosophies of good-will, freedom, justice, equality and liberty, a murder-crazed mob of taxi drivers in Greenville, South Carolina, seized a Negro prisoner from the city jail and lynched him. This incident keynotes the beginning of the 1947 series of "Horrors for the Negro" throughout those sections of the United States where such displays are in vogue.

In Portland, a prominent department store recently had for sale in its shoe repair department a shoe polish manufactured in England which features a color advertised under the label of a six-letter word that is genuinely insulting to all Negroes. During the war, Negro troops stationed in England resented the presence of this product to such an extent that the assistance of Walter White and the NAACP were brought into service to have distribution of this polish sharply curtailed. The war is over now (so it is thought), so the various American retailers who have no consideration for the feelings of Negro customers are stocking huge supplies.

In addition to this, there is the *Oregon Journal's* Pacific Parade section where the utmost contempt for Negro people is shown by the continued publishing of the the Roy Hennessy flower advertisement. (See page 6, *The Observer,* January, 1947.) See also Dr. Joyner's letter under Interesting Correspondence, *The Observer,* February, 1947.

Negroes are witnessing a steady decline of the meager privileges and scarce opportunties to which they have become accustomed. It is unfortunate that these people are inclined to remain passive in the face of the most dastardly insults that can be conceived by the master race. Lynchings have for a long time earmarked the essentially barbaric culture of the noble supremacists. It is not compatible with contemporary social demonstrations to believe that this atrocity will disappear from our lives at some reasonable date.

For those who are honest with themselves, the following facts are in constant evidence:

Every medium at the command of the wily forces of reaction has been brought into play to establish universal contempt for the Negro people.

Movies, powerful national publications – as well as the local dailies – are aligned in this singular program.

Another objective appears to be to convince Negroes that they must learn to accept insults, derogatory references and humiliations without evoking any bitterness, because this is what America wishes. After all, it is precarious and oftentimes disastrous for the word Negro to be used in its contemptuous vein by the superior people, when the possibility for correction is within the power of a Negro listener.

THE OBSERVER, APRIL 1947

It's Getting Late

THE NEGRO POPULACE OF PORTLAND has witnessed first hand for the past few months what can happen to minority communities where economic planning is lacking. During the war years, huge sums of money passed through the hands of Negro workers. Legitimate and nefarious businesses under the control of Negroes profited during this era. Vice was wide open, and hustlers of all types ran rampant in every sector where Negroes were concentrated. The city fathers and their gestapo winked their eyes at the abominable violations of the law that have at long last proved to be the economic undoing of the Negro people here.

Contrary to the ideas advanced by wishful thinkers, many of the Negro people left in Portland are persons of few skills and limited talents. In order to survive in this stronghold of white favoritism, they must avail themselves of the meager earnings they can amass from participating in skimpy gambling and other illegal operations.

Now that a pseudo-cleanup campaign is in progress throughout the city, a business recession has set in. This recession is rapidly reaching the stages of a severe depression for Negroes.

As a result, welfare units and progressive groups concerned with the uplift of minority groups have run into serious obstacles in their efforts to improve the status of the Negro people. Tensions have been lessened considerably. However, there have been no substantial improvements in job opportunities. Exhaustive discourses can be prepared on this theme, but there is a more serious aspect to ponder now.

The fact that most of the established businesses of Portland (Negro owned) have a history steeped in vice and racketeering, even if at the present such endeavors have been sharply submerged, lends an indelible stigma to the business acumen of the Negro. It is deplorable that the factions who were established before the war did not have the foresight to develop enterprises that could offer industrious Negroes postwar employment.

Rapid financial turnovers from illegal maneuvers designed to exploit other Negroes made lasting impressions on the early entrepreneurs. Many individuals with a degree of influence in local circles have rendered themselves impotent in business matters because of their subjective programs. Long-range objective planning will have to be resorted to before the economic situation will be altered. The Negro or group of Negroes entering into a sound business undertaking that will furnish employment and advancement opportunities to other Negroes is long overdue in this area. Let us hope for a benefactor in this respect. SOON!

THE OBSERVER EDITORIAL, SEPTEMBER, 1947

Spotlighted

CONSIDERABLE ATTENTION IS AGAIN DIRECTED toward the Negro people here and the roles they are to play in the labor theater. Varied trade union groups in this area are revising their strategies to resist the potential adversities to result from the recently enacted Taft-Hartley labor law. Already, reactionary elements have reached out and usurped the uninformed Negro to serve as an anti-labor agent.

Help Please

The benefits that Negroes are supposed to derive from the continued campaigns and crusades of social welfare programs are sharply restrained because of the programmatic incompatibility of many functionaries. Needless to mention is the fact that the vast degree of distrust, selfishness and egotism predominant in this circle must be alleviated before the masses of hopeful Negro citizens will notice any definite social improvements. Much of this conflict and confusion could be eliminated, if there was an effective method of convincing some of these self-designated racial stalwarts that a perpetual monopoly on social prestige is impossible to acquire.

Lesson Learned

Notice has been given to the fact that continued Negro attendance of segregated dances featuring name bands at a local ballroom is a matter to be regarded with contempt. Even the various orchestra leaders and members are prone to regard such affairs with sharp distaste.

It is encouraging to see more and more music lovers are refraining from giving support to such assemblies. Eventually, public jazz concerts may entirely replace this form of disgusting entertainment.

THE OBSERVER, JANUARY 1948

New Teacher . . . Old Lesson

"I'm Sorry That Governor Hall Still Believes In Racial Discrimination." — *Wardell Henderson.*

History Repeats Itself

The subject of this discourse is a strong indictment of the moral code underlying majority group political control in the state of Oregon. It is strongly reminiscent of the last words of another Negro, Robert Folkes, who paid the death penalty in the gas chamber at Salem for a crime it was never conclusively proven that he committed. Folkes departed this life with the farewell comment: "It's easier to convict a Negro."

The fact that the Folkes' case eventually received much attention and analysis by eminent legal authorities, which revealed it was unquestionably an "all time great" among the miscarriages of justice, influenced many people into believing that the factors leading to a gross recurrence of this incident would be forever erased from the history of this state. It was hoped that Oregon had now arrived at a point where it could be announced that legal guarantees to minorities were strong and durable. The downtrodden citizens of this area began to take hope that their lot in life would be on a more nearly equitable basis with those who enjoy full American citizenship privileges. The execution of Wardell Henderson, January 23, 1948, dealt a staggering blow in this respect to the recuperated faith of the masses of Negro people and their sympathetic white friends.

What He Died For

According to the October, 1946, edition of *Shadows,* a monthly magazine edited and printed by the inmates of the Oregon State Penitentiary, in an article entitled "I Am Next," Wardell Henderson wrote: "I was born in a southern state, and I have worked for white folks all my life, mostly in their homes, or in the gardens, or taking care of the children...I'd been overseas in the Army, and I wanted to go home...Anyhow, I am next to go to the gas chamber. They tell me that there is no pain to the way they kill a man in there. I don't know about that. I don't even want to find out. All I want is for somebody to believe what I've tried to tell folks. I haven't killed nobody, and I don't want to die."

The editor's note at the conclusion of the article states: "Wardell W. Henderson's greatest crime seems to be his having been born a poor man, with a black skin and with a most pitiable belief in the honesty, integrity and supremacy of the white man."

Case Summary

On December 25, 1945, the body of Walter H. Poole, a white man, was found by Wardell Henderson, a Negro. Henderson, who was wanted because he went AWOL, voluntarily surrendered himself to military authorities. While in their custody, and confined in a stockade, he was extensively interrogated, and he ultimately signed several statements implicating himself in Mr. Poole's death. Thereafter he was indicted, returned to Portland, charged with murder in the first degree, convicted, and sentenced to die. He was never previously convicted of crime.

Two Portland attorneys, who had been appointed by the Court to defend Henderson because he was without funds, gratuitously appealed the case to the Oregon Supreme Court. During the pendency of the appeal, the article in *Shadows* came to the attention of the Oregon Prison Association, The National Association for the Advancement of Colored People and the Urban League, and a committee from these three organizations interviewed Henderson in the penitentiary. So impressed was this committee with his insistence of innocence of the crime that the NAACP filed a brief *Amicus Curiae.*

Although, as previously stated, there were no known eyewitnesses to the manner in which Poole's death occurred, and although the case against Henderson, aside from the signed statements, is based solely upon circumstantial evidence, nevertheless the Oregon Supreme Court, on September 9, 1947, affirmed the conviction and imposition of the death penalty.

The fight to save Henderson's life became more intensified at this point. The efforts of Attorney Irving Goodman and the NAACP to gain clemency for Henderson led to the drafting of a petition listing six reasons for a commutation of sentence. One-hundred Portland attorneys signed this document before it was sent to the Governor. The six reasons were:

(1) Henderson's conviction, aside from alleged confessions, was based solely upon circumstantial evidence;

(2) The foreman of the trial jury recently stated he would urge executive clemency;

(3) The youth has steadfastly maintained his innocence, and if his life is spared, additional evidence may be brought to light;

(4) Henderson, 25, was never previously convicted of crime and, in view of his past record of good conduct, every effort should be made to effect his reformation as is required by the Oregon Constitution;

(5) Henderson volunteered for service in the Army when 19, or six months before Pearl Harbor, served honorably here and overseas over three-and-one-half years and was promoted to the rank of Sergeant, before he went AWOL and became involved in his present difficulty;

(6) Consideration should be given to the fact that several persons were convicted of murder in Oregon in 1947, some of these crimes being of unusually atrocious character, but that in no instance was the convicted murderer executed. Regard for the constitutional requirement of equal protection of the laws urges that the penalty in this instance should remain consistent with the policy followed in the prior cases. Special care should be taken in this case, since Henderson is a Negro; meticulous endeavor by the State of Oregon to avoid an unequal infliction of penalty in like circumstances is required both by the principles of law and morality.

This petition, as well as numerous letters, telegrams and other appeals from various persons and organizations, were sent to Governor Hall. Like his predecessor, the late Earl Snell who denied clemency to Robert Folkes, Governor John Hall refused to commute the sentence of Wardell Henderson.

This action on the part of the Governor, who is also a respected Portland lawyer, reduced the whole issue to the level of a basic incident in a class struggle that has been an integral part of America's infamous history. Henderson's life became a tragic pawn in a game of conflicting professional legal maneuvering between one lawyer with the viewpoints and power to protect his class interests, and the other lawyer, a distinguished social thinker and champion for the rights of the underprivileged. The Governor, in denying executive clemency, said in part in his statement, issued January 20:

"There has not been received any recommendation from the trial judge or from the district attorney. Nor has there been any expression from any of the jurors, except for the foreman, who recently wrote that had he to do it all over again upon the same evidence, he would have voted to convict the defendant but would have recommended life imprisonment.

"The vast majority of the letters received on behalf of the defendant are based upon the fact that the writers are opposed generally to capital punishment. If these individuals and organizations feel so keenly about this, they should resort to our initiative law and place before the electorate of Oregon the question of whether the death penalty should be invoked in capital offenses. However, until such time as capital punishment is removed from our constitution by the voters, it must remain the law of this state. Another provision provides that the chief executive has power to commute a sentence from death to life imprisonment. My opinion is that it gives us a power that should be used with caution and only in the interests of justice.

Verdict Forecloses

"The question of the guilt of the defendant has been foreclosed by the verdict of the jury.

"The trial judge had no alternative other than to decree a death sentence in the absence of a recommendation from the trial jury. The power to commute should be exercised only for the purpose of preventing a miscarriage of justice, such as a showing that the accused did not have a fair trial or every opportunity to present a defense, the presentation of newly discovered evidence since completing the trial or other extenuating circumstances. In this case, there is no evidence or claim that the defendant did not receive a fair trial. There is no indication that racial prejudice had any part in the case.

"The decision of the jury will not be disturbed and the law will take its course. Executive clemency is denied."

In reply to this decision, two identical telegrams of the following content were dispatched to the Governor's offices in Salem and in Portland: "You have ignored and declared invalid the sworn statements of two jurors that racial prejudice entered into the jury deliberations in the Wardell Henderson case.

"If you deny the validity of these juror's statements, you accuse them of perjury, or deny their competence to render a fair judgement. In either case, simple honesty required that you appoint a special committee of Oregon citizens to review the case and advise you after study whether or not racial prejudice was a factor in the death sentence.

"In our country, it is traditional to make every effort to eliminate race prejudice in passing sentences. Governor Meier (Julius E. Meier, governor of Oregon 1931-35) appointed an advisory committee in the Theodore Jordan case and Governor Fuller of Massachusetts in the Sacco and Vanzetti case in 1926.

"It is especially incumbent on you to take such a step in the light of your long association as an attorney for clients who discriminate against Negro citizens. You are in a particularly different position, because your present responsibility of taking a human life has been thrust upon you as the result of a tragic accident, and not by election of the people.

"The most highly respected judicial body of our land has set the precedent by supreme court justices voluntarily removing themselves from deliberation on cases in which personal feelings or previous identifications prevented them from rendering impartial justice.

"We again urge you to suspend the death sentence on Wardell Henderson long enough for an impartial investigation to be made of the circumstances surrounding the Henderson trial."

Signers of this message were representatives of various welfare and political organizations of prominence in this state.

This was to no avail. As a last resort, Attorney Goodman petitioned the Supreme court for Writ of Habeas Corpus. Part of Mr. Goodman's plea in this behalf before the Supreme court will give an insight as to why the struggle to save Henderson's life reached such exacting detail:

"The defendant, Wardell Henderson, accepted these jurors on their sworn statements given on their *voir dire* that they had no prejudice against the defendant because he was a Negro; that they had no prejudice against the race to which the defendant belonged; that they would give defendant the same fair and impartial trial as to a white person. Upon the basis of those interrogations and answers, or words to that effect, Wardell Henderson accepted this trial jury.

"I say to you that if the affidavit of the foreman is true, and I believe he would so testify, and if the affidavit of the other juror is true, some of the jurors did not truthfully answer the questions on their *voir dire*. Therefore, Wardell Henderson did not know about them. This just came to our attention, just within the last few days.

"I think it is terrifically serious. If some of the jurors were prejudiced, as the foreman swore to, and one of the other jurors swore to, the verdict is null and void, because the defendant did not have a fair and impartial trial as is guaranteed by the Sixth Amendment to the Constitution of Oregon: `In all criminal prosecution, the accused shall have the right to public trial by an impartial jury in the county in which the offense shall have been committed.' Amendment VI of the United States Constitution: `In all criminal prosecutions, the accused shall enjoy the right to a speedy and public trial, by an impartial jury of the state and district wherein the crime shall have been committed.'

"Amendment XIV of the United States Constitution: `No state shall make or enforce any law which shall abridge the privileges or immunities of citizens of the United States; nor shall any state deprive any person of life, liberty, or property, without due process of law; nor deny to any person within its jurisdiction the equal protection of the laws.'

"How can you say that this defendant got a fair and impartial trial before jurors who, if the foreman told the truth and the other juror, falsified under oath? If these affidavits are true, some of them committed a fraud on the defendant and the circuit court and upon the public, and no person, no matter how humble — and this defendant is among the most humble and I am happy to give him my services—should be put to death under these facts."

The supreme court decided that it was unable to give any relief on this matter.

Henderson died. The human elements possessing the power to comply with meager requests for justice had no intention of jeopardizing their political futures by giving the full benefits of American constitutional guarantees to a Negro. These persons realized that any expression of true justice to Henderson might be highly flattering to the Negro people. It might also be construed to mean that they were incapable of protecting the concepts underlying white supremacy. This would be tantamount to political suicide.

These ridiculous and despicable techniques of dealing with the submarginal beings in our national confines have caused catastrophic social convulsions in the thinking of the Negro people. It has thrown them into the depths of depravity. As a result of this type of proscription only two consuming mental dispositions have been developed among the majority of Negroes toward white America. One is hatred — the other is fear.

In the administration of justice, *denial* has been the key-note when concerned with the Negro. Court procedures throughout the Nation are notoriously unfair to Negroes. In letting Henderson die, Governor Hall made sure that Oregon would not set a new and strange precedent.

THE OBSERVER, MAY 1948

New Party For The New Era

IT IS ENCOURAGING THAT BRAZEN EFFORTS to keep alive the atrocious social patterns that have so effectively limited minority group development and expressions in America are becoming more readily perceived by many alert and politically conscious individuals. In turn, these persons are rapidly learning to make themselves valuable to their fellowmen by taking the time to interpret for them the many complex social and political processes affecting our lives. This assists greatly in placing minority group voters on their guard against bewildering influences and is also slowly beginning to result in their supporting candidates and issues that will make complete freedom here for all the people a reality.

If the Negro people are ever to improve their position in American life, they will of necessity have to support those basic progressive political programs that envision and provide for full emancipation and freedom for all underprivileged groups. The New Party, with Henry Wallace and Glen Taylor as its illustrious and distinguished standard bearers, is an impeccable example of what the minority groups of this land should struggle vigorously to develop as their political bulwark against oppression and old party reaction.

Many illustrations having their origin in this contemporary period may be cited as concrete proof of the progressive and uncompromising nature of the New Party in its attempts to bring vital political understanding, practices and philosophy to the American people. For instance, Glen Taylor, candidate for vice president on the New

Party ticket, has not just begun to fight Jim Crow. On the opening day of the 80th Congress, Taylor took the floor when Bilbo's name was reached in the Senate roll call and introduced a resolution demanding that Bilbo be refused his seat. He delivered an hour-long attack on Bilbo, who was subsequently never seated. In the Senate, he paired for the FEPC (Fair Employment Practices Committee) appropriation in 1945, voted against all measures designed to block a vote on FEPC in 1946 and voted for cloture to FEPC for a vote. He also voted for cloture to permit debate on the anti-poll tax bill. This is the same Senator Taylor who was arrested in Birmingham, Alabama, fined $50.00 and given a suspended sentence of 180 days in jail, because he refused to honor the Jim Crow sign on a door of a church where a political meeting was in progress. If this case is carried to its logical conclusion, it should result in the certain destruction of the Truman-led Democratic party.

The history of Henry Wallace as a courageous and indefatigable progressive is legendary. His refusal to speak to segregated audiences in the South drew the respect of all decent-thinking Americans. His forthright defiance of hoodlums, intent upon breaking up a recent political meeting where 5,000 Negroes and whites heard him speak in Columbia, Mo., indicated a trend is now underway in American politics as new as the party that gave birth to it.

His sound criticisms and denunciations of the Truman military clique's foreign and domestic policies have stirred the interest of all peoples who feel that another war is unnecessary. It is Henry Wallace and the New Party who state unconditionally that the Taft-Hartley Act must be repealed, that there must be a FEPC, and that price reductions be instituted by Congress in order that inflation may be curbed now to avert a serious depression. All of this and much more spotlight the hourly activity of this people's movement.

From time immemorial, the social system with which we are most familiar has been a cradle for patterns of life wherein there must always be underprivileged peoples. Now we are beginning to learn that often this condition results from legislative and political disadvantages. The New Party proposes to correct this state of affairs and to remove those distinctions that have gained prominence through operation of an economic process that is grossly inequitable.

THE OBSERVER, OCTOBER, 1948

Double or Nothing

MUCH EMPHASIS HAS BEEN LENT to the political corruption and economic instability of this country by the campaigners and crusaders seeking power and prestige in the coming election. One commentator has recently remarked that he "didn't realize this United States was in such bad shape until time for the election drew near. Anyway it will all be straight after November 2."

This is not true for minority peoples and especially Negroes. Acknowledging that the financial strength and general social influence of the reactionaries will preserve for them all of the important posts in government, the role of the Negro people should be regarded in a practical light now more than ever.

From all indications, war and its accompanying horrors are truly in the making. As yet, no changes of any significant social import have been registered as far as a Jim Crow military arrangement is involved. There is no federal FEPC in effect. Housing is deplorable. Civil rights are non-existent. Educational facilities are still gravely unequal. Courtroom injustices still run rampant. Therefore, regardless of the outcome of the election in any section of the country, a struggle must be continued to bring about these necessary political and social revisions.

In war or peace, the efforts of our people must be doubled and redoubled to remove the age-old hindrances to our progress, or else all previous struggles have just been so much proverbial water under the bridge.

THE OBSERVER, JULY 1950

Comment

THE NEGRO QUESTION IS AGAIN GAINING IMPETUS HERE. Only a few weeks remain before voters will go to the polls to indicate whether the positions of non-Caucasians in metropolitan Portland are to become full-fledged citizens. A bill providing for complete civil rights for all persons regardless of race, etc., is to be voted upon in the November election. So far the speculative odds in predominantly Negro sections are that customary Americanism will override the higher principles of fellowship and brotherhood of man.

Now that war *[The Korean War. Editor's Note]* and its kindred atrocities are underway, the efforts of our leaders must be redoubled to remove all of the time-worn hindrances to our progress and general uplift. The President of the U.S. and top brass advisors are preparing to draft laws that inflict severe penalties upon saboteurs and persons guilty of treason. It is likely that conscientious Negro functionaries in all walks of life will find themselves faced soon with the choice of setting aside their programs of advancement for the Negro people or risk being penalized for attempting to increase the coverage of democracy. Southern politicians and their allies in Congress will again find it possible to declare any effort to extend full democratic privileges to Negroes a threat to the nation's security.

Not near enough emphasis has been placed upon the political corruption and instability of this country and how it affects 15,000,000 Negro people. Needless to say, with all the social changes that have been proclaimed, there is much left to be desired and fought for. Jim Crow still is the predominant pattern of life in America. At the same time Negro troops of the 25th division were acquitting themselves valiantly in Korea, idiotic statesmen in Washington were making unprecedented headway in their political careers by shelving a federal Fair Employment Practices act. Believe it or not, it's going to be awfully tough just holding on to a second- and third-class citizenship.

III

The Search for Quality Education: The Struggle in Portland

A Suggested Plan of Organization For All Minority Workers

OCTOBER 15, 1944

[This article, first published in The Negro Quarterly: A Review of Negro Life and Culture. Vol. 6, is based on excerpts from a speech delivered in San Frandcisco and Los Angeles, February 10-15, 1944, by William H. McClendon. Editor's Note.]

Editor's Comment and Introductory Note

IN DEVOTING THIS SPECIAL ISSUE of *The Negro Quarterly* to a discussion of Pacific Coast race relations, we wish to direct attention to certain new emerging racial patterns which indicate two possible solutions of racial conflict in postwar America. Based upon extensive research into the attitudes, customs, prejudices and fears growing out of economic competition among the immigrant population and the "natives" of the Pacific Coast, we have concluded that of the two emerging patterns of racial adjustment, one of them will become fixed law governing the relations between Negroes and whites immediately following the war and for many generations to come.

First, it should be noted that prior to America's entrance into the war, conflict between Negroes and whites remained within certain boundaries of control, and with the exception of scattered instances of open violence, the problem was more psychological than real. This was due to the fact that the 134,000 Negroes who lived principally in the Pacific Coast industrial centers of Seattle, Portland, the Bay Area of San Francisco, and Los Angeles in 1940, did not constitute a large enough segment to threaten the economic status of the white group.

Second, from 1940 to 1943, the problem had become more real. With the Negro population increasing to approximately 500,000 in the Pacific Coast Area by 1943, the matter was now one of a life and death struggle. This westward shift of large numbers of Negroes marked the closing of the last frontier for racial adjustment in America.

The difference in cultural background, and competition for jobs, revealed on the one hand that large numbers of the white population were not decided as to how this problem would be settled. On the other hand, resentment and fear of the Negro's presence caused immediate reaction from the white group which regarded the Negro's migration to the West as an intrusion and an attempt to step out of the "place" that is fixed for him in every American community.

This conflict is more dramatically reflected by the various white groups and individuals who have contended that if we are fighting a people's war for democracy, the Negro must be integrated into all phases of American life and allowed to contribute his full share toward winning victory over our enemies, and the efforts of certain individuals and labor groups to force the Negro to accept an inferior status in life.

One distinguishing characteristic of Pacific Coast racial attitudes is the fact that the strongest opposition expressed publicly against the Pacific Coast Negro immigrant has been spearheaded by reactionary leaders of American Federation of Labor unions. This is indeed a strange phenomenon when considered against the background of organized labor on the Pacific Coast and its fight to win the recognition that it has today.

Testimony presented in this issue from the hearing conducted in Portland, Oregon, by the President's Fair Employment Practice Committee, as well as other material related to the subject under discussion, is but a reflection on the nature of the racial conflict on the Pacific Coast.

No attempt is made here to portray in specific detail how this issue of race will work itself out in postwar America. We are merely concerned here with those basic factors which measure the difference between the ideal and that which is real. The facts show clearly enough, however, that in the years previous to the war, the Negro question existed in the Pacific Coast Area only in its psychological aspect, and that following the attack on Pearl Harbor, the traditions, customs and prejudices of the South began gradually to move West.

If we take the shipbuilding industry as an index of how the matter of racial conflict will be met in America now and after the war, the prospects are far from encouraging.

First among attempts toward the integration of the Negro into American life is to permit him the right to work and earn his living. This is a basic and fundamental right which determines whether a people are free indeed or slaves in fact. Although patterns of segregation and discrimination have not been definitely established on the Pacific Coast, as for example in the East, the facts presented here show that they are rapidly becoming fixed and set, and that if the forces contending for such segregation and discrimination succeed on the Pacific Coast, such an adjustment of the Negro-white situation will become more universal throughout the country.

The employment figures of Negroes in the shipbuilding industry in 1943 as contrasted against the number of Negroes employed in the same industry during the last war, is proof enough that the war we are fighting against Hitler in Europe will have to be fought all over again at home, and perhaps for a long time after Hitler will have vanished from the scene, if we do not begin now to face the issue of racial conflict realistically. — W.H.M.

As late as 1850, few Negroes resided in the states of Oregon, Washington and California. However, even at that time their presence was a great political issue. The slavery question was at its zenith nationally. Negrophobia was given added significance and emphasis. Southern custom, laws, restrictions and attitudes were rapidly transplanted to the West Coast. Residential restrictions, special legislation, and anti-Negro statutes plus separate educational facilities were given undue expression here. After the close of the Civil War, the Negro question gained impetus.

Attitudes and expressions of the South and East were simultaneously reproduced on the Pacific Coast. The present day aspects of Negro life in this part of the United States assume a more enlightening appearance, since we are able to understand the racial prejudices that have been prevalent in this area prior to Civil War days. The laws which were passed in this area barring Negroes, free or slave, are in large part responsible for the vast proportionate discord between white and Negro citizens today.

Negro workers vs. the Boilermakers litigations have been aired in courtrooms on both the Atlantic and Pacific Coasts. Two distinct examples are the decisions rendered by judges in Rhode Island and California. These decisive court orders restraining the Boilermakers from forcing Negro workers to hold memberships in auxiliary unions comes as a warning to the un-American and reactionary union monarchs that their powers are not unlimited where matters of harassing and persecuting minority peoples are concerned. Negro labor functionaries have known for a long time that eventually various judiciary and legislative branches of our government would be driven to set up warning signals and stop signs to control the widespread oppression that some union heads practice toward Negro workers.

All of the people of the United States are now acquainted with these controversies which have arisen between the ignoble personalities of the Boilermakers and Negro workers holding jobs in the various defense industries throughout the country. Many social struggles have sprung forth as a result of the vitriolic attacks made upon the Negro people by the unsavory leadership of the Boilermakers union.

Their determined position of absolute refusal of Negroes to membership in the bona fide lodges has been seriously questioned and contested by Negro workers and their organizations in a most significant manner.

Although confronted with intricate problems arising from limited financial resources, scarcity of qualified strategists and able organizers, an abundance of Uncle Toms and renegades, and interference from titular heads of glory-mongering political groups, these fighters for freedom have been able to attract the attention and win the respect of liberty-loving peoples everywhere. And though the tangible gains are not many at this time, the basic issues for which we have fought courageously and valiantly have not been suppressed to a point of despair. The uncompromising position which some Negro workers have taken on these matters will send a ringing challenge down through the years to all fighters for freedom. Ample evidence exists now to prove that some of these issues which have been fought, heard and decided upon here on the West Coast in the past 18 months have made definite indentations into the wall of prejudice that some labor leaders have attempted to construct throughout the ranks of the working class.

But we cannot afford to revel in these momentary accomplishments. Before the Negro workers now lies a problem of tremendous importance — a problem whose magnitude is so great that if its positive solution is delayed or even altered, the destiny of the Negro people as workers and as citizens, for centuries to come, will be submarginal and inferior.

Intelligent thinkers have recognized the need for racial amity and have come forward with various proposals for the purpose of purging racial prejudice from the ranks of labor. However, most of these plans are based upon the fallacious doctrine that "Education will take care of these matters. A day will come when there will no longer be any prejudice." As a reply to this, remember that not one obstacle to a people's social and economic advancement has ever just vanished or dissolved of its own accord.

It would be redundant to recount at this time the courageous battles waged against the establishment of auxiliary unions for Negroes. On the West Coast Negro and white workers from every environment imaginable have met on an industrial frontier of confusion and disruption. One fact is outstanding, however. Despite the bitter antipathies that have been developed, such as race against race, person against person—union chiefs have not found it possible to stultify the burning obsession in the minds of some Negro workers to become fully integrated into the American labor movement.

Many factors have favored this integration. Military necessity and productive expediency have definitely compelled a relaxation of tense restrictive barriers. The degree of acceptance has still not been satisfactory or gratifying to politically developed thinkers. For this reason, it becomes imperative that a program of organized activity be mapped out for the express purpose of channeling this fight in the directions that will bring more direct economic and social advantages.

So far, the leaders of the Boilermakers and their machines continue to rule the Shipbuilding Industry in this area with an IRON FIST. It may be said here though that the shipbuilding corporations desire this arrangement, for they are obviously powerful enough to force a change if they were disposed to do so. These labor racketeers have seized this war crisis as a splendid opportunity to ignore application of the basic principles of trade unionism. Negro workers desiring to become full-fledged members in the Boilermakers Unions have been shown that the rank-and-file liberal element of this union have no unity or cohesiveness that will effectively alter the present policies of race exclusion. Moreover, Kaiser Company claims it would be a violation of the rulings of the National Labor Relations Board for them to retain Negro workers on the job if the Boilermaker heads ordered them discharged.

The National Labor Relations Board has recognized the right of all workers to bargain collectively. It has also issued unconditional refutations to the claims of the Kaiser Company that they are forced to discharge Negro workers because "to look beyond the union so far as employment of Negroes is concerned" would be "to interfere with the internal affairs of the union" and lay themselves "liable to violation of the National Labor Act." The decision of the Board in the Bethlehem-Alameda Shipyard Case, No. R-5693, shows "That an employer who has a closed shop contract with a union which excludes Negroes, far from violating the Act if he ignore the union's request for discharge of a Negro employee, will violate the Act if he gives effect to the request."

You have seen how the various shipbuilding corporations, as well as the union, have proceeded to go counter clockwise to the most potent agency's decree that this government affords for working people. As a last and final resort, we have but one way to turn for relief. It is mandatory now that an organization be founded whose scope will be broad enough to embrace and offer to all discriminated against laboring people those basic, fundamental things that are denied them in this antiquated American Federation of Labor scheme. The proposal to be considered is simply this: A Minority Industrial Organization must be formed. Name it what you wish as long as a specific nationalist connotation is not imparted.

This organization will have as members white liberals and progressives, Negroes and all other workers regardless of race, nationality, political affiliation or religious convictions. The purpose of this organization will be to serve as a *bona fide* bargaining agent for all workers who are compelled to work in jobs and plants where labor contracts are held by unions that practice racial and other discriminations, and deny membership to minority peoples. It would welcome with open arms those workers who are ushered into auxiliary rackets. In any and all matters pertaining to wages, hours and working conditions, this organization would be the representative of all workers who today are not considered as human beings by the anti-labor clique of the International Brotherhood of Boilermakers, Iron Shipbuilders, Welders and Helpers of America. It would not be possible any longer for patriotic and devoted American workers who toil for democracy and victory to get discharge slips marked "Order of AFL."

On the basis of its memberships and intent, in addition to the atrocious conditions motivating the building of such an organization, application for recognition and sanction by the NLRB, WLB, and all other appropriate bureaus could be made. It is practical to believe that under the conditions which these assorted agencies operate, they could not thwart the existence of such a body.

This would create a dilemma for the prejudiced union officials whose fascist practices have aroused in the minds of Negroes the desire to effect changes in their sub-standard work status. The ultimate aim of all this vast organizational program is to begin an infiltration of Negro workers into the trade union movement; to furnish the Negro people and other minorities with an important role in production; to remove Negro and other minority women from isolation; to thwart any and all unnecessary reverses for all minority peoples; to assist in the emergence of a new Negro leadership springing specifically from the ranks of workers; to furnish higher per-capita incomes for minority groups, thereby improving their health, living standards and culture; to lend support to all war aims which are designed to bring about equality of races.

If the union heads who have sought to visit economic and social inequities upon the Negro people through union exclusion suddenly realized the vast influence such an organization could wield on the entire labor front, it is quite likely that auxiliaries and all other similar devices would disappear overnight.

It is important to keep in mind that if national recognition could be acquired for an organization of this type, workers in every occupational endeavor imaginable would be eligible for membership, coverage and protection, providing their occupational status in plants or union is that of an oppressed or discriminated worker. By no twist of thinking should anyone feel or believe that this means only shipyard workers' problems are to be considered.

This medium of protection for underprivileged workers has many decided advantages from the course of action we have been following. The fact that Negro workers and other groups of progressive peoples have consistently tried over a period of two years to change the thinking of demagogic heads of the Boilermakers and other outfits is ample proof that the methods of attack are not in keeping with the nature of this particular phase of the class struggle. It is apparent now that we must adopt a plan of action that is unified, concerted, determined and aggressive, and well-established in American democratic procedure.

Attempts will be made to portray this new organization as a divisive factor in the trade union movement. However, this should not hinder or hamper the immediate building of this organization. For it is an irrefutable fact that the fascist elements on the labor front have dictated the division that now exists. We should remap our strategy according to the demands of the struggle which today compels us to prepare to furnish honest, sincere and full protection for all workers whom the American Federation of Labor monarchs have decreed are unfit for their brand of unionism.

Sanity, Silence and Social Justice

TEXT OF SPEECHES TO ROTARY CLUB, BEND, OREGON, APRIL, 1964 AND TO JAPANESE-AMERICAN CITIZENS LEAGUE, PORTLAND, OREGON, 1965

AN OLD PERSIAN PROVERB is of prime concern to me as I ponder the statements which are to follow. It is, "Two things indicate weakness — to be silent when it is proper to speak, and to speak when it is proper to be silent."

One of the great impediments to progress in the relationships of mankind, in a limited or general sense, is the difficulty in communication. It is hoped that these remarks lead to a better understanding as to what the sharp dissatisfactions are which blacks in every walk of life are expressing now.

Here are some random impressions which blacks have shared about the Japanese Americans: Japanese prior to World War II were living largely on the West Coast in the major cities in districts that were ghettoized to a strong degree. Some Japanese worked at farming and were very successful. Others were operators of small businesses, and some were engaged in the professions. On the whole they were satisfied and adjusted to their patterns of living, although many obvious discriminations were directed against them because of race and national origin. The rich Japanese cultural and national heritage was assumed to be a strong force in sustaining them through periods of punitive American laws and abuses. The dispersal of Japanese Americans which followed after World War II led to an increase in Japanese obtaining higher education, engaging in a wider variety of professions, operating a larger assortment of businesses and gaining footholds in industry and commerce. All of these are commendable. On the other hand, not much is known about how Japanese view the issues that are the heart of civil and human rights. It is possible that the comfortable and uncomplicated existence of most Japanese has caused them to be apathetic and indifferent to the harassment, persecution and injustice affecting many other Americans, of whom blacks are a very large percentage.

In bringing to you some of the information about the position and thought of blacks in the American social structure, it should be said here and now that the rights of citizens which are contained in the laws of this land, including the Bill of Rights, Declaration of Independence and the Constitution, have to be re-identified, fought for and reclaimed in every generation. This is the realistic affirmation and application of the indisputable adage, "Eternal Vigilance is the Price of Liberty."

For citizens who have never enjoyed equal rights, the efforts to obtain them can be a series of the most terrifying, agonizing and brutal ordeals. The public policy of this country, for much too long, has been to allow inequalities in citizenship, but it is the intent of the blacks who are concerned to create the national awareness that will make social justice a reality.

The American black is an integral part of American History. However, blacks have been continuously portrayed in an insignificant and derogatory light. They have been forced into a completely subordinate role that began 346 years ago. However, for every minute of this time, blacks have been a challenge to the application of professed and proclaimed American ideals. This is best explained for the sake of brevity in the fact that the history of the black in the United States is contained in the struggle to aim at and obtain freedom and equality and the degree of equality that has been achieved.

The black is the only immigrant to have come to America against his will, and when this first happened, it was under the condition of slavery. Slavery is a practice in which human beings are owned and held captive by other human beings. The slave works and serves his master without pay. The slave status of the black lasted in practice and as a matter of public policy for 246 years, and blacks were branded with a dehumanizing stigma that has not yet been obliterated. Many white minds in many important places remain tyrannized by the concept of slavocracy, and many of the debilitating and constricting social injustices of today that affect blacks are holdovers and reruns of bitter dramas that permeated the slave era. No section of this country is devoid of those Caucasians who continue to give vigorous support to that noxious pattern of living which is satirically referred to as the "White Southern Way of Life."

Thoughtful blacks and their allies throughout the history of this country have assumed the stupendous tasks of focusing more and more attention on the alarming amounts of inequities suffered by blacks because of the failure of local, state, and federal governments to guarantee them civil and human rights. Despite the fact there are blacks with influence who would adhere to an insane diplomacy of silence on such matters, there are an overwhelming number who now take pride and joy in making a continuous assault and battery against the theories and practices which sustain notions of the black's racial inferiority.

De Tocqueville, writing in 1835, pointed out that the white southern aristocracy and the slave-holding oligarchy "spiritualized despotism and violence, and they have violated towards The Black all of the rights of humanity." To this day, America is still trying to choose between "equality in freedom" vs. "inequality in slavery." So far, the black must realistically view his lot in America as living under a condition where the inequalities of custom are replaced by the inequalities under law.

The architects of the "White Southern Way of Life" began before the 1870s to redraw the format that would assure white advantage for the next 100 years plus. To maintain this image, the white manipulators were compelled to use subterfuge, corruption, atrocity and perversion. And most damaging of all was the emergence of a social system that was based on racial segregation. For this, the whole nation has paid and is paying dearly. The vast economic and social problems of today do not cause segregation, but segregation is in itself the cause of these colossal difficulties.

Black people who are given to humane considerations can recall the horror that was felt when approximately 110,000 Japanese Americans (including 70,000 citizens) were herded off to concentration camps in 1942. Some voices were raised in feeble protests, but little else could be done because the status of most Blacks at this time was equally insecure. Blacks had been confined to living in slums and backward rural areas at less than concentration camp standards for several decades. Black people did admire and respect the courageous and distinguished performances of the American Japanese troops in the European Theater of War. They are not unmindful of the supreme sacrifices and exceptional gallantry of those soldiers of the 442nd regiment—Japanese American Volunteers, and know that they established a war record unsurpassed by any other units of the allied forces. News accounts have repeatedly reported the 442nd to be the most decorated unit in the entire military history of the United States.

Because of their forced evacuation in 1942, Japanese Americans suffered losses in businesses, houses, lands and savings in excess of 400 million dollars. The final settlement of claims under the Congressional Evacuation Repayment Act of 1948 totaled 38 million. This, in essence, is the kind of shortchanging which has affected blacks in America for 350 years.

New forces are now engaged in the attempts to bring solutions to the many problems that remain unsolved and the human rights tasks that are uncompleted. These are best illustrated by blacks having assumed an aggressive posture in the direct action programs for civil rights and ceasing to rely on the intermittent expressions of benevolence from some few influential whites of goodwill. The black is now active, mobilized and militant. There is complete impatience with social improvement geared to the white man's timetable. This is being demonstrated daily by members of new organizations and their forceful, uncompromising leaders. New pressures are being exerted for change and improvement.

There have been street processions, sit-ins at restaurants and lunch counters, boycotts of segregated businesses, freedom rides, voter registration drives, determined resolute efforts to use the ballot and now the irreversible commitment to bring about an equal integrated public education for black children. The people involved in these programs are not submissive and have no intention of adjusting to white plans that suggest the Declaration of Independence should not be taken for exactly what it means. There is no doubt among responsible and concerned elements of humanity that blacks are going to win the battle to complete their emancipation in the foreseeable future.

A few examples of the contemporary connivance and machinations on the parts of the whites which have placed the black in a distressing position and further impeded his enjoyment of equal rights are to be found in the areas of housing, employment and education. Attention will be centered on these items and their relevance to our own community.

Since World War II, 117 billion dollars has been granted in loans for housing by the Federal Housing Authority (FHA) and Veterans' Administration (VA). Less than two percent of new homes insured by FHA have been for non-whites. The vast majority of these are in all-black housing developments in the South. The VA's record is no better. In the matter of public housing, the policy of choosing open occupancy, or segregation, has been the prerogative of local housing authorities, and most of them, North and South, chose segregation. More than 80 percent of all federally sponsored housing remained racially segregated as of 1963. No man is free unless he can freely decide where he will live. The integrity of the democratic system is at a deplorable level until this right is recognized and protected. At the turn of the century, most cities in the United states did not have racially distinguishable districts, but by World War II, every major city had a rigidly specified black district. The one major commodity on the American market which a non-white cannot purchase freely in accordance with needs, means and desires is *housing!*

Long years of promoting segregation by the realty boards throughout the country have resulted in interracial public housing being viewed by many whites as a threat to what they imagine as their exclusive privileges and superior status. This has presented serious problems in carrying out integration policies in public housing, as many white and black families would rather remain in substandard housing than live in racially integrated settings. Further complications are that many whites often regard living in a racially mixed area as a loss of esteem in the eyes of the general public. This happens for both whites and blacks by virtue of living in public housing. Many of them often feel that they have achieved low status — in their own estimations and among their friends and acquaintances.

Credit reports and investigations are notoriously slanted to restrict the financial functioning of blacks in property buying. Their purchasing rights in areas where realtors and mortgage companies consider them as intruders are effectively frustrated. Some of these credit reports are unusually persecutory, and even gross errors are never erased or removed. Any credit facts of an uncomplimentary nature are presented in language so detrimental that the parole reports of convicted felons appear as banquet testimonials by comparison.

In giving attention to the subject of employment, many jobs (skilled and unskilled) remain closed to blacks. Unions continue to discriminate in their membership provisions, especially in the higher paying crafts. Employers are to a large degree indifferent and seldom motivated to give serious attention to revisions in personnel policies that will be of any real benefit to blacks on the labor market. Apprenticeship programs are notoriously discriminatory and infamously rigid in their nonacceptance of blacks. Several studies recently appearing in professional journals pointed out that in unions and industries where blacks manage to be upgraded in their jobs, this happened because of the initiative, organization and power of the blacks involved and the amount of pressure they could bring to bear on management, unions — or both. Almost no cases exist where *indiscriminate upgrading is a matter of democratic policy.*

In professional job settings, the practice of keeping the black "in his place" is carried on with effective subtlety. For example, a black employee ascends to the point of replacing a white in a status position and the job is suddenly reclassified or abolished. The black then inherits the work but not the job title and salary. Blacks are frequently used in the leg work routines to establish new projects, etc., but when success becomes apparent and permanent assignments are contemplated, the black becomes an expendable factor.

Customary and Contemporary Racism in Oregon and The Black Experience

SEPTEMBER 28, 1967

THE PRESENT DAY ASPECTS of the life of black people in Oregon will be better perceived if the prejudices which were reproduced here from the South are better understood. Even before 1850, when only a very few blacks had been able to get inside the borders of the Oregon Territory, their mere presence was a serious issue of gigantic social and political proportions. The transplanting of white racist attitudes, customs, laws and restrictions was evident among the very first white settlers. After the close of the Civil War, the negative expressions towards Afro-Americans gained impetus, and this led to many more anti-black statutes, legislation and residential restrictions being incorporated into the basic policies governing racial relations in Oregon.

On November 9, 1857, Oregon voted 8,640 to 1,081 to refuse admission to black people to the Territory under any conditions. This was followed by the leading paper of the state opposing the emancipation of slaves and labeling the abolitionists as the violent enemies of the Republican party. (*The Oregonian,* May 19, 1860)

Black people in Oregon were frequently the victims of violence, and they were ostracized and excluded from all areas of professional, business and occupational life. They were tolerated in only the most menial, servile and servant jobs.

The early theater in Oregon witnessed the appearance of minstrel shows around 1880. Minstrel shows are the caricatured antics of lazy, jovial, ignorant and stupid blacks as conceived by whites. For people who had little or no contact with black people, this was effective propaganda for propounding notions of black inferiority. As late as 1950, this type of theatrical entertainment was a favorite among some whites in the Portland vicinity and was offered as an annual fund raising presentation by a prominent white fraternal and civic organization. Protests on the part of black residents, which led to these shows being discontinued, met with considerable objection from a large number of whites of all political and religious affiliations.

In May, 1905, a court decision upheld the right of the Star Theatre to revoke a box seat ticket purchased by a black patron, because theater policy restricted black people from sitting in box seats. This decision was later upheld by the Oregon Supreme Court on March 6, 1906.

Newspapers in June, 1909, took stands against equal opportunity in employment. There has been no departure from this position up to this time. The thought was expressed that it would be out of the question to expect whites to work side by side with blacks or to admit them to unions. The employment situation and apprenticeship program in Oregon today reflect the same attitudes.

Segregated public schools were an issue in 1905. The parents of black students prevailed upon School Superintendent Henry Failing not to segregate their children, and he gave his promise that this would not happen for as long as he was superintendent. The school board and superintendent today should exhibit this same level of adherence to democratic social principles.

Oregon was, by custom, ideologically suited to provide in 1921 an ideal haven for the Ku Klux Klan. The Klan was anti-semitic, anti-Catholic, anti-Chinese, anti-Japanese and anti-black. There are known cases of severe Klan persecution of black people in Roseburg, Oregon City, Grants Pass and Medford and also of strong Klan intimidation in Portland. Most of these cities, plus many others, also had sundown laws which were applied to blacks specifically. There are still towns in Oregon where the local police enforce the spirit of the sundown laws, regardless of whether the laws appear in the local statutes.

Black people still do not have even the elemental civil and political rights proclaimed to exist in this nation. This includes individual liberties, equal protection, the right to work, equal access to a home, education and public services.

Black people in Oregon are still generally viewed by many whites as members of an alien group that is inherently inferior because of doctrines to this effect that have prevailed from the beginnings of American slavery. It has been only in recent years that black citizens have been acknowledged as human, and to this day they are permitted to occupy only the lowest of human positions on the American scale, and any departures from this are still not routine but exceptional. All relations between whites and blacks in Oregon are still carried out with blacks in subordinate positions. Equitable police and legal protection is not yet available to black citizens. Police are still regarded as instruments of persecution and death, and most black people describe policemen as a force against whom they need to be protected. Police are not believed to have any positive interest in the affairs and well-being of black citizens, and any exhibitions to the contrary are believed to be for ulterior motives.

Newspapers of the Portland area have followed a rather reluctant course in providing for their readerships social interpretations favorable to improving the status of black people in Oregon. For example, in 1948 the Washington High School assembly heard the school chorus sing a song containing the passage, "Some folks say a nigger won't steal." Forty-four black students in attendance summarily walked out of the assembly. This matter was reported to the Urban League. Efforts were exerted by the League to have the school administration apologize publicly to the black students for this insulting and abrasive incident. Newspaper criticisms which followed were leveled at the League for expressing its displeasure, rather than at a negligent school administration for permitting programs to take place that humiliated some of the students.

During the 10-year span (1950 to 1960) there was a 400 percent plus influx of blacks to take up residence in the Albina district. It is estimated that by 1960 more than 78 percent of all of Portland's black population had been herded into this area. Fifty-two percent of all blacks in the state were living in this district whose dimensions were one square mile. This population concentration was six times greater than that of the city of Portland, and the density is believed to have exceeded that of any other area of the state. This happened because realtors, in following the customary practices of the realty board (sanctioned by the Real Estate Commissioner of the State of Oregon), made available for purchase to blacks only the deteriorating and near dilapidated houses in Albina which white owners were ready to dispose of. A City Club report of 1957 verifies that this was official realty board policy, and more than 90 percent of the brokers would not sell a home to a black in the more desirable neighborhoods. The League of Women Voters conducted a survey in 1961 which revealed that 35 percent of the black prospective buyers of property had been discouraged by realtors and 27 percent were outright refused when they attempted to buy homes in other areas.

Many factors, positive and negative, demonstrate that black people are a potential power segment in this country. Whether this power will be used positively or negatively is directly related to what is available in public life for black people to enjoy and in education for black children to learn.

Albina Moods vs. Public Social Service Attitudes

MAY 17, 1967

BOUNDARIES OF ALBINA ARE NOW DRAWN to include as far as possible all identifiable clusters or concentrations of black families. As a result, every black in this area is viewed by the outside community as needing special consideration, and in many instances, charity. The stigma of blacks being culturally backward, socially inadequate, politically ignorant and educationally deficient is given wide and unlimited application. Thus, some of the most respectable people in Portland are generally held in low esteem.

Black people of Albina who have no problems with their identity are aware that blacks anywhere who have survived the class rigors and racist horrors of life in this United States are unquestionably very strong people. This fact is indisputable regardless of whether blacks fall in the category of affluent, intellectual, culturally disadvantaged or impoverished. Here, The White Power Structure, the racist system and the racist culture have contrived for every black person to be more or less disadvantaged. If some blacks fail to perceive this or are reluctant to acknowledge same, it is because they have fallen victim to the dominant population's propaganda and accepted white definitions of the black circumstances. Sadly, it can be said they are the blacks who are content to wait for white solutions to the complex social problems that white attitudes and planning have created.

Albina is reported to have the largest concentration of poor people within its boundaries of any community in Oregon. Out of an estimated total population of 36,000 in the greater Albina district, 10,000 are poor people, and of this number, black people comprise more than two-thirds. This means that there are numerous special problems, such as inadequate food, clothing, parental supervision and beneficial activities. The children are physically, emotionally and intellectually deprived. Most of them are affected by an inadequate diet, especially if they are in families receiving public assistance. Because welfare standards, so far, do not provide sufficient money for marginal diets, many times people in this bracket are just hungry.

All blacks who are known to public welfare have low status and are in need of financial assistance. Other needs such as legal aid, medical care and professional counseling are often very evident. Black people, more so than any other group, have had whites devise for them what is commonly thought of as a virulent social pathology, and this is something that the most skilled social workers are unable to help with. Most social workers fumble in this area and invariably say or communicate all of the wrong things at the wrong time in the wrong way. This has led to the existence of a marked social distance between many black clients and some white caseworkers. On the other hand, when the genuine, helpful motives and services of a caseworker are misinterpreted or distrusted by clients, the worker may consider this a routine rejection, and from this point forward all relations are hesitant, guarded and cautious.

Black families in Albina who receive public assistance need a thorough understanding of their problems by the persons rendering professional social services. Caseworkers will have to become more knowledgeable about public policy factors that contribute to the continuing deterioration of these families. Stereotyped notions of blacks are shared by people in many occupations and professions who should be free of such false concepts. Not the least of these are some persons working in the social services. Without question, too often some caseworkers accept the long established, stigmatizing interpretations of black inferiority. Underneath a veneer of pretended social concern they act as advocates for some of the most noxious of racist doctrines. Frequently some of them also manifest similar types of contempt (where race is not a factor) towards any person of the poverty category. These are the workers who add traumatic emotional distance to the social distance that already exists between themselves and their clients.

Generally, the policies of public welfare, nationally and at the state level, show an intent to provide assistance for all people in need. This includes blacks, but there is a reasonable likelihood that man will have reached the moon long before the philosophies of many functionaries at various levels of social services will have developed to the point of accepting blacks as human beings without any reservations. This is also true for all other sources of public and private professional services.

Most recipients of public social services require assistance because the social disabilities from which they suffer are too awesome for them to manage. When blacks are involved, a great deal more understanding and insight is needed. Significant matters such as public education, housing problems, employment discrimination, police attitudes and practices, publicly flaunted vice and crime and selfish performances and immoral involvements of influential community status figures have to be better understood by those who are going to work with blacks needing assistance. More insight should be gained about the damage and harm done to black families because some blacks in all strata prefer to seek their social niches by acting out the roles of "Toms" and "Aunt Jemimas."

Most poor blacks are politically weak and without effective organization. When organized, they are sometimes able to compel some minor community changes. They have even been known to show concern for civil rights, but the "Toms and Jemimas" make these hard to come by. Fortunate economic circumstances permit some blacks to withdraw into a world of suburban fantasy, but their insecurity remains in a thousand ways, because they are still black and live in America. They spend their lives trying to act in ways that will earn them the approbation of whites. Wherever this type of person is living in the largest numbers, these are the places where blacks have made the least progress. These persons are truly the "Bastards" of the American Social System. They cannot have durable association with blacks of any class because of general mistrust, enmity and conflict of class ideologies, and they are automatically rejected for their color by most whites who are their middle-class counterparts. In most communities there also are some blacks who function only at undercutting those who are politically black in their thinking and direct action efforts. Those who do this assure their continued prestige as leaders with the whites.

America is a racist country, Oregon is a racist state and Portland is a racist city. Some sections of the deep South have made greater progress. This means that from the cradle to the grave, most of the attitudes, thinking and behavior with which an individual will be confronted throughout his life will be racist in nature. This is unavoidable, because this is unequivocally a racist system of government, a racist culture and civilization. Until the social work theorists and practitioners can come to grips with these facts and deal with them without evasion and deviousness, the low level of present day social rapport is doomed to further deterioration. Much of the abuse and harassment to which blacks are subjected results from the attitudes shared by whites who express their prejudices without restraint. Laws, while designed to restrict behavior, are rather ineffective in changing the basic morality of a racist. More commitments to moral principles that allow for the defenseless to resist the powerful should be a visible part of social service programming from the topmost levels of administration to caseworkers.

Just a brief mention about education. Recently a panel of youths had one of its white participants tell an audience at an Urban League meeting that Jefferson High School, while having 46 percent plus blacks enrolled is a segregated school because the tracking practices prevent the inclusion of blacks in the larger and broader academic areas of school activities. This school's administration and faculty had been presented with these facts in an address by an NAACP spokesman long before this meeting. A black faculty member along with whites voted against having this NAACP spokesman ever speak at a faculty meeting again. Their feeble explanations were that an overwhelming number of black students come to Jefferson from elementary schools where they were graduated with severe deficiencies in all essential areas of subject matter. They are unable to handle mathematics and are three or more years behind their grade level in reading. This situation is worse now, even though the Model School Program was established under the pretext that it would correct these deficiencies by offering the necessary compensatory specialists and resources. Recent news releases stated that the school board and administration are confronted with the trauma of more than 60 teaching vacancies in the Model School Program for the next school term. In order to lure more teacher replacements into this segregated cesspool of academic degeneracy, teachers will be given $1,000 in bonus pay. What more public illustration of vile racism is required to clarify the level of concern which the rulers of this school district have for poor children?

The school board has gone (and will go) to any lengths to practice its own brand of apartheid. More than 90 percent of the black children in the Model School Program remain in segregated classes. They are being compelled to stagnate and fester in the corruption of stigmatization and ostracism. Black people should consider who are the most dastardly and criminal influences on black life in Portland—the anti-social, misbehaving street hustlers, or the school board defenders of the "White Racist Way of Life?" The welfare administration and staff should become better apprised of the circumstances and ramifications of this educational system and begin to apply its advisory and counseling services to helping inept parents on assistance obtain better education for their children. Currently, certain policies may restrict an expression of this kind of interest on the part of caseworkers, but perhaps the time has arrived when community pressures should be applied to bring about desirable policy changes.

It is reasonable to expect social service employees to understand that blacks cannot be held, in this day and time, accountable for themselves unless the society which controls them does so without malicious discrepancy and discrimination. Blacks cannot be expected to give the right reactions to wrongful, psychological prejudices which public service agencies and white society exercise against them.

E. Franklin Frazier once stated that one of the problems preventing many social workers (black and white) from working effectively with black clients was their using an approach of "Tender Condescension." Also, many caseworkers view behavior that is different from their personal values as deviant and that which conforms as acceptable and healthy. Nevertheless, people who need help should be encouraged to seek it. This should be the purpose and commitment of all persons in the community who know of people living under undue stress and hardship.

Public Welfare has some knowledge and techniques for working with human beings beset with difficult problems. In many areas a great deal of experience has been amassed in working with deprived peoples. Social service representatives often realistically assess the waste in human resources that results from community indifference, apathy and neglect. Tremendous amounts of time, plus immense sums of money, are required to provide services of the quality that can reduce client frustration and hostility and encourage better behavior. In spite of the many baffling perplexities that result from insufficient funds for social programs, less than satisfactory salaries, vacillation on the part of those in political control, and inadequate staffing and resources, social service staffs continue to offer the best services they possibly can. In this respect efforts are continuing, but they can do more!

The question is, WHEN?

The NAACP and The Model School Program: Community Problems Produced from Racial Segregation in Portland Public Schools

William H. McClendon, *Chairman,* Education Committee, Portland Branch NAACP

ADDRESS TO JEFFERSON HIGH SCHOOL TEACHERS' MEETING, 1968

FOLLOWING THE NAACP REQUEST of September, 1962, for the school board to change the deplorable pattern of black pupil segregation in those elementary schools in the Albina District, the response from the school board and the press was negative and hostile. Persistent efforts to bring this matter to the attention of the entire community eventually obtained the support of benevolent and concerned white people who prevailed upon the school board to at least study or investigate the complaints voiced by black spokesmen. The answer to this, after prolonged verbal prattling along lines of the most illogical formations, was to establish a committee of 40-odd persons to investigate: 1. Unequal education opportunities; 2. Cultural deprivation areas of the city; 3. Racial prejudice among students.

As a side comment, it should be noted that the failure of the Portland School District to hire blacks during the '50s as teachers in the high schools, despite their possessing secondary certification and training, was believed by many blacks to be a matter of racist policy. Also, it was believed that the employment of black teachers was conducted on a quota basis during the years of 1950 to 1960. These impressions were often expressed among blacks concerned with problems of discrimination. Naturally, when a former school board member *(Herbert Schwab),* who had served during the aforementioned period was named as the Chairman of the Race and Education Committee, this shattered the hopes of the more thoughtful blacks that the committee would give any serious attention to the real needs of black school children who were the victims of segregated education. The Race and Education Committee is now a community legend that will be remembered best for producing a work which developed a brisk breeze of fallacious thought that strengthened, expanded and compounded the segregation of school children in this community. This was accomplished by grouping nine elementary schools, including those in the Albina area, into what is called a Model School Program.

The one result of the Model School Program has been the hardening of existing school segregation (black children in the MS program remain segregated), and this in essence is a social disservice to the entire community and culturally crippling to the children. Thoughtful black people must continue to condemn the Model School Program because of its calculated and continued debasement of black children and also the flagrant manner in which they remain stigmatized. These factors in themselves serve to socially constrain and circumscribe the children to the point that they can seldom perform adequately.

The fact that black children in Portland remain in segregated classrooms in such large numbers 13 years after the U.S. Supreme Court decision outlawing segregation is a galling example of the racial contempt and snobbery that prevails in high places of local and state government and at the authority vested levels of the school district. This in itself is sufficient to emotionally convulse the entire black community.

Civil rights are those rights which a citizen has simply by virtue of being a citizen. These are the rights to use and enjoy equally all forms of public services and accommodations without being discriminated against. Public schools without reservations are to be included. Unequal segregated education is an indignity to all blacks, and when human indignity exists, the issue of civil rights is at stake. The Model School Program denies to black children of Portland their civil rights. School Administration spokesmen for promotion of the Model School Program are constantly gearing their remarks toward explaining and advertising half-truths to imply black inferiority and prove the inadequacy of the black child. Invariably, they overemphasize the negative aspects of black family life, poverty, fear and social rejections. Reports received by various persons and groups concerned with harassment of blacks have noted that expression of harsh discriminations against many black children have been expanded, and teacher and principal contempt for black students has increased. Many cases of sheer physical abuse of students are reported frequently to the

NAACP, the Urban League and the various ministers.

The public function of the Model School Program is now regarded by most blacks as an institutional process for the frustration of social justice. Its highly perfected system of racial segregation and its applied inferior education is considered evidence that those persons responsible for public education are indifferent and continue to evade keeping abreast of the social directions that are honorable and legal, and which the whole nation is recognizing as expedient to follow in some degree.

The Model School Program is a contrived device for holding in careful, isolated containment 90 percent of its black pupils, so they can stagnate and fester in the corruption of segregation and its accompanying intellectual shortfallings. This assures a complete social and academic mortality for black children by the time they reach the age of 16. The failure of Judge Schwab's Racist Education committee and the Portland School Board to come to grips with the need to end the miseducation of black children is now regarded as the in-place symbol of real South African apartheid in Oregon – and possibly in all of thc United States.

In principle, there is no difference in the emasculating effects of segregation on the minds of defenseless black children in Portland and the mutilation of children's bodies in the gas chambers of Auschwitz! America's greatest scandal is still the treatment of American blacks, and Portland's Model School Program ranks at the top among the types of maltreatment, neglect and abuse directed at black school-aged children to be found anywhere in this country. Until this school system can offer equal, integrated public education to black children, this state is in essence an undeveloped country. The really developed countries make the best social use of nature, including people.

All segregation since the passage of the Civil Rights Bill of 1964 is *de facto*. Segregation is a violation of the laws of the United States, and in public schools it matters not whether its causes are through innocence or intent. When children in PSD #1 are prevented from obtaining quality non-racist educations, this assures that they are automatically placed at an intellectual disadvantage. Under segregated, or so-called desegregated arrangements, no matter how loaded with the promises of remedial and compensatory devices, the real education of the black child is provided under different, unequal and stigmatizing conditions. Examined from a black perspective, this ensures that most of these children will continue to occupy a subordinate place in the social order. The slave system of this country was not designed or intended to prepare slaves for freedom; it was directed toward making each succeeding generation of slaves better slaves. In the same sense, the segregation and desegregation schemes of public education are not directed toward preparing black children for an equitable status in American life. On the contrary, it operates to continue their subjugation.

Segregation provides the psychological basis for making the segregated believe they are inferior, and the end result is that many are unknowingly influenced into accepting inequitable tracking in society. This is perhaps the greatest evil of this immoral practice, and it is the reason black people are seeking quality, non-racist public education systems. Already, there are far too many who will never be cured of the disease of inferiority. This number includes blacks with no degrees to Ph.D.s.

Oregon: Haven, Dilemma or Tragedy – The Black Experience Recounted

JULY 16, 1973

AMERICA IS A RACIST COUNTRY, Oregon is a racist state and Portland is a racist city. This means that from the cradle to the grave, most of the attitudes, thinking and behavior with which any black person here will be confronted throughout his life will be racist in nature.

Earlier this year, a panel of youth had one of its white participants tell an audience at an Urban League meeting that Jefferson High School, while having around 40 percent plus blacks enrolled, is a segregated school, because the teaching and administrative practices prevent the inclusion of blacks in the larger and broader academic areas of school activities. School officials had been confronted by me (as a representative of the NAACP) on this matter long before this meeting. Explanations offered were that an overwhelming number of black students come to Jefferson from elementary schools (Model Schools) where they were graduated with severe deficiences in all essential areas of subject matter. They are unable to handle mathematics and are three or more years behind their grade level in reading. This situation is reported as worse now.

Recent news releases stated that the school administration was confronted with the trauma of 60 teaching vacancies for the coming school term in the Model School Program. In order to lure replacements into this cesspool of academic degeneracy, teachers in the Model Schools are to be given $1,000 per year bonus pay. It is impossible to conceive of a more vile public expression of racism. The entire black community becomes the victim of defamation and denigration because the school board feels that the teachers of black children in segregated schools, which it maintains against the dictates of social reality and progress, should receive combat pay or lucrative financial rewards "for services above and beyond the call of duty . . ."

Pessimism, bitterness and criticism which may seem to creep into this discourse can hardly be avoided, because there are countless documents in evidence to support this analysis. For example, in the years prior to 1941, Portland had a black population of approximately 2,000. These people, in direct ratio to their percentage of population, educated their children in all degrees (high school, college, and beyond) comparable to whites. All through the 1930s, each year witnessed enrollment and graduation from college percentage-wise as the same for blacks as for whites. From three to seven Portland blacks would graduate from college each year. Now, twenty-seven years later, with a black population estimated at more than 18,000, numerically there are no more blacks graduating from college each year than during the '30s – in fact, sometimes not as many. And if you are of the impression that there are more, it is because of the increase in black students from out of state who have been completing their education in Oregon.

This change in academic follow-through on the part of black students can be attributed to the severe decline in aspiration and motivation that has occurred since 1950. This symbolizes the point in time when segregation of black children became a school board policy and was revealed with the rebuilding of the Eliot School more than 25 years ago, at a location that was even then destined to be a slum.

A study by G. F. Boyd, "The Levels of Aspirations of black and White Children in a Non-Segregated Elementary School," *Journal of Social Psychology, Vol., 36, 1952,* found that children of the same intelligence level from a non-segregated Portland Public School – 25 white and 25 black – the blacks had a higher level of aspiration. This was before the existing problem of school segregation had been so rigidly established. It is of the utmost importance that this previous level of aspiration be restored. It is apparent that the difficulty of segregated education is the segregation itself – nothing more, nothing less! This is borne out by studies and observations of the highest academic quality, including the recent Civil Rights Commission report entitled "Racial Isolation In The Public Schools, Vol, I."

It is hoped that civil rights groups can be encouraged in the near future to launch strong assaults against the grading system in schools, a sore black observers are perceiving to be a racist and class defining device which is too often used capriciously to limit or advance students in accordance with the opinions, attitudes and prejudices of teachers. This has undoubtably served well the supremacist notions of many elements of white society. The vulnerability of black children in northern segregated schools is readily perceived. Since more than one-third of all black students drop out of high school before graduation, it appears that abandonment of the prevailing grading system is a necessary prerequisite to bringing civil rights into the schools.

In Defense of Black Life

SEPTEMBER, 1980

Sometimes America has been right for public education. Now public education has to be made right for black people.

IT HAS BEEN CLEAR FOR SEVERAL DECADES that the quality of education, non-racist in content and context, the American public school districts will offer to black children — all children — is not going to be any better than the political efforts the black communities extend to make real the fulfilling of school boards' long-overdue obligations. Public school systems have the responsibility to providc thc vcry best academic environment for students and nothing less. As the black population insists that programming and planning include black children, school administrations in many localities are seeking any stooges who can be duped into accepting and advocating preposterous compromises that will continue to obstruct better education for black children from coming into existence.

Blacks are demanding that schools become academically authentic and that teaching competencies be accompanied by attitudes and expectations that are genuinely humanistic. These are major requisites for making education beneficial and should be in evidence without question. This requires that school administrations not allow their systems to degenerate into settings for tokenism, just to keep the heat off inept principals and unfit teachers.

America's Greatest Scandal

Segregation was put into operation first in a "Jim Crow" context. It was applied as a means of separating or ostracizing blacks by whites on a physical basis in public transportation and other sectors of public services. Segregation now has grown far beyond just being a plan in the platform of white racism; it is the major pillar of support and maintenance for the individual and institutional white racist structures that operate in every niche and crevice of this nation.

Fallacy of Integration

Racial proscriptions as delineated in white vs. black relationships are based on beliefs in white supremacy and have been extended to cover virtually every human activity from birth to death. Segregation is no longer confined to arranging human body placements according to white racist color schemes. It is a deeply imbedded, diabolic conviction prevailing among most of the white population, including all classes, that the natural place for blacks in America, whether at close range or considerable distance, is at a visibly lower status than that enjoyed by whites. In order for this to have been and to continue as the legal structure and public policy of this nation, the controls over blacks in every context are vested in white people. This is a major cause for blacks being incensed over the public education game-playing of many school boards and administrations.

The problems in education faced by black children are compounded, because most white educators are caught up in the complex and confused dynamics of segregation and are unable to deal honestly with the reality, nor are they able to extricate themselves from it. In addition, arrogance and contempt are coagulated so strongly behind much of the fallacious rhetoric of integration that it is difficult for supporters or critics to fathom the impact of ridiculous fears and abominable ignorance that may seem to have unwarranted influence. The more planning that involves confused school boards and manipulating administrations, the more hurt, dissatisfaction and disappointment to be felt by those blacks who seek and need improvements in public education.

An Absence of Virtues

The aforestated and more have led to many public school systems being viewed by an increasing number of observers as having an absence of virtues and a mass of sickness. All of these coincide with the recorded history of white racist thought as the philosophical force guiding the growth and development of education in the United States. This may explain why school boards and administrations across the country have often acted as sneer centers toward the black population. The results are that the most legitimate proposals for non-racist education coming from blacks are defined and treated in ways that reflect the most hateful, sterile and static preferences of the reactionary elements of the dominant population. The major thrust of white racist attitudes, policies and behavior has been to provide more often than not the most degrading environment imaginable for the black population. In the present era, this is increasingly noticeable in the area of public education. Many discouragements and frustrations are consistently produced for black parents and children through the tactical and strategic deviousness of school administrators. Often these are blatant and frequent. Ironically they are passed off as constructive social therapy.

Despite the many expressions of a contrary point of view, in America at this time black education is a politically advanced component in the area of multicultural education that does not fall into second place when compared to white racist indoctrination. This is not stated to suggest or infer that black concerns should take precedence over those of the dominant or other non-dominant ethnic populations. It is a reminder that black people throughout the course of American history have been the avant-garde to affirm and demand that American public education systems do more to effectuate non-racist education and cultural pluralism. Black survival, along with the preservation of identity, culture and diversity despite the dominant population's chronic inhumanness, provided most black people with a unique legacy and capability for resistance, struggle and perseverance. Blacks for more than a century have fought against systemic and systematic segregation, and those continuing battles have made clear their opposition and antagonism to the virulence of implacable white racism. The dominant population has reacted by highlighting with political pomposity that integration should be the goal for black people. This was/is of course a "Catch-22" concept, because the unattainableness of integration is kept concealed. As a result, poorly publicized elements of blacks and whites are produced who remain in varying states of confusion and conflict over issues and procedures springing from a myth. Some social theorists have shown that integration was developed as a substitute for assimilation, because integration creates the illusion that blacks can become part of the society, while assimilation means that blacks would become swallowed up by the dominant population.

Segregation, Integration Interlocked with White Racism

Any inclusions of black people at any time, anyplace, anywhere in America has never been on an equal basis, and the qualitative differences in every situation and every environment have brought about increased anger and alienation. These have had the irreversible effect of clarifying the deception built into an abysmally bad social fallacy: racial integration. For social pragmatists, there are no doubts about the realities contained in this analysis: the black population has never received any measurable benefits from any of those activities, programs, schemes and plans structured by whites to conform to their mythology of integration

Blacks have learned from long involvement in deceptive struggles the word value of integration. Its greatest service is to conceal from blacks that the dominant population does not intend to share authority or permit the establishing of equity for blacks anywhere in the national life. Integration for whites is an assortment of sociopolitical tools used by those who intend to continue the oppression of blacks. Integration is a means of teaching and persuading blacks to believe that they can escape other blacks by slipping off or "up to" the white milieu. Blacks who are susceptible to these overtures are never beneficiaries of genuine white largesse. They become the tragic victims of well-organized, sophisticated chicanery.

For those who are politically black, there is only one goal to be achieved, and that is to acquire without question or interference the right to be liberated within this nation. This means that members of the black population, wherever they are, will be free individually and collectively to make decisions about their own lives without any limits or frustrations because of the distance or proximity of white people. Blacks must have the right of self-determination here in the American nation. It must be the same as that exercised by the most privileged and fortunate sectors or settlements of the dominant population. If black people can not have these choices and enjoy these rights, then America has no merit and must be judged as ranking minus one on a justice scale of zero to ten.

There is determination now to make it possible for black children to reduce learning impediments and provide more emotional comfort through exposure to non-racist, non-sexist education. In the struggle to reach these objectives, supporters and opponents should understand some black perspectives as they relate to segregation and integration.

Segregation and integration in America are interlocked with white racism. They are inseparable. Their assorted functions collectively frustrate the black population (all non-dominant ethnic populations) from having any success in liberating themselves from the horrendous circumstances created by the barriers and constraints which are the social constructs for their racist rejection.

Percentage Formula Capricious

Segregation sets the stage for its targets to be vulnerable to any negative social excesses, abuses and proscriptions which segregationists wish to impose. It provides the social climate for segregationists to feel a collective obligation and duty to preserve the status quo. To accomplish this, laws, public policy, attitudes and custom are utilized in some of the most appalling ways. Consequently, racial discriminations are stimulated and maintained that seriously interfere with interpopulation communication and understanding. This assures that any percentage of black students in any school operating under the racist mandates of the dominant population may be segregated with impunity. This does not become altered if the black student population is 1 percent, 50 percent, 99 percent. In a word, the theory of correcting the educational problems facing black children through racial balance is a joke.

The racial attitudes among many school officials are inherited and remain fixed, with few exceptions, throughout a lifetime. There are very strong correlates to these attitudes in evidence throughout the dominant population, and for many they have been in existence for several generations. This brings us to face the long-held adage that all education up to this point for black people in America, no matter where it is offered or acquired, is alternative education. There is no valid challenge to this, because America as a system and its educational structures, always deal with blacks as outsiders. American education, as much or more so than any other institutional area, is a colossal bureaucracy and bastion of exclusivity, selectivity and status quo maintenance. It has been very effective in providing and sustaining the most damaging negative definitions of black people, their culture and history. When arbitrary and capricious determinations are announced by any school administration as to the percentages of blacks that will be admitted to certain public schools, these are not expressions of interest in the education and intellectual development of black students but are dominant population contrivances to erect new structures of paralyzing selective segregation under the pretense of fostering integration.

White manipulation for segregation and for integration are not put in place as mutually agreed stipulations. They are not covenants entered into with the black population having equal input, influence and authority. Consequently, arrangements are never reached that make possible the even and balanced functioning of society.

KGW: Free Bias, Fettered Speech . . .

SEPTEMBER 19, 1980

THE THEMES OF "OPEN FORUM" and "free speech" have been used by the advocates for white racism to direct uncountable assaults and indignities at the black population. KGW-TV has now openly joined its many predecessors in such endeavors. The station manager, in his proclaimed concern to offer opportunities for public discussion and enlightenment, revealed an appalling insensitivity to the normal daily concerns of the black population. Every expression and explanation indicated that his understanding of the doctrine of free speech is grossly deficient. He failed in an attempt to dignify as theory what William Shockley has plagiarized from age-old white racist myths and propaganda. KGW invited Shockley to espouse this repugnant garbage to the viewing public and implored blacks to be on hand *gratis* to help him achieve credibility. Without blacks, any exposure given this individual is invalid.

The station manager is confused, if his notions of free speech assume there exists the constitutional right and freedom to denigrate and slander. The awesome KGW resources in personnel and technology are misused when they carry the messages of defamation against black people from an internationally known racist. This is an inexcusable display of unconscionable racist contempt on the part of KGW management and ownership.

Other recent news accounts have illuminated the racist inspired disservice, disregard and discriminations of other broadcasting media in this area. National network television also, is no exception. In presenting Shockley, KGW boldly declares its ingrained commitment to revitalize one of the sickest segments of white racism's tired and dissipated vitriol. This should concern all decent persons. The fact that KGW is involved in disseminating the empty, unsubstantiated and pernicious opinions of Shockley is an unparalleled insult to the entire black population. It is absurd and disgusting that the station manager has the gall to see himself as doing blacks a small favor by offering them a chance to debate white racism. For the socially developed persons of this world, this is a non-debatable issue. Only the mentally ossified would seek to exercise such prerogatives.

This kind of programming on the part of KGW should be considered in violation of FCC regulations. If there were not an absence of empathetic racists at the federal monitoring level, this station's license might be subject to revocation. This point is well taken, because Shockley has no contribution to make to any social order that includes black people. The sounds he has made up to this time consist only of hate-filled insults, and these consistently lack reason. It is not unusual but it is surprising that KGW would brazenly show admiration and shower attention upon an individual whose chief business is to diminish and jeopardize the limited esteem that exists in this nation for its black population. As a medium serving the public, KGW should show responsibility to provide the materials and information which also reflect the goals and values of black people. But instead, fees and facilities are provided so that Shockley can recite and re-emphasize his phony anti-black dogmatic distortions. This boils down to being an insidious KGW strategy for creating societal polarization and increasing disrespect and repression for black people.

The showcasing of Shockley holds up the entire black population for defamation and disrespect. No rationalizations can explain convincingly that this is done to reduce tirades against black people. It must be seen as KGW affirming that all who share notions of white supremacy should assert themselves more. Therefore, from a black perspective, KGW used Shockley to provoke black reaction and to arouse indignation. KGW shows itself to be a safe haven for white racism, and it is doubtful if the dominant population it serves will be critical of any subsequent scurrilous offenses that are directed at the black population.

KGW and Gerry Pratt were first perceived as only interested in winning support for Shockley and his views. Minor modification in their verbiage became apparent after organized black opposition was expressed at a press conference September 18, 1980. However, prior to this, many citizens informed KGW via telephone of their objections.

KGW in all probability will be able to establish that it has not violated any laws. Despite this, the truth is the publicized sentiments of Shockley do damage and violence to the sensitivities and the humanity of black people. These are not undone or altered by challenge, confrontation and refutation. Thus, blacks are correct in asserting that the failure of KGW to be cognizant of these far-reaching implications for black people throughout this nation is a matter of immeasurable gravity.

KGW in serving the total population should avoid threatening the social tranquillity and well-being of any population sector. In foisting Shockley upon the black public, KGW was not displaying interest in social betterment. This was a cold, forceful, disturbing white racist anti-black political statement.

KGW is distressingly limited in its capacity to provide sound social focus. This is clearly revealed in its failure to respect the black population as another intelligent, complex, human entity. This compels blacks to reject without reservation the put-down implicit in the capricious thrusting of a white racist sensationalist before us the same as a slap in the face.

In addition, black people cannot disregard the fact that Shockley's beliefs and attitudes as disseminated over the past dozen years have comforted millions of whites and confirmed their tendencies to treat blacks with contempt. Blacks are rightfully incensed upon discovering that KGW has openly joined the hordes of the racially cruel and barbaric. An even more appalling aspect is that the FCC is not likely to develop a will to correct any of this as the black image is ground to pieces in the racist mills of television's commercialism.

White racism is the pervasive ideology of this community and this nation. Many whites do not deny this. This Shockley thing enables blacks to see KGW as intending to deprecate black life and culture, cloud the black presence, increase degradation and compound misery for black people. At the same time, the dominant population will be made to feel "normal".

A note for the uninformed: Shockley was dismissed from serious attention by thinking blacks more than ten years ago. The question: "Then why this commentary?" The answer: "The American nation at this very moment is victimized with magnitudinous social problems." If the social and political consciousness of the television media can reach no higher level than what we have witnessed at KGW, then oppressiveness and inhumanness surely will propel the total society into a state of unsurpassed decadence. Count on it!

Some Black Perceptions of Public Schools in America

OCTOBER 26, 1981

THERE IS A NEED TO LEARN ABOUT AND UNDERSTAND the clamor among black people for political, cultural and social liberation. Once such understanding is acquired, there still remains the need to develop qualified personnel to provide black perspectives on the literature, music, art and history of black people. However, more is required than a superficial awareness of the role of culture in the rising level of socio-political maturity among the black population. For this to be accomplished, teachers and students must have no unresolved questions about the black identity.

1. Introductory Factors

The dual identity of blacks must be comprehended in terms of their being black and also American. The procedures for correctly categorizing and combining these distinct identities are complex and, for the untrained, immensely difficult. For those skin-priviledged persons whose experiences do not include being targets of warped, racist social theories, myths and presumptions, gaining these insights can assume awesome dimensions.

Duality in the black experience is imposed by the system of white racism. The criterion for this was indelibly reiterated in the U.S. Supreme Court's *Scott vs. Sandford* (Dred Scott Case) decision in 1857, with the judgement: "A black man has no rights a white man need respect." At this point the entire black population was branded with an inferior status, socially and institutionally, in every sector of America. To this day nothing has been developed to alter, remedy or correct this punitive judgment of black people.

Black political movements, black Studies and black commitments geared to realizing limited personal and group aspirations have been the major black efforts and responses to offset the negative impact of living as an oppressed group. Blacks are not fooled by frequent promises to improve the education of black children. They regard these as just more adornments on a long train of deceptions.

The duality of black life in America brings into clear perspective that white educators do not motivate black children. Black parents, relatives, friends and peers motivate black children. The black identity is much more than just a by-product of a racist socioeconomic system erected to accommodate the avarice and greed of European adventurists. Blacks in America today are the descendants of a captured people, who were forcibly subjected to slavery and debasement in the Western hemisphere for more than three centuries. The cultural tics of blacks in North America were severely ruptured, but they managed to transmit to succeeding generations that their origins and heritage were African. This, from the beginning, enabled the masses of black people to recognize that between them is a common condition of which a common consciousness remains.

2. Dominance as the Norm

Most blacks see public schools in America as bureaucratic devices maintaining the status quo. This will not be altered until teachers understand clearly that from most black perspectives the conservative ideological mold of education here is geared to implementing the continuation of uninterrupted racism. Most of America's school systems' operations reflect clearly the determination to practice unequivocally white domination and black subordination.

Perceptive blacks insist that these educator-controlled systems must change those guidelines that treat black children as deficit models. There has to be a muting of opinions, beliefs and attitudes at the administrative, principal and teacher levels that approve or ignore the steady stream of attributions implying social, genetic and cultural inferiority of black children. The instruments of education—materials and personnel—must be redirected toward teaching students to aspire to reach the highest possible levels of humanism. Racist myths, mores and customs passed off as American values must be removed from the entire academic circuit. The psychological and social dynamics of the black existence must seriously be considered objectively.

3. Unamended Inequities

Most blacks believe that there are few, if any, commitments at any of the administrative levels to protect black students and to treat them humanely. Based upon the history and evidence of maltreatment of blacks, many blacks view educators the same as they do some police.

Both schools and police departments are seen as organized bodies from whom blacks need protection. Most black people (parents and students) are highly sensitive to the travails of living in communities (a nation) where the laws, regulations and public policies are specially structured to give maximum benefit to whites and offer maximum disadvantage to blacks, making them the dupes of illegalities and the victims of inequities. When blacks seek to use laws, they learn first that most of their efforts and energies must be directed toward injecting humanism into the law prior to judicial consideration. This requires painstaking maneuvers that in many situations are unable to produce justice. Historically and customarily in America, when black people seek to obtain justice through legal processes, formal, positive rhetoric receives only harsh, negative interpretations.

4. Pluralism versus the Myth of Multiculturalism

Most public school districts do not have a real commitment to provide quality, non-racist, non-sexist education. Currently, some emphasis is being placed on the label "Multicultural Education." For blacks and other non-dominant ethnic populations, cultural pluralism in form and substance is the relevant and acceptable academic component. Most so-called multicultural programs are understood to be and are carried out as assimilation and amalgamation schemes. On the whole, these have amounted to little more than perfunctory, limited excursions for blacks to exhibit cultural values through types of food, music, dance and specially selected art forms. Establishing quality, non-racist public education is the first step in insuring that black students will no longer be targets for numerous assaults that historically have sprung from white racism.

Public school boards throughout the nation employ the customary pattern of stonewalling, evasion and double talk when faced with questions and challenges initiated in the black community. In these times, the main thrust of black awareness and consciousness must be to confront head on those racist forces responsible for heaping indignities upon black people. Now blacks in many sectors of the United States believe it is no longer necessary or worthwhile to acquiesce to the insults, discriminations and abuses that earmark the major policy patterns and activities of whites in authority and control of education and other public institutions. For some blacks, there is an increased appreciation of the adage, "Anything a slave does to end his slavery is justified." Slave buying and slave holding are the legacies of white America. Any present-day public policy practice symbolic of these practices have earned long ago the contempt of black people, a thousandfold.

5. Intransigence of White Racism

Blacks are concerned that the nation's public school systems do not take into account that black people reach their destinies by handling the contradiction between their own cultural traditions and the dominant population's customs of brutality and exploitation. History clearly shows that this racist system persists in oppressing blacks, because it can; black tradition teaches blacks to remain in a perpetual state of resistance and involved in an eternal quest for justice and liberation, because they must.

America's public schools for too long have indulged their staffs in human devaluation and punitive action towards black students and parents. There is now a belief among many blacks that the American academic environment is dysfunctional, and its deficiencies and failings are protected by arbitrary and capricious authority. There is a catastrophic potential in the anger that seethes in many black conclaves because of the imperious arrogance displayed by many school district personnel. Now is the time to end those frequent manifestations of indifference, insensibility and contempt toward black people, black perspectives and humanistic values.

Living situations for most blacks in this country are fraught with obstacles and hardships produced and maintained by white racism. This truth has not escaped the various boards and administrations of America's public school systems. In recent years, momentous protests have been conducted by members of the black community to address and correct some of these aggravating conditions. For the most part, the responses of boards and administrations continue to be more intensive maneuvers to evade abolishing an educational environment that black people often classify as heinous and barbaric. Black students and parents want educational offerings that treat the black experience on a comparable basis to the curriculum that buttresses white nationalism. And most settings' administrations have not removed those sanctions that have been exercised overtly, covertly or inadvertently to prevent blacks from learning about themselves. For as long as black students are prohibited from receiving these academic experiences, they will remain immeasurably weak in challenging and confronting the ever-multiplying forms of white racism. As long as there is no well-developed Black Studies component in school curricula, public schools will be depriving black children of meaningful and purposeful education. The absence of Black Studies means that for black students, only white ideological positions and directions precariously perched on deceptive cliches and false promises will continue to be used as charades for education.

There is an obvious dearth in most of the nation's public schools of managerial staff with adequate training, study and experience in ethnography and comparative sociology. This poses immense problems for school districts to structure the analytical and methodological capabilities to come to grips with the fact that America is a nation of alienated and polarized people. Also, it is unlikely that white racism will be perceived as largely responsible for this. It is not expected that institutional white racism will be acknowledged as the system of government in the United States. No attention may be directed to the fact that the vast majority of political leaders are those who appeal to the worst facets of character in people. Therefore, no thorough comprehension will be obtained as to how this energizes and continues the scapegoating of blacks, and because they are the non-wealthy and non-powerful, this makes them maximum victims of deprivation, maltreatment and violence.

The Socialization of Black Youth

MARCH, 1994

OVER AN EXTENDED PERIOD, there have been frequent indications of seriously flawed and misguided policies in several public education sectors. Some analysts attribute these in part to delays in structuring programs committed to meeting humane and humanitarian requirements for large student constituencies when the needs were early in evidence. Where crucial situations developed, many spasmodic experiments with crisis management schemes began to dot the national public educational landscapes. Often these did not have the benefit of broad professional and community collaborative study and preparation. Most were conceived under pressure, designed in haste and limited in scope, offering little more than semblances of stop-gap damage control.

A large number of families in this last quarter of the twentieth century are faced with unprecedented difficulties in coping with problems of dependency, deficiency and delinquency. Many frequent arguments are being made emphasizing that some of the battles for the preservation of youth are being lost. One need is clear: Caring for children has to be a life-long process in order that they will not reach puberty and adolescence in a state of unmanageable social, psychological and physical disorder. At a very early stage and age, value structures must be provided and instilled that will enable children to develop ego strengths, strong internalized concepts of personal worth and a capacity for positive, independent decision making.

Reforms are sorely needed in many public education formats. Education offered in many standard and existing alternative programs should be constantly evaluated to distinguish the inappropriate and unproductive content from the substantive and useful. For example, for much too long teachers have been expected to affirm and reinforce basic social training that presumably occurred in-family for students prior to their arrival in school. Now it is broadly recognized that many teachers find it extremely difficult to carry out basic tasks of student-in-school socialization because of warped and imprecise concepts students already have about behavior and personal responsibility.

The socialization of children is an immensely complex task today. Life in America across the entire spectrum has become an uncertain and unpredictable macro-system of social and psychological experiences. Many elements of these are in conflict with or contrary to values, customs, traditions, relationships and behaviors commonly acknowledged as traditional, conventional or regular. Many entrenched methodological socialization processes are no longer certain to be adequate for preparing children from myriad circumstances to assume responsible and humane roles in society.

The appealing political adage expressed during the 1960s that "those not part of the solution are part of the problem" cannot properly be applied when correctly assessing some basic problems and solutions for troubled students of today. Development and implementation techniques and skills to effectively influence the will of youth to seek more out of life than being scapegoats, victims or outcasts is of the utmost concern and importance. This requires acquiring understanding of this system from black as well as other cosmopolitan perspectives, coping with the complexities of life, avoiding a destiny of sub-marginal living and rejecting the unexpected seductions in situation hazards that impair many youth in their routine life experiences. On balance, many programs are created to help broad sectors of America's student population engage in constructive developmental activities.

It is not uncommon, however, for some individuals and groups to use this to reject other individuals and groups. Many educators have worked diligently to prevent education from being perceived by any category of the broad constituency of youth as an exercise in futility. Now, this demands additional careful scrutiny of the larger social environment to identify negative influences having an impact on the lives of youth. Schools have to assume major roles in challenging, check-mating and counteracting.

School administrators and boards are aware that academic improvement demands they deal forthrightly with personnel attitudes, practices and competencies. Also, expert attention must be given to student problems, difficulties and behavior. To do one without doing the other is useless. In assuming responsibilities for eradicating incompetencies and correcting improprieties, educators now know they cannot wear blinders and cater to biases. Extra-special attention is required to help those not enmeshed in antisocial activities to expand their academic and social potentials, to set higher goals and reach them. Stronger and more intensive efforts must be made to assist those who have been immersed in difficulties to increase their endeavors to achieve more productive social and academic adjustments.

Counseling techniques and practices, even when of superior quality, should be persistent to influence students to counter unacceptable behavior and perceive the risks of social deterioration and alienation that result from criminal activities. These must complement the teaching of ethical decision-making and training in the acquisition of social skills and negotiating behaviors.

Rethinking and restructuring school programs are receiving the utmost concern because of the imminent demands to meet the awesome responsibilities involved with educating effectively the troubled, troubling, troublesome and in-trouble children of the nation. Also, society and its institutions cannot afford to ignore any longer the appalling numbers of unproductive citizens at large in the total population. In many communities, these people are serving as some of the major role models influencing nonchalant attitudes and indifference to normative and significant values among many school age youth. Educators are now keenly aware that schools will not be able to avoid becoming primary sources of student socialization. Some rather rapid adaptations have to be made in this direction to reverse and correct the assorted student-attributed disorders and instabilities in many schools. These should be followed by planning and implementation of public educational services to those families and communities where there are diminished social and cultural supports.

Many social categories exist among the diverse populations of this nation. Some by their very nature give rise to sustained feelings of social distance. In many instances, these are highlighted by strong animosities and frequent hostilities. Often, reconciliation requires adjustments that many affected groups and individuals are unable to make. Children whose earliest interpersonal experiences include scarcity of necessities, physical-emotional-mental abuses, cultural rejections, negative or non-educative exposures, atrocious environments of anti-social conditioning and behavior usually encounter more difficulties in adjusting to the formal requirements of routine school operations. For many children whose intelligence levels are very high, there are no guarantees that perceptive and skillful teachers will be in sufficient supply to assure academic attainment and successes. The fact that some students commonly exposed to negative social influences infrequently distinguish themselves academically is viewed often with amazement. However, those who fail are not regarded as surprises.

Many crises are constantly being created for the people of America. Most of these are systemic and systematic, and more than ample evidence exists to support this assertion. Consequently, there is a need now to focus more upon the matter of caring for children. A vast number of youth do not receive any care that seriously involves commitment to their preservation with emphases on values, standards and stability. Many children are becoming the products that derive from emotional immaturity, confusion and negative peer-group emulation. Their expressions and behaviors are indicative of increasing emotional disintegration and hardening of contemptuous attitudes. These are generating more vandalism, bizarre sexual proclivities, physical violence and wanton murder. Many of these behaviors can be related to the shortage of sufficient consistent human-relations examples to demonstrate effectively uncompromising moral concerns with humane and qualitative improvements in the human condition.

A pressing need exists for structuring intensive social programs to counter the accommodations governmental administrations have made to ignore the expanding debasement of defenseless children and other less resourceful members in diverse sectors of the total society. An increasing number of communities throughout the American nation are acknowledged now to have more youth who are targets of poor (or no) education, diminishing employment opportunities and greater susceptibility to damaging social experiences. The detrimental results from all of these are incalculable.

Routinely, a large number of people in their daily existence are subjected to great pressures. Many now live under conditions of unprecedentedly severe stress, and in many settings socialization processes are severely crippled. In some situations, they appear to be absolutely numb or paralyzed. For most persons who live under such conditions, the deprivations and disadvantages permeating their living situations are almost always beyond their control. Inconveniences, discomforts and hardships are intensified for them because of too few or a total absence of material resources. Academic interest and scholarly motivations are often much more difficult to inculcate among many of the students who have been locked into these circumstances. Frequently they create insurmountable obstacles that deter efforts of schools and communities to better educate students whose life experiences are characterized by antisocial behaviors, crime, substandard living, excessive negative predicaments and poverty. There is long standing belief that schools should fill a leadership role in American community life. In many situations, this is not questioned. However, many episodes and incidents of the present era have aroused serious concerns over whether this expectation for some schools is realistic. Some of these disquietudes have emanated from quarters where there are real professional anxieties over the diminished achievement and slow or no intellectual growth among broad categories of students.

In the student socialization techniques that may be developed and implemented, there should be substantive methodologies for alleviating student feelings of inadequacy, insecurity and indifference. Aspiration levels have to be raised and any suspicions of cultural lockouts removed. Most youths who continue to have serious problems in schools are more the victims of on-going and severe confusion than of prior social conditioning. Intellectual development is a serious matter for any and all students who are not adequately prepared to meet the social and academic challenges they face at school. At this stage there are no agendas, programs or school communities that meet the socialization needs of all student constituencies. However, public schools must endeavor to function and serve better as socio-academic complexes where students irrespective of diversity, ethnicity, gender and social class can experience functional improvements in academic competence, cultural enrichment and social relations proficiency.

Today, the professional, humane and moral demands of providing public education compel educators and supporting sources to be irrevocably involved with carrying out unending tasks of social reconstruction. Now these have to include the design and implementation of social and technical functions that will meet the needs of students who enter school without any cognizance of need for self-regulation, orderly participation and stability. When some students are away from schools, their lives are affected by many seriously disordered relationships. Increasing manifestations of interest and concern about such matters have come from a wide assortment of lay people and professionals. These have, in several instances, produced social atmospheres of broader mutual respect for some students, parents and communities.

Family circumstances, living situations, education, employment/unemployment and scarcity are dynamic forces in creating behaviors, habits, beliefs, concepts and attitudes that, as they continue, take on the characteristics of culture. As recognizable manifestations of unpalatable antisocial behavior move beyond responsible constraints, the matter of instituting some measure of effective social reorientation becomes much more difficult. A constant concern in rearing children today is that it is a difficult and stupendous process.

Educators cannot take the place of parents and family. Educational systems do have more of the resources, skills, psycho-educational professionalism, organizational structure and methodologies to move children and their families toward more viable social futures. This suggests that in time, school systems will be perceived as having the responsibilities for providing more ongoing socialization instruction and monitoring for students throughout their school life experiences.

Many youth identified as troubled, troubling, troublesome or in trouble have internalized aspirations that prevent them from being trapped permanently and stifled by their difficult socio-economic circumstances and living conditions. For others, marked disadvantages often hamper and restrict their making satisfactory adjustments to community life and school routines. Sometimes this occurs because negative attitudes rampant in many sectors of society overshadow appeals to modify behavior and continue education. Some students do not share (have never shared) in the educational and other social development offerings in a manner comparable to those whose heritage and endowments are described as adequate, privileged and wealthy. The results are that many such students do not find it possible to set aside their feelings of alienation. Personalities and attitudes shaped solely within the milieus of poverty, scarcity, insecurity and disadvantage frequently reflect levels of socialization that are conditioned by these experiences and exposures. Many children from these settings acquire perspectives and attitudes that are shockingly incompatible with the societal expectations of those whose assets, supports, and opportunities are stable and sufficient.

Regardless of the undertakings of education systems to educate, students with broad gaps in their preparation sometimes exhibit behavioral disorders and learning disabilities that result in their being pathologically labeled by some educators. Also, many of these children for the first time are made to realize that the status of themselves, their families and their communities is in dire need of change in this country. Those who are conscious of lower-class status also become aware of the real meanings of "later" or "never" more so than other children.

America is widely publicized as the land of tremendous promise for all peoples. Politicians and bureaucrats are among those occupying positions that are symbolic of how promises have been and can be fulfilled. The history of the poor and defenseless in this nation reveals that many in such posts are not genuinely interested in supporting humane educational policies and politics. Those must change to the extent that everyone can receive equal protection and justice. One reality that needs to be acknowledged: There is no protection in poverty and there is no worse condition.

Children in some schools in America have encountered a declining quality of education that ranges from bad to worse to disgraceful. Nevertheless, some school systems, in their operations, merit the privilege to serve as criteria for direction in delivering pedagogical services and as exemplars in selection and use of methodologies for improving the social development for all students. This has occurred despite the national educational environment being fouled because of the Reagan and the Bush administrations and their politics for polluting educational programming and planning with doctrines of "more for less" and "better with nothing."

American public school systems must be dedicated to evolving from fair to good to better mediums for conducting effective communication among parents, communities and schools. Education offered should not treat any children as deficit models and indicative of student academic unpreparedness, social maladjustment or material limitations. Socialization skills should be met with determination to stimulate scholarly aptitude and competence to overcome obstacles. The most careful monitoring does not guarantee that all students will substantially improve their academic performances, but as erratic or negative tendencies are discerned, carefully considered corrective procedures are put into place to adjust irregularities. There are no attempts to evade or avoid meeting head-on questions, challenges or criticisms. Complaints are dealt with forthrightly, whether they are real, cloaked in innuendo or surreptitiously introduced by critics as a means for attracting to themselves more public and personal attention.

Professional deficiencies, incompetencies or derelictions among staff should not be treated as accidental aberrations. There must be real commitment to help students improve their academic performances and make better personal adjustments. Serious efforts should be made to teach students about rights and responsibilities, rights they may not have and responsibilities they must not abandon. Many parents and children must be helped to comprehend that most failures to reach levels of success in the future often are linked to past antisocial and/or criminal behaviors. Students must be prepared to solve problems and assume responsibility regardless of complexity or difficulty. There is critical urgency for education (at all levels) for teaching and learning that will increase the number of students acquiring greater consciousness of self-regulation, participation and social stability.

IV

The Foundations of Black Culture

The Black Perspective of Frederick Douglass

MARCH, 1972

FREDERICK DOUGLASS IS ONE OF THE VERY RARE and outstanding examples of these black persons who consistently regarded blackness and the black experience with seriousness and respect. He demonstrated from the day of his decision to escape slavery that the defining of the black situation and taking control of black life were matters that rightly rested only within the realm of black people. This awareness along with other facets of his social and political consciousness are the stimuli that impelled him to carry on for fifty-five years an unfaltering and unyielding battle to remove the white oppression of black people.

It is well documented that the contrivances, contradictions, brutalities and atrocities of the slave system combined and produced circumstances of living for black people in America that can best be described as a veritable hell. Also, the accompanying prejudices and attitudes which were expressed toward non-slave black people were equally as vicious and caused them misery closely akin to that endured by the slaves. As black people began to acquire recognition as formal communities in some places within the American scheme, there were corresponding expressions of resistance from an impressive number of black spokesmen. Of these, black history and other fields of black social concerns concur that Frederick Douglass was one of the most courageous, dynamic, prolific and articulate.

Douglass was born February 14, 1817, and lived as a slave for the first twenty-one years of his life. He knew firsthand the cruelties, indignities and degradations of slavery. During his youth when he resisted and fought a brutal slave breaker to whom he was assigned, he learned, "He is whipped oftenest who is whipped easiest." He escaped from slavery in 1838 and shortly afterwards was married to Anna Murray.

From the time Douglass removed himself from bondage and

became part of the abolitionist movement, he undertook establishing a new set of ground rules for attacking the slave system. The most important was that the anti-slavery causes could not be best asserted and championed by whites. Douglass held this to be a violation of a general tenet of human conduct. In making his position clear on this point, he said, "There is no royal road to perfection, certainly no one must wait for some kind friend to put a springing board under his feet, upon which he may easily abound from the first round of the ladder onward and upward to its highest round. If he waits for this he may wait long and perhaps forever. He who does not think himself worth saving from poverty and ignorance, by his own efforts, will hardly be thought worth the efforts of anybody else."

Douglass thus placed clearly before the blacks and the whites of this nation the perspective from which the black struggle for freedom would be launched. The starting line in the battle for the liberation of black people was to be drawn by the blacks themselves, and their resourcefulness toward this objective would have to be consistently demonstrated. This did not preclude acceptance of the cooperation, help and philanthropy to be offered by whites, but it was necessary for all blacks seeking an end to slavery to show their allies and collaborators the direction to be taken to obtain freedom. This level of thinking was exhibited by Douglass when he was just 21 years of age.

Douglass had heard of the abolitionists while in Baltimore, and after moving to New Bedford where he first subscribed to the *Liberator,* he began to attend Abolitionist Society meetings. On March 12, 1839, he spoke in favor of resolutions condemning slavery and also delivered an inspiring denunciation of the African colonization efforts of the American Colonization Society. "That we are American citizens, born with natural, inherent and just rights; and that the inordinate and intolerable scheme of the American Colonization Society shall never entice or drive us from our native soil." It was thus that Douglass emerged as a black spokesman, and his leadership capabilities were immediately recognized by the white abolitionists.

Douglass' first speech of note was delivered when he appeared with William Lloyd Garrison and forty abolitionists at Nantucket on August 12, 1841. His unquestioned authority and eloquence elicited amazed responses from the audience. In this and in subsequent appearances, he gave a new spirit and drive to the anti-slavery movement.

Douglass possessed an excellent speaking voice, masterful appearance and incomparable intelligence. Through the skillful use of mimicry and magnetic elocution he could: transfer his listeners (entire audience) to a slave compound; dramatize the slave-owners teaching obedience to slaves by using Christian dogma; depict the horror and humiliation of black women being subjected to the lusts and rapings of slave-owners; illustrate the grief of mothers, fathers and children when separated by slave-sales punishments. He was able to create sorrow, sympathy, repulsion, anger and rage over the slave system. William Wells Brown said no one could talk against the slave system on a level equal to Frederick Douglass.

When Douglass spoke to the Plymouth Anti-Slavery Society in December 1841, he came to grips with the malevolence of white Christianity and white education in America. He said, "Church, God, nor Christianity removes prejudice . . . blacks are to be kept in a special place in the United States. A placed decided upon by whites. Blacks do not choose or make the decisions. Whites degrade blacks and then ask why they are degraded. Colleges and Seminaries are closed to blacks and you ask why we don't know more."

Douglass avoided directing his sharp critical rhetoric at persons and kept it aimed solely at the slave system. His thesis was centered around the master and the slave alike being tyrannized by slavery, both stripped of dignity. On this same occasion, Douglass said there is a twin battle to be fought, one against Southern slavery and the other against Northern prejudice. In supporting this he cited his "Jim Crow" ordeals in riding trains in Massachusetts, the job discrimination to which he had been subjected and the degrading treatment that was directed at blacks by the white Christian churches. These personal experiences removed from Douglass the label of being a mimic of the thinking of white political opportunists.

Douglass soon tired of relating his own slave experiences. He was determined to examine issues, question morals, make inferences, express principles and develop social concepts. John Collins, general manager of the Anti-Slavery Society, was opposed to this. He instructed Douglass to speak with a plantation accent and just tell his sad story; the whites would take care of the philosophy. Douglass in response asserted that the North could not be committed to abolitionist purposes unless the fullest expressions of black manhood were in evidence, and this included the intellectual and the learned. Douglass refused to accept or be a party to any attempts to portray the informant, meek, stupid, clown black as a stereotype. He raised the question that has convulsed deceitful white liberals ever since: "Do you think of black men as causes and as sentient, intelligent beings, or as the raw material of crusading righteousness?"

In 1845, Douglass went to England to crusade and lecture in the cause of the abolitionist movement. After he returned, he began publishing the *North Star* in Rochester, New York, in 1847. A breach occurred between Douglass and Garrison, because Garrison and his followers insisted on following a line of non-violence and passive resistance and using only appeals of moral suasion against the slave system. Garrison was opposed to any nationalistic indications or expressions among blacks, such as having their own churches, lodges, schools, newspapers or conventions. Douglass was determined to follow a program of political action and to exercise an unmatched and unrelenting zeal in his assaults against the slave system and all of its proponents. This meant that he would lead blacks in setting up programs to take control of their own lives.

Douglass pioneered in structuring the logic which black people in subsequent periods of their existence in the United States could use to evaluate the roles of white political functionaries. His succinct assessments of Abraham Lincoln, Henry Clay, John Calhoun and Daniel Webster are deserving of recall as these figures wore some of the most common faces of white racism with which blacks have to deal. In explaining the feelings of Lincoln towards black people, Douglass said, "President Lincoln was a white man and shared prejudices common to his countrymen towards the colored race."

Douglass commented that Henry Clay in his support of the 1850 compromise used soft, gentle diction and exemplified the spirit of compromise and conciliation. This served to increase Clay's political stature tremendously and provided him with an image of working to end the sectional conflicts between the North and the South. Clay managed to be publicized as preparing the way for unity for the nation while using deceptively every guile he possessed to strengthen the position of the South. Douglass perceived and disclosed that Clay was ambitious beyond all comprehension, and that he lacked the intent, capability or skill to remove the deeply imbedded antipathies that had developed between slavery and anti-slavery forces. In reality, Clay was committed to giving all concessions to the Southern slave holders. Douglass summed this up by stating Clay's plan "gives everything to liberty, in words, and secures everything to slavery in deeds."

In describing the customary performances and ideological expressions of John Calhoun, Douglass evaluated him as "Truly representing the slave holding spirit of his state (South Carolina)." In considering Calhoun's 1850 speech to Congress, Douglass categorized it as a despicable diatribe, filled with evil proposals but candid and forthright. Calhoun expressed directly his wish for slavery to continue, although it could hardly have escaped his awareness that slavery was inhumane and sinful. Douglass revealed that Calhoun had the attention of the nation because he was the most effective political voice of white supremacy, but once his speech had been heard, "The mighty man of slavery is found to be mightier in his silence than in his eloquence." In speaking of its actual worth Douglass said "Something brilliant and powerful was expected; something dim and weak was given." The Calhoun speech was expected to cause a tremor throughout the land and strike terror to the opponents of slavery, but the speech revealed that the power attributed for so long to Calhoun had ended, as the language of his discourse was actually shallow and should be viewed as lacking in moral substance. (This is true of most of the rhetoric of the oppressors, whether it is uttered by the whites or blacks.) Such rhetoric is never a force for or a source of morality, strength and liberation; it is always modified, ambivalent or assaultive and spoken by those who are servile and obedient to the forces of repression. Its purpose is to intimidate and to announce that other instruments of harm and authority are to be used if and when power chooses. Those persons who speak sincerely for liberation and against oppression employ the language of freedom, which is for the oppressed a commitment and for the oppressor always a threat.

Of Daniel Webster, Douglass asserted that his celebrated oratorical capabilities were misused and his talents wasted in supporting the 1850 Compromises. Webster was pictured as being endowed with intellectual powers but seriously deficient in moral integrity. Douglass exposed him as adept at distortion: "Mr. Webster presents us with a specimen of his skill, in the art of substituting darkness for light, and bitter for sweet, and of the manner in which he can confound ignorant bigotry with uncompromising and intelligent fidelity to principle."

By 1851, Douglass was assuming a position of "ballots if possible, bullets if necessary." He demanded integrated institutions, but if racist opposition was overwhelming, he would establish special or separate facilities for blacks. Numerous accounts of Frederick Douglass quote his classic call to black people to struggle. "The man who has suffered the wrong is the man to demand redress, that the man struck is the man to cry out and that he who has endured the cruel pangs of slavery is the man to advocate liberty. It is evident that we must be our own representatives and advocates, not exclusively, but peculiarly — not distinct from, but in connection with our white friends."

Frederick Douglass was distinguished by his flexibility in dealing with the various dilemmas and concerns of his time. He was always willing to reverse himself where new evidence and information revealed the errors of any previously held opinions. Douglass interpreted the "freedom concepts" of Jefferson, Lincoln et al. to mean that blacks were human, and any abridgments or denials of their humanity deserved repudiation. He was aware of the white racist prerogatives that were woven into the fabric of the Declaration of Independence and the U.S. Constitution, just as he also fully comprehended the racist content of white Christianity in America. In his deliberations and political action crusades to shake this white racist nation away from this confidence in the infernal slave system, he embarked upon a program of his own to politically propagandize the U.S. Constitution as an anti-slavery document. This was done specifically to win the minds of as many people and nations as possible to black causes. He claimed that the preamble was specifically avowed "to secure the blessings of liberty." He followed through with many telling arguments that slavery was thus incompatible with the fundamental principles of the U.S. Constitution. To many, he seemed to regard the American nation as being a white racist system with firm ethnocentric convictions to classify blacks as property rather than as persons.

Douglass became the most vigorous and effective political abolitionist. Garrison became even more aggravated with him and charged him as being an apostate. In turn, Garrison was labeled by Douglass as an abolitionist politician.

Frederick Douglass was the epitome of leadership and he led superbly — both the enslaved blacks and the enslaving whites, in the direction of freedom. He offered firmly and judiciously solutions to the greatest social and political problems of this nation. He was an ardent and uncompromising crusader of unrelenting zeal for the inclusion of black soldiers in the Union armies; a forceful and determined advocate of enfranchisement for freedmen and in efforts to extend and expand the coverage of civil rights to include all Americans. He earned the respect which is typical of the life he lived.

Douglass made compelling statements to encourage blacks to fill the roles they had to play; to show abolitionists that there were spokesmen among black people who recognized their responsibilities; to warn pro-slavery forces of slave unrest and the ultimate violence that could develop. He expressed in philosophical terms the morality underlying all of man's struggles to achieve liberty. Black people were being taught by a black man that they had to be activists for their own liberation, and the messages of Douglass were being carried to all black people, including those who existed under the most horrendous circumstances.

Two excerpts from Douglass' many dissertations were of significance at this point: "The limits of tyrants are prescribed by the endurance of those whom they oppose," and, "Find out just what any people will quietly submit to and you have found the exact measure of injustice and wrong which will be imposed upon them, and this will continue until they are resisted with either words or blows, or with both."

Exposure of slaves to the teachings of Douglass caused much unrest. As they began to understand better, many situations developed in slave-holding areas that were difficult to control. There was widespread feeling among blacks that the tyranny of slavery must end. In obeisance to Douglass' statement, "He who would be free must strike the blow," many slaves resolved that any effort expended in the quest for freedom would be an honorable way to die. This philosophy was relatively easy to teach to some slaves and even more so to many of those blacks who were not held as chattel.

Douglass as a slave saw slavery as evil, a violation of human beings and out of harmony with nature and conscience. As a slave, Douglass thought and acted as a free man. He believed man should have freedom of choice and that slavery was a denial of this. Whatever a slave did to end his slavery was moral, and the slave could not and should not be held responsible. All slave actions are reactions to the brutalities of slavery and are justifiable! This he learned from ten years of serious study and from his association with John Brown.

From Frederick Douglass, the country began to learn that liberty and slavery are both considered in the U.S. Constitution, but an oath to support slavery should be unthinkable. He emphasized that if there is acknowledgment and acceptance of the preamble of the Constitution and its concerns with liberty and justice, then slave holding, fugitive slave capture, and the kidnapping of non-slave blacks must be condemned. Douglass saw the Constitution as having some radical defects, but these oppressive features must be rejected by all honorable people in the North and the South, because as it stood, slave holders would continue to get the strongest defense for their way of life from the Constitution. Those people who see justice and freedom as a purpose of the Constitution are in opposition to slavery.

Douglass' arguments illuminated further that "The wickedness of the slave system and its evils were not victimized and all Americans were responsible for its existence. If the right to liberty is self-evident then slavery is a sin. It is ridiculous that people of the North can claim as friends people who hold slaves in the South. Slavery is a system of lewdness and piracy and the slaveholders are but keepers of houses of ill-fame. Slave breeding is the chief source of the business wealth and income in Virginia. The blood of the most prominent slaveholding families is for sale in the slave markets of New Orleans." Douglass charged the criminals in this endeavor as including the lawmakers and ministers. They were forces of evil.

Douglass' response to the Fugitive Slave Law of 1850 was vigorous and vitriolic. He pointed out that blacks in the North were in a panic; free blacks now had no more defense against slave hunters than slaves; no black was to be given a court hearing if he was claimed by slave chasers as a fugitive; so called freedmen of the North were now literally being thrown into slavery; the law was disruptive, threatening and demoralizing; family life, jobs, houses, communities were placed in jeopardy for blacks everywhere; many settlements of black people began to fall apart as the inhabitants were forced to flee and scatter. Many distinguished black activists and leaders (also fugitives) were forced to seek other places of refuge such as England or Canada. Among these were Samuel R. Ward, Henry H. Garnet, and Daniel Payne. Douglass did not waver in his stance nor did he withdraw from any of his previous positions as an abolitionist, although his personal safety was far from secure. He committed himself to create in the North an anti-slavery awareness and a conscience about the injustice of the Fugitive Slave Law.

After the Compromise of 1850, Douglass became aware of the additional difficulties of shaping white opinion to favor blacks. Also, black communities became further divided over the issues of emigration and segregation. Douglass emphasized that sectarianism, patriotism and male supremacy were divisive and destructive. The emigration movement among blacks was gaining in numbers, but he was opposed as were the majority of blacks at this juncture. Between 1847 and 1853, he determined that the black condition in the U.S. needed considerable analysis and that long-range goals and strategies must be delineated. The 1850 Fugitive Slave Law convinced Douglass that these could no longer be delayed. Douglass saw blacks as being of two groups: those who felt inferior to whites in status and ability, and those who believed that more black professionals and intellectuals would provide the only solutions to black problems. He labeled the latter as a negative quantity as they were disregarding the masses. They were charged with being disillusioned with the ignorance of other blacks and despairing of the prejudice of whites, and thereby losing their courage to continue to battle for the status and conditions to which they should aspire for all of their people.

By the late 1850s Douglass was moving towards a position where he would assert that men were moved by practical interests and not necessarily by appeals to logic and morality. By 1850 twenty-five percent of the Northern blacks were mulatto. Whites feigned more tolerance for them and their economic opportunities were slightly better, as the whites would hire them with the notion that a lighter skin revealed a white genetic input; thus they were likely to be a bit more intelligent. This was very damaging to some blacks. They actually accepted it and began to use such judgments in setting their own standards. The color factor began to influence some lighter skin blacks to feel superior to those of darker complexions. The irony of this is that mulattos were never accepted as white and had to share all of the legal and public policy discrimination of their darker brothers. This was an era when blacks failed to apply the lessons taught by Douglass. The black experience is centered in and results from the peculiar status and the bizarre and brutal treatment imposed upon all known African descendants by white racists in America. There are no reductions in the intensity of these merely because there may be visible residual effects of Anglo-Saxon lust in the skin coloring and hair texture of some black people. Blackness is the commonality and the basis for communality for black folks, no matter what the variations may be in their appearances.

More than 130 years ago, Douglass was organizing and participating in sit-ins on trains and railroads in Massachusetts. Later, he was actively involved in protests against segregation of black children in Rochester, New York, public schools. He faced squarely the issues of separate (complexional) institutions and organizations. He advocated and fought unequivocally for complete inclusion of blacks in the public life, but when the white racist political manipulations and legal evasions prohibited this, he would immediately demand special institutions.

These were in many respects the initial steps towards local control. He taught black people that the Fourth of July had a very special meaning and significance which could not be overlooked. In "The Meaning of July 4th for the Negro," delivered on July 5, 1852, he said of the black man, "it is a day that reveals to him, more than all other days in the year, the gross injustice and cruelty to which he is the constant victim. To him your celebration is a sham, your boasted liberty an unholy license — a thin veil to cover crimes which would disgrace a nation of savages."

Douglass was a man in the most real and concise meaning of the word. His presence gave rise to the belief that a people who can produce a Douglass, no matter how few their numbers, have all of the essentials to triumph over their oppressors. Frederick Douglass knew and taught that manhood is founded on self-respect and self-esteem. He taught that black people in and out of slavery were chained together, and there would not be freedom for one until all were liberated. He added to the anxiety of pro-slavery, racist whites and escapist, middle-class blacks when he said, "The world is full of violence and fraud, and it would be strange if the slave, the constant victim of both fraud and violence, should escape the contagion."

He asserted that an ignorant people cannot support an educated and professional element. Blacks should be developed in the skills and the trades. He saw black skilled craftsmen as a positive force for abolition. In July of 1853 at the Colored Men's Convention, held in Rochester, Douglass reversed his position of 1847 where he was opposed to establishing a vocational college for blacks. He foresaw the difficulties and frustration of getting blacks included in the apprentice system. This remains a major problem for many black workers today. Douglass saw separatism (determined and controlled by blacks) as a defense against segregation and not as an implementation or extension of it. Blacks would make decisions about their lives and do so from a position of strength. Douglass knew this could lead to a higher level of amiable race relations if blacks were in control of their communities and institutions.

After the South had begun the bloody conflict of the Civil War there was a widely held belief in Northern governmental sectors that the union of the states could be contained and controlled without violent military battles.

From 1860 to 1863 the war conducted in a manner that seemed to favor this kind of thinking. Douglass assumed the task of defining clearly and explaining fully for blacks and the whole of America that the ultimate result of the war would have to be the ending of chattel slavery in all of the states. This position was considered ridiculous at the time.

There were strong compromise forces at work in the Union who were determined that Douglass' predictions would never materialize. Secretary Seward was directed to have our foreign representatives and diplomats say to the various governments to which they were accredited that no matter how the rebellion might terminate that "The status of no class of people of the United States would be changed...slaves would be slaves still and the masters would be masters still." Generals McClellan and Butler informed slaves that any efforts put forth by them to become free would be suppressed with force. In addition to this the Union government would not employ under any conditions black slaves who escaped to the Union Army lines; they were returned to their masters. Union troops were stationed on many plantations in Virginia to protect masters who continued to hold their slaves. These troops were much more active in ousting black men from their camps than in fighting against confederate troops.

Frederick Douglass interpreted the Civil War to mean the intention of the North to extend the benefits of democracy. He knew this could never be done unless slave-owning power was destroyed. Because of the manner in which this country had come into being, slavery was an integral part of its creation and development. The extracting of this evil sore from the body of this nation would require the most skilled and determined social, political, economic and military surgery. He was well aware that the system of life in both the North and the South that flourished from the sale, purchase and unlimited free labor of black human bodies was not about to preside peacefully over its own demise.

Douglass regarded the Emancipation Proclamation as a significant milestone to be reached by blacks. He said it was "invested with sanctity," and many celebrations were held. Black people all over the country were jubilant over the proclamation, and those in the slave holding south shared their elation, secretly, in cabins and other gathering places.

Congress authorized the use of the first black troops in July of 1862, and in January of 1863, the War Department gave the order for Massachusetts to accept persons of African descent into a separate corps for combat duty. Black leaders acted as recruiting agents and Douglass was foremost. His son Charles was the first to enlist in the Massachusetts regiments, and soon afterward his other son, Lewis, signed up. Douglass discovered in his recruiting travels that blacks did not fully understand why they should join the Union Army. He wrote trenchantly and spoke widely, explaining:

"(1) Manhood required black people to take sides; (2) The black man was now a citizen of the United States and must serve his country when it was in peril; (3) Arming of blacks would be a calamity to pro-slavery supporters; (4) blacks should learn the use of firearms; (5) It would provide self-respect and establish the right of citizenship; (6) The war was now for emancipation, no matter what else it might be; and (7) It would frustrate the country from a pro-slavery compromise when hostilities should cease."

Militarily the North suffered frequent reverses, and pressures mounted for more vigorous military performances. General McClellan was replaced by General Grant, and President Lincoln invited Douglass to the executive mansion for a conference on planning for inducing slaves in the rebel states to come within the federal lines. Lincoln requested Douglass-organized black scouts to go into the rebel states and inform the slaves that freedom was offered them if they would escape to the Union Army lines. This was a method of guerrilla warfare that appealed to Douglass, and he accepted without hesitancy.

Blacks throughout the country were aggrieved at the unjust treatment of black troops in the Union Army. There were glaring differences in pay and overwhelming assignments of blacks to servant and laboring types of activity. Color discrimination was in evidence everywhere. Black soldiers were paid at laborers wages, and in turn they exhibited overt and vigorous objection to these discriminations.

Douglass advocated active participation of black troops in the military actions, and said that black people must expect annoyances but must not hold back on this account, for before them there was a double battle: they must fight slavery in the South and must challenge prejudices and proscriptions in the North. He believed the black soldier was the foundation of black citizenship.

There was no exchange of prisoners when black soldiers were captured by the South. All black soldiers, free or otherwise, were considered insurrectionists and were sentenced to death for subversive activities. The slave codes of the South applied to their punishment.

In his speech to the Convention of Colored Men in September of 1883, Douglass pointed out that the oppression of people makes cowards of the victims. To reverse this, he explained the necessity for closed black conventions to deal with their oppression. This was in response to those blacks who wanted to include whites at the secret liberation assemblies, which blacks needed so badly. Douglass pointed out that white life in America is a convention of whites against black people. He saw the law as customs, attitudes of white America hostile to black people and serving to prevent blacks from being free.

In reference to the blacks resorting to emigration to remove themselves from proscriptions in the United States, Douglass said the "impossibility of finding any part of the globe free from the presence of white men, conspires to keep the black here and compels him to adjust himself to American civilization."

On the occasion of the twenty-fourth Anniversary of Emancipation (1886), Douglass delivered a speech on "Southern Barbarism." He gave exhaustive attention to the compatibility of the Democratic and Republican parties in all things that work to continue the suppression and subjugation of black people and to lend support to those who would treat blacks as sub-humans. After adding the Thirteenth, Fourteenth, and Fifteenth amendments, the Constitution was destined to remain meaningless to blacks for as long as white racists were the ones to provide interpretation and enforcement of its provisions. Douglass assailed the government for its failure to establish legal and humane guarantees for blacks and focused attention upon the grave need for justice for his people. According to the highest legal authorities, justice is the perpetual disposition to secure to every man, by due process of law, protection of his person, his property and his political rights." In the United States justice is not yet one of the components of black experience.

Douglass was the complete and dedicated libertarian. In addressing the Women's Suffrage Association in 1888, he said, "I believe no man, however gifted with thought and speech, can voice the wrongs and present the demands of women with the skill and effect, with the power and authority of woman herself."

By 1893 15,000 black people were residing in Chicago, a city founded by a black man — Jean Baptiste de Sable — ironically. This was the year of the first World's Fair. The blacks appealed to Congress for the right to participate in this event to show their progress since the end of slavery. Douglass was presented as part of the programs sponsored by the blacks under the auspices of the Prudence Crandall Club. He spoke in his usual spirit to fight on to overcome vicissitudes of white prejudice.

In 1895, not long before he died, Douglass stated, "If the American church and clergy were only half Christianized, if American moral sensibilities were not hardened by persistent infliction of outrage and crime against black people, a scream of horror, shame, and indignation would rise to Heaven."

Kelly Miller, a distinguished black scholar, wrote in 1908 that "Frederick Douglass was the moral leader and spiritual prophet of his race."

The historical significance of Douglass has importance to the whole sequence of education and how it must be made relevant to the needs of black people and serve as a contribution to the social development and humanizing of whites. The life of Douglass provides an example of straight and unfettered thinking and how to view the facts as they really are. Facts must not be distorted out of fear or because by doing so one becomes so temporarily more comfortable. His life furnishes instruction that it is cowardly to abandon a belief or an opinion solely because it contradicts established preconceived practice; it communicates the importance of standing by and defending one's convictions. This nation, in spite of its material strength, is in general short supply of those qualities which would convey to the majority of its members the critical importance of every citizen respecting the abilities and rights of others.

Frederick Douglass was a black man accepted and respected by black people. He was a preceptor and the advocate for millions of blacks who sought and seek liberation. Douglass was the voice and teacher of blackness and the personification of protest and agitation. White America could not avoid him or what he represented and was compelled to give attention. Douglass took black people with him through every door he opened. This probably accounts for whites contriving since his death to prevent this performance from being repeated. Indisputably, Frederick Douglass must be included among those who served and preserved black people in the United States.

Black Studies: Education for Liberation

THE BLACK SCHOLAR, SEPTEMBER 1974

We shall never have a science of history until we have in our colleges men who regard truth as more important than the defense of the white race, and who will not deliberately encourage students to gather thesis material in order to support a prejudice or buttress a lie. W. E. B. Du Bois, Black Reconstruction in America, 1860-1880.

BLACK STUDIES HAS BEEN AROUND FOR A LONG TIME. Any perfunctory review of the monumental scholarly works of distinguished black people such as David Walker, Henry Highland Garnet, Martin Delaney, Frederick Douglass, George Williams, T. Thomas Fortune, William Monroe Trotter, Ida B. Wells, W. E. B. Du Bois, Carter G. Woodson, Alpheus Hunton, Paul Robeson, and others will provide ample evidence of this. Much of what early black scholars produced remained obscured, however, until the struggles of blacks for improved and meaningful higher education were better planned and organized. The earliest efforts for black courses occurred on the campuses of black schools. The more impressive, attention-gathering crusades to establish black educational offerings on white campuses came later.

American education has been viewed for some time by many observers from assorted placements as falling apart throughout the American nation. In many ways this is seen as similar to the disintegration of American imperialism. In considering the conventional roles of American education and its institutionalized discrimination, and exploitation, blacks in many sectors of life came to the conclusion that educators occupied only one of two positions: they were either oppressors or liberators. The response to this by white educators and the media was to label blacks as volatile and incendiary influences. In return, many blacks began to consider black education as having a special mission to challenge and eventually replace white education because it was deficient and corrupt. Out of this grew the realization and acknowledgement for a large number of blacks that all education is unequivocally political and black education can ill afford to be less so.

Throughout the country, public school systems are also strongholds of white racism. There is abundant evidence to prove that in many places they are the early contributors to the currently existing waves of intellectual decline and academic degradation. Most urban school districts now are burdened with more than a controllable share of debilitating social ills of their own making. In all of these systems the overwhelming percentages of administrative and teaching personnel are white and if professionals of other ethnicities are slightly visible they invariable are goose-stepping to white policies, regulations and directions. Those in charge of urban public schools are glaring failures at what they promise to do, which is to educate students. For their failures they are rewarded with public relations build-ups which attract for them more public support. Often it seems that the greater the damages that are done to the mass of defenseless students from poor backgrounds, the more accolades these mis-educators are able to provide for themselves through contrivances with their mutual admiration cliques and professional organizations. There are indications now, that some minor reprimands are to be imposed because the failures to educate are evident among the students from the upper reaches of white middle class affluence. If this condition is corrected the benefits in all probability will not be extended to the less influential.

The development of Black Studies from the very outset was accompanied by blacks being compelled to evaluate the largely racist nature of established education in America at all levels from kindergarten to doctoral. Some of the early organized Black Studies courses began by giving critical attention to those blacks who hang on tenaciously to conventional white racist dogma that in most sections of this country is largely disguised as education. It is believed by many black teachers that the seductive illusions contained in the warped rationale used by those black apologists to assert that "white is right" only serves to lead uninformed and apolitical students further astray and contributes to their acting as morons. In addition to this, a false consciousness is deepened and the students are often imbued with many doubts and fears.

Simultaneously, in a wider context some whites began to recognize that the existing systems of education needed to be transformed. Many of them were quick to learn however, that they were not going to be the ones to perform the tasks required.

Most Black Studies advocates and supporters saw the need for their programs to be intellectually strong and stable, but in some settings whites who were aligned with the forces opposing strong programs (or weak ones) saw every symbol of growth and achievement as threats. Unfortunately, some black proponents of Black Studies were deluded into believing that its purpose was centered around the mere posing of rhetorical threats because by doing so they would have a personal radical experience. It is easily perceived that the practice of such absurd self-deception, if it became widespread, could bring about a disastrous dissipation of the usefulness of Black Studies programs everywhere.

More often, however, politically astute black scholars went about the business of providing certain specific insights for students in how to deal with many labels and definitions coming from white quarters which affected black life and scholarship negatively. An example is the so-called black revolution myth (highly propagandized by the white press) which was analyzed very early on as a white racist attempt to deceive blacks into believing that their ego trips in manure-dipped rhetoric, plus the wearing of funky clothes, dark glasses and disarranged hair were revolutionary weapons that would intimidate less aggressive blacks and terrorize whites.

Black Studies does not avoid recognizing that psychologically the white establishment and the government of this country in many situations are overcoming the need for black people. The recently concluded Presidential administration of Richard Nixon continued to move beyond its previous practices of manipulation, containment, disregard and repression of the masses of the black population. Often blacks were forced out of the position of being able to absorb each other (humanely, politically, protectively) and this contact with themselves is the substance of the communication that gives meaning to all human existence.

Black Studies, in remaining compatible with the assorted needs of black people to obtain useful and purposeful formal education, is compelled to teach contrary to much of what has become customary and routine in a variety of disciplines. This requires a distinct determination not to permit black perspectives, humanistic values and black people to be further denigrated by anti-black academic attitudes that have been developed and nurtured in the hostile quarters of the dominant society. For longer than it is worthwhile to remember, some white social scientists have made a lucrative business out of researching black people. Black Studies has been effective in demonstrating from the standpoint of scholarship that most of this material is nothing more than sophisticated voyeurism.

A great deal of the social searching that is done about black people by whites, even if it is glaringly faulty, is permitted to be used to serve social science as a beginning to leverageeven more deficient social information and social policy.

Daniel Patrick Moynihan may be the criterion of what white sociologists are, but to most black scholars and students he is just another of the intellectual mercenaries. Interestingly enough, most of these social scientists who pride themselves on being unprejudiced never subject their root feelings and gut attitudes to thorough critical analyses by black scholars. When this does take place, as can happen accidentally sometimes, the disclosures are often shattering. Black Studies rather effectively establishes that white social scientists cannot have the black experience that America metes out to black people for the simple reason that whites are not black. But whites can have traumatic and painful ordeals such as America hold in readiness for all persons (white or otherwise) who, for whatever reasons, confront and challenge its basic racist policies and practices.

Many black scholars have been busily concerned with directing their research and teaching proficiency toward developing Black Studies to be a major force to enable black people to take control over their own lives. White-directed and dominated education should not be lamented as having failed black people, because it never promised to do anything for them in the first place. If the educational institutions of this country had been directed towards providing adequate educations for blacks then the white racist system would have failed, because blacks would undoubtedly have brought an end to their subjugation and oppression long ago. Black Studies brings into sharp focus the fact that blacks are not behavior problems, but they are unknown and unpredictable elements of human responses and reactions to the continued abuses offered up so abundantly by the racist institutions of white America.

Black education also addresses the brainwashing that causes blacks to believe they have been restricted from competing in America's proclaimed pluralistic society. This is grossly inaccurate. Blacks were programmed by whites from the beginning to be the property and the servants of whites. As a result, they have never been a part of the self-determining peoples of the world. This what the black struggle is all about! In a racist, capitalist nation only those who are racist and free can compete. All others are forced into concentrating their efforts in a continuing series of survival maneuvers. Blacks are being taught now that they cannot continue to indulge America by persisting in a sentimental attachment for its long-time social blundering.

Black Studies decisively and positively develops within students a patience and persistence to struggle and learn. Dropping out is tantamount to surrender and no dropout wins anything anywhere. Black students especially have to maintain a clear perspective about what they must do in order to prepare themselves to engage in those lifetime intellectual, social and political campaigns that will result in fundamental change. To the dismay of some, Black Studies has not turned out to be the academic trip which gives to the young brothers and sisters those grades of A or B unless they have demonstrated the studiousness and scholarship which merit such rewards. Most black teachers are impervious to color being a passport to grades of excellence. The black community does not profit if Black Studies returns to the community students who have not oriented themselves to understanding the meaning of academic excellence and a commitment to achieve it. Black Studies and its intellectual richness have spread immensely, and the culture and philosophy endemic to black life is being realized (no matter how reluctantly) as a humanistic component the world needs.

Black Studies brings under sharp scrutiny those blacks with white minds who under a variety of circumstances have been selected by white educators to be celebrated and eulogized for their performance on behalf of the status quo. A classic case in point is Booker T. Washington. He understood white racism, but he chose slavery over struggle. His philosophy of survival in itself represented the disgraceful subjugation and ultimate death of his own manhood and if there had been no Trotter, DuBois, Wells, and others the permanent destruction of black people could have occurred. Black people must make positive decisions about their lives. They do not need to worry about being alienated from white people; they must be constantly working to remove their alienation from black people.

Students of Black Studies learn that critical analysis and interpretation are major facets of Black History and there will exist for some time many opposing viewpoints. Critical analysis and its abiding significance for Black Studies does not mean the exercising of calloused and unthoughtful disagreement, nor does it suggest there will be an easy embrace of the varieties of appealing thought covering in range from Du Bois to Soyinka. It means that Black Studies will insist that students examine and comprehend a multitude of theories and teachings. The relevance of each body of knowledge to black liberation can be determined only through obtaining an understanding of the substantive content, and not by practicing avoidance, disregard and indifference, as these are the tools for turning common naivete and simple stupidity into strongholds of colossal ignorance. There is no guarantee that a unity of thought will be found among the various scholars. This does not mean that black scholars will not continue to be able to provide scholarly direction and intellectual leadership for their students.

Black Studies comes to grips with the various social science fabrications used to delineate the alleged inferiority of the blacks. There is emerging now a rather clear understanding of the dominant society's stereotypical tendency to find all other ethnic peoples as hyper-emotional, irrational,sexually irresponsible, and anti- or non-intellectual. But because of Black Studies students are now better able to evaluate from a liberating perspective the assorted materials pouring forth from all sectors of the white media treating of everything black. They are able to recognize the contrast between the black experience and white advantage and to understand that the pathology of white society is the basic reason for black people living in harsher environments and under greater internal stresses. Also historical, political and social documentation clearly reveals the evidence as to why blacks enjoy America less and suffer from it more. Students are developing more care and vigilance and are being taught more effectively to exercise discretion and prudence in using those strengths and resources which must be expended by all peoples whose aspirations are to be free.

The Black Studies impact is apparent in the new directions that are beginning to be adopted by some career professionals in furnishing special knowledge and information about the services and functions of their professions. Black people are aware of the long-lamented inequities throughout the country in various professional services including law and medicine. Legal protection and medical care for blacks have been abominable states throughout their existence in America. While there have been numerous black professionals in the past who have given aid to those blacks who have found themselves distressed and handicapped because of medical problems or legal difficulties, most of this assistance was provided to relieve special crises. Now the larger need of the black communities all over this land is to have professionals in every field involved in those tasks and programs that will enable increased numbers of people to understand how these professions should serve the people routinely. The expertise of more of these professional blacks is being shared with the people in order that they will be able to cope with and offset those kinds of difficulties that are often created by the professions themselves.

Not only white education but all other institutionalized areas of this system follow unwaveringly the guidelines of white racism. All whites are programmed to remain white and blacks are programmed to think and act as white as possible. Black Studies is, without reservation, diametrically opposed to this. This is why courses do not become Black Studies courses merely because a white Board of Education (higher or lower) or departmental chairmen display liberal magnanimity by ordering or allowing the word Black to be used in a course title or label.

The customary exhibitions of patriotism among whites are clearly understood by "politically black" people to be sanctimonious ways of manifesting more white racism. Presently and historically these displays of Ku Klux Klan type nationalism and religion have glorified and sustained horrendous white societal behavior patterns toward all peoples of other ethnicities in this country. These result in black people being born to the conditions which produce anger and dissatisfaction. The creative expression of this anger has made it possible for some long submerged aspects of black culture to expand and strengthen. Black culture is basically rich in the noble, heroic and sacrificial struggles of blacks seeking for hundreds of years to achieve liberation. A variety of cultural treasures has been developed in the centuries-long resistance of some blacks to all forms of subjugation and oppression.

Competition is advertised as the essence of the American way of life. The damaging implications of this for black people are manifold and for those blacks who become indoctrinated to this ideal certain negative social manifestations are inevitable. Competition fosters individualism and for black people individualism obstructs the development of strong group black consciousness. At the same time, this system regards black people as an undifferentiated mass, and this supports and sustains the varied rationales that are employed whenever and wherever the treatment of blacks is based upon mass presumptive inferiority. Students are being given the opportunities to study the possibilities of black people reversing the effects of long-standing white customs and attitudes by thinking of themselves as an undifferentiated social mass in a white racist system. This is a vital step in establishing a humanistic relationship that reduces individual aggrandizement practices and at the same time serves as the foundation for a politicization of the mass of black people around legitimate black protest, reaction and resistance.

Walter Wilson, co-chairman of the Du Bois Memorial Committee, stated in his syllabus for the Study of Selective Writings by W. E. B. Du Bois, 1970, that:

Du Bois was merciless in criticizing any sign of neglect, laxity, rowdiness, or intemperance on the part of his students that might give substance to the accepted stereotypes of black behavior. At the same time, he was tireless in counseling with his students as to their work habits, personal problems, and future professional appointments. Despite some resentment of his strictness, the end result was the creation of a body of trained black sociologists, scientists and scholars, who, in retrospect, recalled his stern admonitions with gratitude and his personal friendship with affection.

Black Studies is in part, of course, a creation of Du Bois, and now in this era which Wilson states is the "age of Du Bois," Black Studies can be no less demanding. There has to be at all times a basic commitment of service to black communities through intellectual preparation and teaching competence of the highest order. The integrity of the learning process must be respected and teachers must have self-respect and acknowledge that there are distinct roles for students and teachers. The responsibilities of each must be explicit and filled with honor. Care is to be taken to avoid meaningless rhetoric and uncouth performances that will deprecate these standards.

Carter G. Woodson discovered that almost all education offered to blacks by white America is demoralizing and crippling, therefore, Black Studies must be strong and remain in the forefront for developing and strengthening the intellectual, social and political thought necessary for human liberation.

Black Music: Sound and Feeling for Black Liberation

THE BLACK SCHOLAR, JANUARY 1976

"There is no aspect of the culture of this nation which has not been touched by the black presence."
– Shirley Graham Du Bois

BLACK CULTURE IN AMERICA is truly one produced from a past and present filled with causes. These causes have a single common denominator: black liberation.

However, invidious value judgments by whites in past eras reduced black performances to mere "innovations" rather than artistic creations. For generations, these evaluations were resented and resisted by large numbers of black people, who realized this was refined, sophisticated, cultural discrimination by whites who controlled the aesthetic norms.

Today, the regenerated consciousness of black people has led them to demand that recognition of black art and artists be extended. Black culture in America has grown from the efforts of blacks coping with social constraints placed upon them. If a people are to be cultural contributors, they must have some measure of self-determination.

At the vanguard of the black struggle was found the black musician. Thus, in this essay focus shall be upon contemporary black music and the assortment of persons who produce it.

Black music was once viewed as being primitive sounds of despondency and defeat. Carl Van Vechten, a self-appointed white patron-overseer of blacks in the arts and regarded by some as the custodian of the Harlem Renaissance, voiced this belief during the 1920s. Other descriptions of black music at the time were: "Their kind of music helped them to survive"; "It sustains them"; "It is a record of the tortuous journey and bitter struggle of their lives"; "It helps them to endure pain"; "It's sexy and wicked."

Even today, demeaning characterizations continue. For more than a quarter of a century, Leonard Feather, author and contributor to *Down Beat,* has written commentaries on black musicians depicting them as apolitical zombies and uncomprehending of the real America. Throughout the past three decades, he has revealed no perception of black life, black music and the quest for liberation which are inseparably interwoven into the black existence. The preceding is not to imply that all of us can sing, play and dance.

Gospel, Spiritual, Church, Jazz and Blues are all labels that can be identified with the various segments of the black population that gave them their origin and sustenance. However, sounds of dismay, submissiveness and acceptance of atrocious social conditions common to the existence of large numbers of black people is not the music that will be given attention here. This music, though sometimes beautifully rendered by blacks, is essentially a music of accommodation rather than liberation.

Black music of exuberance is closely related to the spirit of resistance and struggle. Concepts of black liberation are strengthened by music that is mind expanding, sophisticated and exhilarating. Moreover, it is personal, intimate, erotic, discreet and tasteful. It reveals in its rhythms and harmonies that it is not a music of grief and despair, but it is symbolic of the steps which blacks take to remove themselves from disabling emotional and spiritual debilitation.

White critics of black music have first emphasized the typology and then attempted to discover blacks as a creation of the music. This has been characteristic of many articles appearing since the 1940s in *Down Beat* and the now-defunct *Metronome.* This is to be seen also in those efforts to link the Blues, Jazz and Gospel as having their origins in the racist American relationship of captor to captive.

In actuality, the basic elements of real black music (rhythm, intonation, spirit, defiance, self-determination) have a common base in African backgrounds that are centuries old. The work of Dizzy Gillespie and Chano Pozo almost thirty years ago brought this into sharp focus. The music of blacks in America is a conglomeration of sound and feeling that is unique to the black existence here, but the sociological and psychological environments of the United States did not spawn black music, they only furnished the settings in which blacks would create distinct kinds of politically melodic reverberations. Excellent examples are contained in the compositions and renditions of Miles Davis, John Coltrane, Stevie Wonder, John Blair and Charlie Parker.

The significance of this escapes many of the non-black persons who have assumed the role of being analysts and critics of black culture and its art forms. Most of them seem eager to recall only those eras when this country was subject to less effective criticism for its harsh treatment of blacks. In a manner similar to the practices that have been followed in all other areas of social relationships between the dominant population and black people, weird distillations of warped information continue to be passed off to the naive as knowledge and wisdom.

Black music serves as durable cultural and social evidence that blacks have survived America. Black music is a lasting symbol of sanity for black people. It has been a potent force to confuse many who struggle to maintain unreserved conscious hostility towards people of black and other ethnicities. With some certainty it can be stated that in those few areas where the white barriers erected against blacks have partially fallen, it is quite likely that black music helped open the way to straighten out some disoriented social thinking. Along with the gradual widening of black cultural awareness into broad areas of social thought and action, some of the most effective sounds to confront the bitter language of white racism are the beautiful tones of black music.

Black music became one of the effective modes of communication for conveying the messages of black abhorrence and resistance to the repressive living arrangements created for black people by the American practice of segregation. Few, if any, white writers have understood that the spirit underlying black music is sometimes the articulate profaning of the practitioners of white racism. Blacks did not and never have needed to find themselves and learn of their humanity in order to produce music. Their music is the product of their humanity and their resilience. Witness the self-assurance of superb artists such as Mary Lou Williams, Michael White, Donald Byrd and Bobbie Humphrey.

Lena McLin, a black music teacher in Chicago, provided a succinct explanation of the difference between two categories of black music, Spiritual and Gospel, when she stated, "black people sing spirituals when they tell their troubles to God; they sing Gospel when they tell their troubles to each other." It seems to follow that in the Blues blacks talk to themselves (individually or collectively) and then give notice to all others of what they are concerned about. Black music is one resource developed within the black cultural reservoir that has been copied in some form by many entertainers of the dominant population, to the extent that they often claim this music as their own. But blacks who are aware of the reality of their blackness and the realities of America remain unperturbed and continue to play music in idioms easily recognized as distinct black creations.

It should be kept in mind that black musicians who are angry because they are black play something that is quite different from the music played by blacks who are angry at the system for what it does to people because they are black. Bobby Hutchinson, Idris Muhammad and Charlie Mingus are just a few of those who belong to the latter category. Some black musicians of extraordinary talent and seriously adroit in their artistry (but who are apolitical) frequently have suffered the worst mental slavery and torture this country could inflict. The results are that many have split the scene through death or in living patterns that are equally as terminal for their talents.

America is generally vociferous and bombastic. Many noises are made about the right, the middle and the left, plus individual freedom. Frankly, there is very little personal liberty. When black musicians first began to flex their imaginations, explore and innovate, they achieved very little, but some of them became personally liberated. This is essentially the saga of Scott Joplin, Duke Ellington, Ornette Coleman, Eddie Harris, Les McCann. In assessing the music some blacks have produced, to some listeners they have strayed far; to some of their similarly situated colleagues they did not move nearly far enough. In finding new ways to continue affirming their personal freedom, blacks continue to discover new frontiers of sound and to write additional musicology. Black musicians discover upon achieving instrumental facility that they can view themselves as no longer powerless. This happens regardless of the severe difficulties and complex problems that are always a large part of their lifetime in this country. For them the heart of black music is in creation and improvisation. These are important artistic elements, and the more highly perfected they are, the more they contribute to black music being recognized as a powerful medium. Whenever black musicians get their "thing" together, many fantastic things happen. The music of any event will to some extent adhere to structure, but most idioms of black music are tonal and rhythmic examples of structured freedom.

The cultural establishments of this country still largely ignore the black presence in their artistic and professional journals. Nevertheless, black music has been a major force in effecting some social enlightenment and attitudinal adjustments toward blacks.

This music has sustained and increased the appreciation for and teaching of black culture and its components. These are rewarding in themselves, but when combined with a review of black music, especially the Blues, they are of even greater relevance to black people, and communication with the whole of humanity becomes more meaningful.

For some black musicians in America, freedom was realized in terms of creativity, expression and performance long before participants in other art forms and fields were expressing this concept as a part of the real meaning of their works Thus, as an avant-garde and progressive social symbol, the music created and produced by performing black musicians occupies a place of unusual significance in the social and political history and culture of America. Many of the changes and innovations in black music inspired, involved, violated, and disturbed a wide range of Euro-American concepts concerned with rhythm, harmonics and instrumental deployment. Distinguished black musical determinists (McCoy Tyner, Charles Mingus, Max Roach) have musically anticipated the efforts by blacks in other endeavors to claim justice and freedom in the social and political areas. This is often apparent in their unique and dynamic musical styling when they are given public exposure.

Black musicianship is most often earmarked by intriguing patterns of ideas. The articulation is sometimes not thoroughly comprehended, because receptivity to improvisation is not always wholly favorable. Black musicians have contributed and installed in the realm of black music the basics and the dynamics for bringing changes to the entire scene of music. Since the advent of John Coltrane, black music is better understood to represent the black knowledge of self, love for the black community, a well-directed sense of personhood and most significantly, a direct artistic renunciation of the historic injustices that are the real America. The lessons implicit in this are tremendous! Despite being one of the most persecuted of the non-dominant ethnic populations of this nation, blacks have established themselves as the creators and proprietors of a music that is one of the most widely applauded and respected art forms throughout the world.

Black music has its own origins and its own directions. It is moving and emotional, intense and uncompromising, soulful and serious, dedicated and tender, clinical and therapeutic, and for those who comprehend its mysterious messages and sense, its enchanting essence, it is almost always a marvelous experience. Black music is not passive. It is explosive and dynamic. No matter the categories or the artists, i.e., Herbie Hancock, Esther Phillips, Kool and the Gang,

Ron Carter, Chaka Khan, Hubert Laws, Earth, Wind and Fire, The Crusaders, there is, even in the most subtle presentations, an obvious element of power. It is a power that frequently has the effect of moving listeners to give spontaneous demonstrative responses of appreciation to a degree that equals the electrifying sounds and feelings provided by the performing musical artists. These visible functional interactions, in their own contexts, are often novel but nevertheless valid examples of spiritual liberation.

Countless other examples of this exist. B. B. King has sometimes stood out prominently. His early adventures into the music field have been reported as occasions where he generated unequaled dynamism, instrumentally and vocally. His music of the '40s, '50s, and early '60s was enthusiastically awaited and responded to by black audiences. There was little, if any reception for this performer in any quarters of the dominant population. This was a common experience for most black musicians. The performance of Jim Europe's orchestra in Carnegie Hall in 1913 was a notable event, but it received only passing mention in a few reports of critics and columnists.

As black people became more immersed in social concerns and developed greater political activism, noticeable changes began to occur in their music. In the black music idioms, there are discernible impatience, courage and assurance. Unmitigated contempt is often expressed towards distasteful and abusive facets of American life.

Many masterful black musicians empathize with black struggles for liberation. They perceive the need for a broader commitment to freedom. In and out of the music game, they are frequently confronted with discrimination and undiminishing racism, but in the music area, they can and do disregard white rules, regulations and orders. In this context they are self-liberated. Black musicians also can be impervious to critics, whether they are "white blacks" or "black whites." The spirit of liberation which many blacks express in their music often has been (less perceptibly but just as surely) imported to blacks in other areas of life, i.e., the economic, legal, political and social. Some black musicians are quite frequently harsh social critics. A few black musicians have been known to rake unprecedented steps to assail the foul practices that have characterized political machinations against defenseless people. Some of the music of Nina Simone performs this service.

Much of black music is uniquely situated, uncannily prophetic, painfully personal and shockingly intimate. As such, it is fascinating, magnetic and totally enveloping. From these standpoints, the communication quotient of black music to receptive audiences defies explanation. In addition to this, the black music sets patterns in its structure that other areas of black intellectualism and education can regard as compatible. Black music is in reality black particularism. It is not a reiteration of anything imposed, as is so frequently claimed by those propagandists for the Euro-American ethos.

Before the close of the 19th century, the National Association of Colored Women dedicated itself to fight for black causes, and black music was one of its concerns. This group took an unequivocal position on this matter, saying to the nation that, "Music in the black is a heaven-born gift that should never be allowed to degenerate into a low and unseemly amusement calculated to degrade rather than to elevate the race."

In keeping with this, black music is one area where black people provide their own definitions and make their own judgments. These prerogatives have been maintained to a noticeable extent, regardless of the persuasive commercial activities that have been carried out by an assortment of exploiting dollar-worshippers. Black music, the same as everything in America, has been the target of supercolossal efforts of profiteers and tradesmen to deal with it and in it, but it has not yet become just another set of shopping center sounds.

On many occasions, black music has been promoted by non-black marketeers as a product of sound effect produced by substandard apprentices. The truth is, however, black music relies upon musicianship and not gimmicks. It is organized but not overly arranged. This provides a rapport among musicians that encourages and stimulates invention.

Black music is an amalgam of black life. It is the music black people from a variety of living situations feel, hear, sing, talk and play as an indigenous expression of collective black experience. Black music frequently reflects virulent anger towards the disgraceful and horrendous aspects of America's racist way of life. Listeners who comprehend the various satirical nuances in this music can also recognize that many black musicians are to be counted among the few truly healthy persons in this very sick world. Their imaginations remain unrestrained, and inevitably a cruel social system is musically assailed without fear of consequence.

A few years ago, David Baker, a celebrated black musician and educator, called attention in an interview to the fact that very little is known of the black musician as composer, conductor, concertizer and administrator. He described the need for courses in black music to bring into perspective the effects and works of black musicians and composers in other cultures. He offered the reminder that black musicians are also distinguished in Latin America and Europe. In defining black music, he said, "black music is by black people, black composers, black artists and embraces everything that speaks in any manner for the black culture."

Some black musicians, such as Quincy Jones and Gerald Wilson in their composing, arranging and instrumental competence, frequently reflect the awareness of the black experience, and then proceed to articulate what black musicians feel about it. Thus, the experience is extended through the sounds that are created, and cultural expressions emerge through unprecedented and beguiling harmonies, produced with voices and instruments.

Liberation concepts and liberated attitudes are detected in black music in any category. Black music is produced by musicians who know that being black in this oppressive society is inseparable from being part of the martyred human constituencies living under this system of white racism. Not all of these musicians survive, because too often the struggle exacts a bitter toll. Nevertheless, black people have been and continue to be the producers of incomparably pleasing musical sounds.

As knowledge increases about the black existence in America, revelations about black struggles on many other fronts also disclose that there is an expanding confidence in eventual black liberation. To be liberated is an important facet of black music, but as a concept and as an objective, it is not an exclusive property of the black musician. Unparalleled contributions and sacrifices for justice and freedom continue to be made each day by blacks across the spectrum of American life. However, in the sphere of sound and feeling, the black identity as the substance and the communality of blackness is the spirit inextricably at the heart of black music. John Coltrane's immortal admonition, "The music has to speak for itself," describes clearly what has preserved self-determination in black music.

W.H. McClendon Interviews Dennis Banks

THE BLACK SCHOLAR, JUNE 1976

Interviewer's Note: *America's racial oppression is an integral part of any and all cultural facets that are or may be claimed since the arrival of the first European search parties. Since the late 19th century, Euro-American imperialism and colonialism have become ready-made topics to receive attention when the plights of assorted ethnic peoples are being reviewed. Detailed theoretical explanations of imperialism and colonialism as frontal structural problems in capitalist national organizations are often labored to the extent that the neo-colonialist phenomenon is under emphasized. Also, the catastrophic impacts of long-standing Euro-American imperialist behavior involving invasion, conquest, pillage, plunder, murder and ultimate exploitation receive tragically inadequate disclosure.*

In recent years, it has been registered impressively at varying intervals that some Third World peoples do not accept passively their subjugation. More specifically, within the national borders of the United States during the past decade, some startling and momentous struggles have been waged by Native Americans to protest and remove many of the barriers that have been erected to contain them in a state of existence commonly perceived as "prisoners of war." Living situations for most Native Americans in this country are acknowledged as brutal, horrendous, and unconscionable. These, in addition to numerous other grievances, are being articulated now by a dynamic, courageous Native American leadership cadre which is committed to correcting these atrocious conditions. In response, the forces of reaction in this nation have extended and intensified their capabilities for assault and repression. As the differences sharpen and the conflicts continue, some special hardships inflicted upon Native Americans have surfaced which the total society can no longer disregard.

This interview with Dennis Banks, one of today's important Native American activists, offers insights on some unique indigenous ethics applied in dealing with some of the social, economic and political problems springing from this racist culture.

W. H. McClendon
June 1976

McCLENDON: *Would you discuss the background of The American Indian Movement and its political philosophy?*

BANKS: The background of the American Indian Movement is this: We formed AIM in 1968 to combat racist discrimination in the urban areas of Minneapolis and St. Paul, including police brutality, discrimination in housing, discrimination in employment and discrimination in the courts. We began a real concentrated program to bring about social changes, to bring about changes in these areas. We began first with a police patrol which helped end the massive arrests of Indian people in the Minneapolis area. Prior to our formation of the patrols there were as many as 200 arrests every weekend of Indian people; after the patrol got started we knocked that down. We went through 22 weekends without any Indian people being arrested for drunk charges; there were other arrests, but not the kind where people were picked up for just walking along the streets.

McCLENDON: *These were really racial harassments against Native Americans?*

BANKS: That's right. And so we began a program to end the unemployment picture, as bleak as it was, for Indian people. We concentrated on a big corporation called Honeywell and within two-and-a-half years we had employed over 450 Indian people in that area with the Honeywell Corporation. In the area of housing, we worked against slum conditions. We formed a housing corporation, and we took an application to Housing Urban Development and we now have built in Minneapolis 241 new homes for Indian people. There are 1-bedroom, 2-bedroom and 3-bedroom homes. These are all funded by Housing and Urban Development with a grant of $4.3 million.

We began to concentrate on having an Indian center in Minneapolis, which is very necessary to cultural identity. I think in every major city you will find Norwegian centers, you will find some kind of cultural center, but rarely do you find real Indian centers. After seven years of working in Minneapolis, the first multipurpose Indian center was built at a cost of $1.9 million. This is a major landmark now in the Minneapolis area, because of what it is bringing together – the Indian tribes in that area.

In the area of education, because the Minneapolis and the Minnesota school boards would not work with us, we began an alternative school approach. We opened the first urban Indian school in Minneapolis, the second one in St. Paul and the third one in Rapid City, South Dakota. What we now have is that the Minneapolis school is going to be considered a model by the United States Congress this year, so that other urban areas can fashion their structures around the concept of the Minneapolis Survival School System.

These are the areas that we have concentrated in from the beginning and, of course, the court system. We went to police captains and the chief of police and finally we had to go to the courts. We initiated some court counselors who were Indian people, and we went beyond the court system and went to the prison system and had counselors installed in positions at the Minnesota State Prison. Even further than that, we finally in 1972 had an Indian person elected to the Minnesota State Parole Board. That is the background of AIM and why it was formed.

McCLENDON: *Do you consider the urbanization of Native Americans a matter of continuing grave concern?*

BANKS: I certainly do. The American Indian Movement really began to express serious concerns in this area when we realized that urbanization was part of the downfall, part of the destruction of the Indian community, and we have to go back and examine the reasons why Indian people were being forced off the reservations. Naturally, the term reservations itself is – we know that they are concentration camps designed in the past to confine Indian people and keep them corralled. But now looking at it objectively, it is the only land that we have left, so we have to protect it. There is a lot of encroachment of Indian rights by non-Indians who desire Indian land right now. So we have to fight very bitterly to protect what is ours.

Beyond that is the process of Indian people leaving the reservation and then accepting employment. Certainly we have to be employed to live in this society. Certainly there has to be a place for Indians to go once they get into the urban areas. Now that process is very dehumanizing for Indian people, because there are very few standard homes, very few places where they can go, you know, where they will be accepted. So they are forced to live in substandard conditions; they are forced to go through a process of near selling out.

McCLENDON: *It is obvious from your comments that you see the presence of Native Americans in all environments as being under the control of external forces. On this basis, what do you see as the American Indian Movement's role in challenging and confronting these situations in relation to the* Third World *movement nationally and internationally?*

BANKS: I think our role has been one of generating, first of all, the awareness within our own people of what lies directly in front of us. That is one part of our program, to re-educate ourselves as to what the obstacles are; then secondly to infiltrate into the international community so that the other Third World communities, other Third World groups, will recognize that our fight here is their fight also, including people in other countries, in South Africa, in Central America, in the black countries in Africa. Bring together unified efforts so that we can begin mobilizing worldwide efforts to bring about change. I think this is working, because the American Indian Movement began to work effectively with the World Council of Churches in Geneva. Through this effort, we were able to touch base and make very good contacts with black nationalists. We were able to make contact with Indian groups and other Indian tribes in South America and also in the Philippines and Australia. I think so long as the American Indian Movement is able to effectively communicate our desires and the desires of Indian tribes to them, I think that we will pull together a worldwide organization that will eventually begin to correct the wrongs that face each and every one of us, no matter what country we are in.

McCLENDON: *Do you think that you have devised any strategies for improving techniques of communication and understanding for those with whom you are working?*

BANKS: I think the effort in the three schools that we have operating in the Midwest is a very good tool for organizations, for organizing our own people. You have to look at what has impressed us, and we have to really sort of unbrainwash ourselves. We have been brainwashed for many, many years to "the melting pot of America," to democracy, to the Republic, these kinds of theories which have actually failed the American Indian, who has actually been near destruction. Christianity has been part of that effort also. We have to begin to re-educate ourselves so that we will learn to step around these obstacles and to go forward in a united group that leads itself to where we were almost before the white man came here.

McCLENDON: *The mass media in this country is notorious for its informational distortions and its social dis-services to non-dominant ethnic populations. Does AIM have any strategies for coping with these kinds of practices?*

BANKS: Well, we have tried to do it. We have tried to put out our own newsletter, our own newspaper, and we submit all of our information to *Akwesasne Notes,* which is an Indian-owned, Indian-operated, Indian-edited newspaper, but unfortunately we can't reach the world population with such meager funding.

Another problem in this area is that many of the journalists that we have become officers of the government; they are officers of the FBI. Just recently, we even see revelations where half of the journalists working overseas are CIA officers. So, we can understand why the distortion comes from the journalists in this country, much the same way the textbooks have been used to distort history and to portray Indian people in a negative sense.

So what we have done is that we are devising alternative methods of communications. No longer can we rely on an Associated Press, no longer should we ever rely on UPI and these media which are controlled by non-Third World people. I think, because of that, we are going to have to devise our own system of communications, and even going back to the movies that are stereotyped, the smoke signals being Indian communication. One thing about Indian smoke signals is that white people couldn't distort smoke signals. That is the only way to be able to bring about corrective understandings, so that there are no middle-man interpretations, and then he starts to put in his opinions.

One of the worst pieces of journalism in news reporting that I have ever seen in my life was when the massacre in Attica came down, and the journalists were saying that the convicts had slashed the throats of the guards. They were reporting this as a fact, because it was the police officials who were giving them the information, and you know a lot of people were confused about that issue when it first began to break. Fortunately, they were later able to piece together what really happened, that no convicts began slashing throats. It was the guards themselves who killed a lot of their own people.

McCLENDON: *Over the past several years, there has been a great deal of attention given by some writers and commentators to the fact that there is some likelihood for spiritual reunification of Native Americans, and a large effort has been put forth to revitalize the spiritual attachments of various nations. What do you see as some of the pressing problems preventing this from happening?.*

BANKS: First of all, the federal government has always been active in trying to prevent spiritual direction from happening. Going all the way back to 1880, 1890, there was the Massacre at Wounded Knee, which was conducted only because the government wanted to suppress and finally kill off Indian religion. As a matter of fact, it was a federal law passed in 1890 that prevented the practicing of Indian religion. That law, incidentally, lasted until 1933.

As long as the Indian people are directed spiritually, they are willing to move forward no matter what the cost, no matter how much blood flows from Indians' veins. They are going to keep moving forward. I think the very fact that we have endured great injustices is proof that no matter what the government puts up, we are going to move forward in a positive manner. What has really happened is that spiritual direction will move forces, spiritualism will move people together, and as long as the government cannot control spiritualism, they know it is a threat to them, and I think that they will use everything in their power to try and hold down the spiritual direction.

That's how Martin Luther King began a mass movement, based upon guidance from his beliefs, and we saw Malcolm X coming from another direction, but he was coming from a different side. We saw Crazy Horse in the 1880s asserting that spiritual direction will lead the people again. He was killed. So as long as spiritual direction begins to lead forces, no matter what beliefs you are coming from, the government is going to kill that.

I think that we really have to continue as we are. The Ghost Dance, that was in the 1880s. The Sun Dance is going on now. The American Indian Movement is going on now. AIM is a spiritual movement. AIM itself is not an organization. It is a movement, a movement led by spiritual leaders, such as Crow Dog (who, incidentally, was thrown in prison, who is now out on appeal), but it is the same principle that's applied throughout history. You get the leaders of the spiritual movement, and you try to kill them, nail them down.

McCLENDON: *Many ethnic peoples as well as many members of the dominant population are to be counted among your supporters. Do you believe that you will have sufficient spiritual force and political guidance to inspire a kind of durable commitment for them to stand firm with you in these struggles until success has been achieved?*

BANKS: I would hope that the kind of spiritual direction that is emanating from the American Indian Movement and from Indian people, Indian spiritual direction, that we could sustain a long battle and come out on top. I firmly believe that the future of the United States, of this country, lies in the hands of Native Americans, lies in the direction of spiritual direction. I firmly believe that. Not for people, 200 million people to get up and support and say, "well, I vote for this man here," and "I vote for this man here," or "I vote for this woman here" – not that kind of support. Let's get up and say that this country needs spiritual direction, and we need it bad. If any country has needed spiritual direction, it is the United States.

McCLENDON: *There are a lot of people in this country who are not what we night call flagrant activists, but they would sincerely wish to support a movement with spiritual direction and guidance such as the American Indian Movement. Now, how is it possible for these people, who may not have any special kinds of contacts or informational sources, to learn more about how they can aid your organization?*

BANKS: Well, I think the way, if these people want to help, there are things that we are asking people to help us out with. That is to write to the members of the U.S. Senate. The Senate actually has control over Indian affairs. The House has some control. We are asking, first, that the Congress establish a treaty commission and begin enforcing the rights of Indian people. Number two is to remove the Bureau of Indian Affairs from the Department of the Interior, because of the tremendous conflict of interest in responsibility. The BIA is controlled by non-Indians, because it is controlled by Interior. You take the BIA out of Interior and establish it as a separate agency so that you would have a Secretary of Indian Affairs, and that Secretary would be an Indian, a Native American. Let that happen.

Number three is to amend what is commonly referred to as the Indian Reorganization Act of 1934. This is the Act that sets up tribal governments on the reservation, which actually are puppet governments of the BIA. Amend it so that Indians could have control of the reservation. Amend it so that the reservation does not look like a giant checker board with Indians on this line, whites on this line, government agents on this line. So that Indians could have absolute control over the lands that we possess, which is the least that the government of the United States should allow. The least that this country could give to Indian people is that we control our own land. It is not that way anymore.

If they do these three things, if they write to Congress and say that is what the Indians want, give it to them. Let's support them. In that way they will in effect support the spiritual movement. That way they will support what Indian people have wanted for many, many years.

McCLENDON: *What do you see as some of the more significant factors that have influenced the AIM organization?*

BANKS: I think, first of all, what has – it is unfortunate that what inspired AIM to get moving was the many deaths in this country of Native Americans — inspired us to get off what we were doing, which might have been nothing for many of us, and to get up and stand with the people who were standing already in this country. Malcolm X was standing, and god damn it we should have been standing right along with him, no matter what his beliefs, because this man was fighting for social change in this country.

When Martin Luther King was standing, we should have stood with him, no matter what his beliefs, because we know objectively he was also asking for social change in this country. Corky Gonzalez is standing in Denver, and we should be standing with him. The Asian people who are standing up; we should be standing with them.

I admit the movements have had faults. I have had contact with Corky Gonzales. I have had contact with Asian Americans, and I have had contact with black Americans. I think that we are ready to go forward in a very united stand now. I think we are going to win this. We are going to win a major victory pretty soon, and we should, after so many hundreds of years. We have been divided. Indian people are being killed, and we are the only ones fighting for Indian people. Blacks are being killed, and only blacks are fighting for blacks. Poor whites are fighting for change in the poor white section. Asians and Chicanos are the same way. I think that inspired AIM to stand up finally and say look, we have got to pull it together, and that is where we are right now, trying to bring non-Indians and the Indians together and bring about massive change in this country.

McCLENDON: *In your discussion you have more or less indicated that Native Americans are victims of colonizing influences by white rulers of America to the same degree as is true in many quarters of other Third World populations. Many Third World peoples have discovered that liberation struggles are filled with danger, and there are varying thoughts on the role of martyrs. One is that martyrs are not liberated, that dying for freedom is a trick bag of white propaganda. Liberation can be realized only by the living. How does this fit into the philosophy of struggle and liberation from the standpoint of the American Indian Movement?*

BANKS: Well, I think the way we view that is that liberation to Native Americans means that this land itself, at least the land that we control on the reservations, must be liberated from the strip-mining, must be liberated from the fear of land reclamation and unnatural use of the land, where there is a raping of the land. When we talk about liberation, Native Americans consider the liberation of the land itself. We are just not misusing and raping the land as they have done in Cumberland Gap in Kentucky.

Going further towards your question of dying and martyrdom: we can liberate ourselves without shooting one bullet; we can liberate ourselves and liberate this land without shedding one ounce of blood. This can happen, and I hope that this kind of course could develop. Unfortunately, it is the non-Third World people who are willing to kill for what they believe in, and if necessary, they say, we will die for what we believe in. So, they are doing all the killing and they are doing the dying. Unfortunately, we are dying also. There has been no real movement to enter into a conspiracy to begin killing, or massacring people. What we are going to do then is to make sure that we're going to close the doors to the kind of oppression that has been brought forth in this country. Close the doors to the oppressors on the reservation, starting from the reservation and working onward from there.

I don't want to die for my cause. I don't want to die for my people. I want to live for my people. I want to fight and live for my people, and I want to live and fight for my struggle, so that I myself enjoy some of the benefits, so that I myself begin to see an end to the discrimination in employment. So I could walk into a job. I could walk into any factory and say, "I would like a job here," and they say, "good, get to work." So I could walk into any office and say, "I can type, can I have a job?" And they will say, "get to work right now." Or, so I can walk into any restaurant and sit down and be served without being questioned as to why, if I am Indian, black, Chicano, or what. So I can go into any hotel and be served and get service. That is the kind of thing, that is what I want to be able to do. I want to be able to walk down every street in the United States of America and people will say, "They don't make any war whoops," so they don't start gawking and coming over and touching my hair and stuff like that. If they respect my visions, then I will respect theirs. That is the way we are going to do it.

McCLENDON: *It has been charged, and I think accurately so, in many Third World sectors of political and social thought that Euro-American, scientific-industrial technology is used mainly to castrate, emasculate and reduce to a state of total dependence all Third World peoples who come under their influence. What is your thinking on this?*

BANKS: I think that is pretty true, when we see what is happening in Argentina, and when we see what is happening in Chile and Brazil, particularly Brazil. There are a lot of native Americans in Brazil. And what is happening in South Africa, where the majority of the people are being ruled by the minority because of the industrialization, because of greed, because of the misuse of people. Sad to say that money has been a controlling factor in who lives and who dies. Fortunately for the people, for the masses of people, that time is coming to an end. Maybe by the year 2000 we will see a major development in world history that will bring an end to imperialism and to that kind of thinking.

We must begin a real examination of how we have treated Mother Earth in the past, so that we can go forward and live in real harmony with all our relations. The Indians have a prayer, and at the end of the prayer they say, "for all my relations." Which means the same. It doesn't mean amen, but it means all my relations: we want the Great Spirit to protect the animals in the forest; we want the Great Spirit to protect the trees and the plants of the universe, because if there is no protection there, we begin to deteriorate as human beings. We look at what is happening with the taconite. They are dumping all the taconite trailings into Lake Superior in Minnesota where I am from. The fish are dying; they are being poisoned, and the fish that live even though they are poisoned, people catch and eat, and they themselves become poisoned. So we are not protecting our relations, and in doing so we are going to hurt ourselves. All the deer that have been tagged in the Northwest and the Midwest, some of them are carrying diseases, and we go hunting and catch the deer and eat the meat and we are going to die. All these sprays and chemicals that we have been spraying on Mother Earth, the fish and the birds are going to carry all that stuff. It is going to hurt us.

Industrialization is to the point where we are trying to perfect society, trying to perfect nature, trying to kill every fly in the world. Sure, the fly can be a nuisance, it can be a carrier of disease, but to kill every fly, every worm, every snake, industrialization to that point, to that degree, means that we are going to kill ourselves. That is where the technology is going to fail. It is going to fail the human race, and the first to go — the Third World people. The first to die — Third World people. That may be a real conspiracy in the end, to kill us off.

McCLENDON: *I will close this by asking you to discuss in some detail your feelings about the dismissal of the charges against you* *in the federal court in Portland on May the 12th.*

BANKS: Well I have always said that this case would never go to court. I know that the government in its effort to jail American Indian Movement leaders will go to every extreme to see that we are jailed. But in doing so, they are involved with misconduct. They are involved with violating their own rules, violating their own laws that they themselves have so generously made and applied to citizens. In doing so I realize that it is an over-kill situation, so what I know is that they will commit crimes against their own government.

The judges have an important role in this. The American Indian Movement is unpopular with the judiciary because in some areas, like in South Dakota, they are jailing us left and right simply because we are movement people. But there are judges who are willing to stand up and say that the laws in this country are being violated. That it is not the duty of this system to jail people. Some judges recognize that if laws are broken, people should be brought to trial; however, it does not mean that laws should be broken on top of laws just to jail them because of who they are, and jail them because they are Indian people. That is where the court is stopping the government and saying we will not allow laws to be broken so that you might put this person in jail. In this case, the government is involved in misconduct, and I think even in the future, they will he involved in deceit.

One of our co-defendants, Annie Mae Aquash, was found brutally murdered on the Pine Ridge reservation. FBI agents initialed the death certificate stating the cause for death was exposure, and yet when our own independent coroner went out there at the request of the family, at the request of the Wounded Knee Committees, x-rays were taken and there was a bullet in the side of her head and her hands were cut off. The shooting of Bryon DeSersa, an AIM leader in South Dakota, was murder. The murdering of Peter Bisonnette, the murdering of Buddy Lamont, the shooting of Russell Means and John Thomas – there is misconduct involved by federal prosecutors against us.

They also thought they had me on October 16th. They had me surrounded in four different cities in the Midwest: Denver, Minnesota, Tulsa and Oklahoma City. Four places where they had me positively identified and had me surrounded all in the same day. And they closed in, and I sat in a place and watched this one incident on TV. They were giving us a blow-by-blow report, that we have Mr. Banks surrounded. All of a sudden I get a telephone call from Tulsa, from this route and that route, people calling up and saying, Banks we just called to make sure you were there, because we understand they have you surrounded in Tulsa. About a half hour later the phone rings and it's Oklahoma City, and it's Denver. So when they said they had an indictment against me for some alleged shoot-out in Oregon, I was not surprised, because I thought they were going to indict me for something in Minneapolis. I thought they were going to indict me for something in Tulsa and Oklahoma City, or in Denver, and it was part of their game, trying to discredit the American Indian Movement, trying to trump up charges against people and things like that.

But I know they are going to go on, and the day that the dismissal here came and I predicted that they will continue the harassment against us, I said no doubt they will try some other federal agony to jail us, and I named the Internal Revenue Service, and god damn it if it wasn't that evening my attorney received a call saying the Internal Revenue Service is beginning an investigation on myself, wanting to know about monies back to 1971, '72, '73, '74, and '75. It is going to continue. I have 15 kids, and I would like to go to court with the Internal Revenue Service, and I would like to ask for an accounting of what they have done with the money in the past 200 years. If they want to ask me for an accounting of my money, I, as a Native American, as a landlord of this country, I am going to ask for an accounting of their monies also.

Dennis Banks, a Chippewa Indian, co-founded the American Indian Movement (AIM) in 1968. AIM is an activist group which has struggled against the oppression of Native Americans in the reservations and cities. In 1973, Banks was with a group of Indians in a Custer, South Dakota, courtroom protesting the murder of Wesley Bad Heart Bull, an Indian shot by a white man. A disturbance occurred, resulting in the courtroom being tear-gassed and Banks being arrested on charges of "rioting while armed without intent to kill." He was subsequently convicted by an all-white jury, but fearing for his life, he fled South Dakota rather than be imprisoned. Early this year (1976), Banks was arrested in California by the FBI and held for extradition to South Dakota. His supporters are trying to halt the extradition. In the meantime, Banks was to face trial in Portland, Oregon, on separate charges, but these charges were dismissed.

The Foundations of Black Culture

THE BLACK SCHOLAR, SUMMER 1983

SLAVERY FOR BLACKS IN AMERICA was not a condition for preparing the slaves to be free. The culture of slavery and its advocates were intent upon teaching blacks to be better slaves. This automatically required that blacks be taught to think of themselves in white terms, culturally and politically.

The conditions to which blacks would acclimate themselves would be those in which their dispossession, wretchedness and subjugation would be perpetuated. Slavery demanded that blacks be educated to accept the living patterns of debasement and accommodation. This would lead to contentment with being controlled by whites. The success of slavery depended upon whites invading and totally conquering the minds of blacks and using their power and advantages as levers to render blacks harmless and keep them obedient.

The entire black population was to be contained in cultural terms at a developmental level approximating that of children. It was intended that black people would never reach a state of mature personhood.

Slavery was unwavering in its aggressiveness and determination to have blacks accept servitude without resistance. Black passivity was the theme of the slaves' socialization process.

The formation of black people into a positive ethnic entity occurred in North America when they first banded together to share concerns and cope with problems related to their captive status. Their common geographical origin in Africa, physical similarities, and skin color were the criteria used by their captors to justify placing them in a common condition of enslavement and servitude. This laid the foundation for the need to organize and establish an identifiable black community. Despite language barriers, vast cultural differences and hosts of other obstacles, blacks soon began to have a collective sense of their slavery and its political and social implications. This led to an irreversible and expansive commitment to be free and grew rapidly to the point where, for blacks, it was the most commonly shared ambition.

Today black liberation remains the cherished objective for the vast majority of the black population. The atrocious circumstances of slavery and present condition of subjugation and degradation do not diminish this aspiration. Most black people from "no degrees" to Ph.D.s are convinced that each succeeding generation of children must be politicized to carry on this interminable crusade. For all who are politically black, this is a major facet of black culture.

White racism on the North American continent assigned to its disciples and subjects the task of continuing in each generation the subjugation of black people. This widely instilled among the dominant population the idea that servility was proper black behavior, and servitude the preferred black condition. Because of the wide application and rigid exercise of this public policy in the decades that followed the founding of the nation, many blacks were overcome by feelings of hopelessness.

After the Civil War, racial segregation became the new public policy everywhere. This assured that blacks would be locked into the bottom of the national societal scale. For white racists, the segregation of blacks was the ideal policy and practice to implement the myths of white supremacy. Segregation, applied in the broadest manner possible, governed black social mobility and made the entire black population vulnerable to unimaginable exploitation, proscriptions and discrimination. Since 1865, blacks have been the most segregated of all the ethnic populations in America. Racial segregation was made viable through laws. It is maintained through custom and caprice.

Black culture is the concept that springs from many forms of black creativity including feeling, thought and action. Black culture is not typified by the findings, impressions, conjectures and analyses of alien anthropologists and other social scientists. The racist societal structures of the United States make it extremely difficult for any member of the dominant population to interpret appropriately or accurately the black experience. Anyone from this group wishing to appear informed, to have influence, exhibit authority or hold power must resort to techniques that define blacks in white terms. For blacks such definitions are invalid.

It is well established that whites can listen to black people and not know what is being inferred; visualize the nuances in black behavior and not comprehend the acts; understand some of the real travails of black life but not the descriptions. Such ineptness has resulted repeatedly in disgraceful caricaturing and intentional defacing of the evidences of black reality. The results are that there have surfaced innumerable intellectually spurious descriptions and definitions placing the black population in zoom focus as simple minded, stupid, childlike, emotionally uncontrollable, culturally backward, sexually irresponsible and genetically inferior.

Nevertheless, blacks retained and strengthened their capabilities to create and develop levels of social thought that clearly identified the sources of racist authority and power in the United States. They pinpointed long before the twentieth century that white racist sociopolitical structures advocating and defending the status quo were intended to make certain that America would remain forever a nonviable environment for black people. Black culture endows black people with insights to recognize these forces in contemporary settings.

Culture is the major force in the resistance of black people to domination by any other external human element. Such culture is the collective base product of the black historical experiences and the black political perspectives that include commitments to achieve liberation. From these evolve the positive intragroup ideological influences that motivate blacks to struggle and exert themselves on behalf of creating determinants for a better history. This is why the dance, the music, the poetry and philosophy emanating from blacks in the United States and throughout the Western hemisphere survived and flourished.

Much of this has been and can be traced directly to the survival of the rich African cultures from which so many blacks (centuries ago) were stolen and captured to be brought as property to the Western part of the world. The most enduring quality of black culture can be witnessed in its clear Africanization of Western music. Aesthetically and philosophically, it is possible that similar cultural strengths in other components of black culture will inevitable find broader expression and eventually raise the level of humanization in this leader of Western societies.

Despite the barrage of abuses and enormous discriminations directed at black people by the American racist system, many blacks continue to manifest ambition and to struggle aggressively to improve their circumstances. More notably many of them have the psychological stamina to refuse accommodating themselves to blatant indignities endemic to the functioning of this system.

Blacks have moved steadily and undauntedly to improve their status to a point where an increased number can experience human dignity and respect. In the black struggle, these are no minor mileposts but for many of the dominant population, they are discomforting and threatening. The evolution of black culture over the last 130 years reveals that disruption has merit. This idea is anathema to most of the dominant population. Propagandists for the "American Way" do not abandon at any point their compulsions to support unconditionally maintaining a system-wide status quo. Black struggle worthy of the effort could not produce a culture deserving of acknowledgement if the objective was not to remove blacks from subjugation.

The culture of black people in America is revealed in social, aesthetic and artistic endeavors utilized to improve in any/every way the conditions of the black existence in this nation. They are clearly manifested in the numerous humanistic needs and moral social demands. These have been and continue to be the major concessions to be extracted from this nation whose most shameful legacy is its treatment of the black population. Cultural awareness has enabled black leadership and its diverse constituencies to oppose steadfastly the forces in this country that plan social disparity as an ineradicable circumstance for black people. The absence of black cultural consciousness is most easily observed among those blacks who feel inferior to whites. These are the ones who lack the courage to battle for improvements in the deplorable conditions under which too many blacks live. They provide rationales for defeatism and set examples for the acceptance of indignities without redress.

In America, white racism is the cultural mechanism for dominance by the dominant population. It permeates every sector and crevice of the dominant society. Its effectiveness is awesome, and most members of the dominant population are its adherents and supporters. In contra-distinction and contradiction, the culture of black people is diametrically opposed to and arrayed against what white racism intends for America's black population. The awareness and consciousness among blacks, wherever they are situated, brings about a recognition of the commonality of the black circumstance. There is broad understanding that white racism seeks to suppress and make victims of blacks under any and all conditions. There has been black cultural comprehension of this for as long as it has been a socio-political fact.

Black culture does not disguise the varied figurations of reality. It reflects and exercises the responsibilities involved with confronting the complexities of the human condition. In the cultural context, black scholars pointed out long ago that "to know black history is painful. For black people not to know it is disastrous." The black experience in History, Religion, Politics, Law, Social Relations, Philosophy, and the Arts comprises the consortium of black culture. Suffering, despair, defeat, and tragedy (of the past and present) are met by blacks with an indomitably timeless determination to survive. The cultural foundations for blacks are frequently subjected to painful and brutal deculturalizing assaults. Wherever the black pursuit for liberation continues undeterred the involved blacks are not afflicted with notions of self-rejection. Even though black people use the same language and have the same exposures to the dominant society's customs, influences and environments, the degree of variance in black encounters with this racist system chokes off any of the system's pretenses that are voiced about its objectivity.

Black culture is heavily endowed with valid instructive materials that teach black people white racism in America cannot exist without resorting to oppressing its targets and victims, blacks and other non-dominant ethnic populations. Black culture affirms that black humanity has as its cause celebre a commitment of resistance to all human oppression. Thus there is placed in clear cultural perspective the eternal conflict that is drawn between white racism (the system) and black people (the resistance).

Frequently, the culture of black resistance moves blacks into a position where their self-respect and personal dignity become a threat and a source of discomfort to all who would oppress us. In a variety of ways America is also a reservation for those of the black population who have been the constant objects of dominant population hypocrisy, duplicity, and oppression. Black culture has managed to expose the problems created by white America to the peoples of the world. Along with this, a higher level of black consciousness has developed. This is to be seen most vividly in those periods where blacks have demonstrated confidence in and support for black creative leadership in varied struggles for liberation. Even though the force of white racism has not abated, the adamance of black culture persists in gradually reducing the effectiveness of those longstanding obstacles to social and political change.

The social, political, economic and philosophical thought components produced from the black historical experience are interwoven into the fabric of black culture in a manner similar to arts, music and literature. The overlapping is so extensive that it becomes impossible to separate one from another. Black culture has its own objectivity which in its most meaning context leads blacks to move in the direction to develop more self-respect and intragroup reliance. Now it is much more difficult for this system to deceive blacks.

Black culture is positive. It is the collective fusion and culmination of black intellectual and experiential substance. It is the durable, dependable, essential force that motivates black people to seek social clarity and humanistic insight. The real autonomy that blacks exercise over their own lives (no matter how limited) springs from dignity as preserved through black social structures and cultural uniqueness.

The black experience in history, religion, politics, law, social relations, philosophy and the arts comprises the consortium of black culture. Suffering, despair, defeat and tragedy are met by blacks with an indomitable determination to survive. Black culture affirms that black humanity has as its cause a commitment of resistance to all human oppression. Thus black culture informs the world that black people are models of humanity and that humanistic concerns are foremost among our priorities.

Civil Rights: Past, Present and Future An Interview by Art Alexander

This interview was conducted by Art Alexander on December 13, 1979 for PBS station TCB, Portland.

"A national culture is the whole body of efforts made by a people in the sphere of thought to describe, justify and praise the action through which that people has created itself and keeps itself in existence." – *Franz Fanon*

ALEXANDER: *Many of us born after World War II have little sense of civil rights history between 1865 and 1955. What do we need to know about that period to better understand the last 25 years of the civil rights struggle?*

McCLENDON: A thorough comprehension of the U.S. Supreme Court decision handed down in the case of *Scott vs. Sanford,* 1857, better known as the Dred Scott case. This court decision signalled for some blacks that the end of an individual ownership system of chattel slaves was now in sight, but for others it caused great anguish. It also revealed the beginning of a wardship over the black population by the U.S. Supreme Court that up to this time does not appear to have an end. The theme of this court decision was/is "No black has any rights that whites are bound to respect."

From this point forward it was clear to astute blacks that black people would have to rely upon themselves to fight for equality and justice, because this would never occur automatically under the law. Many U.S. Supreme Court decisions concerned with human rights and abuses have been rendered since Dred Scott, and most of those of special concern to blacks have been additional fallout to sustain and reinforce the impact of Dred Scott. This is very clearly perceived in the *Plessy vs. Ferguson,* 1896, and *Brown vs. Topeka* decisions, 1954-1955.

A review of the black experience, past and present, informs us that the dominant population maintains the subjugation and subordination of blacks and all non-dominant ethnic populations because it can. The black population remains in a perpetual state of resistance and is involved in an eternal quest for equality because it must. *Scott vs. Sanford* provided the formulation for an atrocious pattern of continuing judicial decisions displaying disastrous punitive interpretations and devaluations of the human and civic worth of black people. In these endeavors, the judicial system remains overtly capricious, conjectural, arbitrary and utterly dysfunctional for the entire black population. This Dred Scott decision assured that American law would be forever the handmaiden of white racism, and therefore it cannot and will not serve as the voice of America's moral conscience in the realm of civil rights. However, if it should do so because of overwhelming public expectations, the total society would be disrupted, because those few among the dominant population who actually dominate will not sanction even the symbolic indication that this could be a society free of white racism.

ALEXANDER: *If it's safe to assume that the movements of the 1950s and 1960s were not in fact monolithic, who then made up the movements? What classes, religions and regions?*

McCLENDON: Participants included members of all races, classes and religions and from all regions.

ALEXANDER: *Was the movement(s) reformist or revolutionary? (A move to join white America or build Black America?)*

McCLENDON: From most black perspectives, the objectives were and are to improve in every way the conditions under which blacks have existed in America. This was more a declaration of humanistic needs and moral social demands. The white racist reaction and response was to brand these efforts as revolutionary.

ALEXANDER: *Is it valid to establish a spectrum of leaders from radical to conservative? If so, who would you put you where?*

McCLENDON: Blacks have made whatever advances that have been durable because of leadership as a collective and not because of the individual. Participants have included persons who fit every niche on the conservative to radical spectrum. Civil rights consciousness will not allow me the prerogative of assigning specific persons to specific places other than to say that some have been judged as negative and others as positive. For example, the Booker T. Washington-Du Bois difference of opinions on some subjects led to white observers of the black experience using their media and forums to blow these issues completely out of proportion to the context in which they occurred. This was not done to advance a black conservative or refute a black progressive. It was done to destroy the credibility of black people who demonstrate superior intellectual capabilities. The dominant population of America has never produced the equivalent of Frederick Douglass, Booker T. Washington, W.E.B. Du Bois, Paul Robeson.

ALEXANDER: *What did America's white (and racist) media ignore or distort about:*

(a) the sit-ins and freedom riders
(b) the black Muslims
(c) the "ousting" of whites from the movements and the "rise" of the Black Panthers
(d) the riots
(e) the white response to the aforementioned events?

McCLENDON: Many bits and pieces of information plus evidence are now available that reveal the FBI infiltration into and influence over many aspects of the civil rights movement and the black liberation efforts of the '60s. In spite of this, much of the activity of this period is still referred to as black struggle. The fact is that FBI and police infiltration were so extensive that policies and performances often were being largely structured outside of those sectors of real black concerns.

Racism is thoroughly institutionalized in this country, and most of the reports and reviews of black activities by the white media were presented by most of the white media sources. In reference to all of the topics you mentioned, the media generally offered highly negative assessments. This had the effect of obscuring the real long-standing grievances of the black population, while at the same time energizing widespread antipathies against black people. The overall result has been to keep the masses of black people in a stressful state of alienation.

ALEXANDER: *Did white America actually give up anything or substantively address problems they began creating in slavery?*

McCLENDON: No. The black population today holds less equity in this nation than it did 270 years ago at the crest of slavery.

ALEXANDER: *Did Afro-Americans gain much, given the amount of bloodshed and destruction we went through?*

McCLENDON: This must be viewed in relative terms, but given the number of martyrs and victims provided by the black population, the results have been minimal.

ALEXANDER: *What crushed the movements? Was it the government – J. Edgar Hoover, the Department of Justice, and the Presidents?*

McCLENDON: The black struggle has not been crushed. Some excitements of the past two decades have subsided. The black efforts to acquire equality, justice and liberation have gone on for the past four hundred years. Black people are at the present time a long distance from their intended destination, but the struggle continues in many different forms. Blacks must continue to pass mileposts and try diligently not to be forced to pass the same one several times. Internal negative factors among any oppressed people do not operate in a vacuum. Blacks must realize that white racism produces victims that seek to avoid suppression by victimizing their own kind.

ALEXANDER: *What should Afro-Americans have learned from the past 25 years? Have we learned it? Are we doomed to be bought off with consumer goods, or is it still possible to achieve a high level of cultural awareness and self-determination?*

McCLENDON: Blacks must have a politically black awareness and consciousness. They must develop a well-organized leadership collective in all of the places where blacks are situated. There must be a thorough understanding of what is meant by the commonality of the black circumstance. There must be a strong sense of communalism related to the problems faced by black people in this land where they have lived for 22 generations. No sacrifice should be considered too great to assure the preservation of black culture and traditions. Joyce Ladner has stated succinctly that for black people "success is measured by the extent to which one cannot only care for himself but help others in the family." Other depressions, the 1930s, were eras of oppressive poverty with the unemployed and their dependents comprising the largest volume of the victims. The depression that is now underway is a monumental milestone for this nation. The domination cliques of global corporate structures in the areas of banking, industry and investments have put into place monstrous mechanisms to create economic hardships and dilemmas for many of this nation's peoples who are not of the establishment. Those who will have increasing difficulties and distressing problems will be comprised of the affluent and employed, as well as the chronically poor and unemployed.

ALEXANDER: *What haven't I addressed that should at least be mentioned before we close?*

McCLENDON:

(1) The black population should no longer be thought of as the property of any white-controlled political party.

(2) An understanding of what segregation is in the United States!

(3) The meaning of the new depression: deprivation and disadvantage with and without employment, a common experience for blacks. Black culture includes ways of coping with poverty that are rich in the imagination and creativity black people have used to acquire resources and resourcefulness to control in some degree their environment. Contrary to the self-serving prophecies of white social science researchers, blacks historically have moved against awesome odds to preserve their self esteem and increase their life chances. These efforts meant the difference for many between enduring oppressive poverty and coping with worrisome deprivation.

Dismal to Abysmal

The Black Scholar, Spring 1992

THE DU BOIS POSITION DELINEATING THE ROLES of the talented tenth within the black population, as resourceful elements to forge the way for the mass of black people to reach an equitable status in American life, has been subject to debate among many blacks for the past 87 years. The same is true for the Booker T. Washington advocacy for black accommodationism. These misunderstood and unreconciled rationales are sources of conflict and confusion that cloud the thinking of numerous blacks, as well as the many whites involved with maintaining influence and direction over black life in America. For a long time, the philosophies of Du Bois and Washington have been highly debatable concepts. In many circumstances these philosophies have been at the base of opinions and proposals that raised civil rights efforts and self-help ideas to levels of intense friction. Often they have slowed the development of positive politicization and social consciousness for many blacks and made more difficult their comprehension of the legitimacy of civil rights and self-help ideas as inseparable essentials for defining, affirming and implementing equity for any oppressed people in America. It is critical for civil rights struggles and self-help structures to be perceived as complementary and not as contradictory doctrines.

The selection of Clarence Thomas as the president's nominee for the United States Supreme Court is widely perceived as a capricious act designed to cripple politically the total black population. There are many areas of American life where there are obvious failures on the part of the people to recognize the ideological forces responsible for such selections. Even more troubling is that many of them surely miss the demoralizing implications. For example, one annoying possibility in this selection process is the belief that the nomination was a reward for the fidelity of Thomas to this nation's competitive, punitive, perverted and inhumane values held in the custody of fanatical conservative zealots. It is not unreasonable to consider this nomination as a token of special recognition for services Thomas rendered above and beyond the most grotesque racist expectations, when he directed the AC mischief against the elderly, as well as his opposition to affirmative action and civil rights. Moreover, as a Bush memorial to Lee Atwater, Clarence Thomas on the United States Supreme Court could be used in '92 to fill a revised role of the infamous Willie Horton which played so well in the Bush presidential campaign of '88. It is possible that Thomas may be useful in obviating the likelihood of any future Supreme Court deliberations that could sustain any interests meaningful to this nation's black population.

It is common knowledge that some blacks openly display political ignorance and attribute any good fortune they have experienced to the mythical good will of the influential members of the dominant population with whom they have a boy- or girl-to-boss relationship. Much of the Clarence Thomas saga seems to follow this theme. It is significant to note that nothing in the Pin Point narrative reveals political aspirations geared to his wanting to make this nation a better place in which to live. Repeatedly, attention is given to docility in manner as a strategy for material acquisition only. The spirit and objectives of struggle for dignity, equity and justice are never referred to or acknowledged as basic values for black people in America.

Unfortunately there has been placed before this nation the record of a nominee to the United States Supreme Court who appears satisfied with and remains passive about the status quo. Thomas is never shown to have engaged in any action to reach higher ideals common to the black struggle. Political thought from Richard Allen and Absalom Jones through Jesse Jackson asserts that the best interests of the black population and America are never served by blacks who think and act as accommodationists. The sojourns of Reagan and Bush in the White House have helped some blacks understand that white racist power and its arbitrary policies are the real recurring obstructions to civil rights, human rights and self-help for any and all oppressed peoples and classes.

For several weeks, frequent media accounts mentioned the endless supernatural paternal supervision Senator Danforth exercised over his protege, Clarence Thomas. These could be taken to be clear messages stating there is never a limit to the care given to assure that blacks are placed where white folks want them. After all is said and done, prior to the Bush announcement of the Thomas nomination at Kennebunkport, no black anywhere (conservative, radical, religious, agnostic, atheist, affluent, homeless) had proposed or suggested that Thomas be considered for anything.

Many explanations, charges and criticisms are at large now focussing on political connivances in high places that gave the Thomas nomination the flavor of a genderized contest/conflict. Blacks and others should weigh seriously whether they are acting responsibly when they avoid facing the realities of those racial and gender antipathies that are omnipresent in all three branches of the American government. Persons anywhere seeking justice and equity continually must be cause-oriented and situation conscious. Ms. Hill provided traditionally defenseless constituencies of the American population with an intelligent and graceful exercise of situation recall. In doing this, she exhibited a quality of leadership that penetrated the smoke screens erected by the Senate to make inscrutable the deceptions and evasions permeating the judiciary committee hearings and their political devastation.

The testimony of Anita Hill is an important milestone in the long journey traveled by black martyrs to improve the quality of life for nondominant ethnic populations in the United States. Her responses to challenges and diatribes coming from judiciary committee members illuminated with shocking clarity that no black can be free as long as one black is making it by Tomming. For those who do not understand the dynamic historical course of uninterrupted and unrelenting white racism, the significance of this assertion may be difficult to grasp. This is why some persons actively support and defend ridiculous aberrant public policies and racist practices imposed upon the black population. Alongside them are members of the dominant population who readily exploit selected black accommodationists to serve as primary voices of expression to bring about mass false impression among other blacks. This influences many apolitical blacks to disassociate themselves from the most painful indignities inflicted upon our people. Ironically, many explain their uncritical stances as acts of loyalty to skin color. They are convinced that because of pigmentation, their support should override any realistic objections that may surface based upon principles of sound social thought. Regrettably, this results in blacks continuing to share a common deplorable condition because of white racism, while remaining unable to weld a common consciousness for effective political resistance.

Political collusionists of the Hatch, Specter, Simpson and Brown class are responsible for making the black existence in the United

States one of life's gravest hazards. As for Thurmond, his expressions, comments and interruptions were probably inspired by his fantasies of Thomas standing firm for the South and cheering for the Confederate Army during the Civil War.

Anita Hill had the misfortune to believe that her concerns would be given maximum protection by the judiciary committee. The history of the Senate is replete with examples of conflict resolution handled to favor the Senate exclusively. Ms. Hill had only her intellect and integrity as bargaining chips. While these are prized qualities among most oppressed peoples, they have little to do with the politics that prevail in elected officials' strategies for maintaining ultimate power.

In the circumstance of conservative vs. liberal positions to assess the fitness and determine worthiness (professional and moral) of Clarence Thomas, the judiciary committee acted as the broker to market the political schemes of President Bush and his White House staff. From this performance came the appalling revelation that, if and when a black woman reports character deficiencies of anyone selected, designed or mentored by rancorous administration and senate manipulators, it is futile to expect that among the plotters there will be awakened any conscionable interest. Anita Hill's mistake may have been her misplaced confidence that she could strike an arrangement for fair play with any part of the Senate of the United States.

The Thomas and Hill testimonies offered excellent opportunities for viewers to distinguish the differences between self-esteem and self-aggrandizement. Moral issues did not affect the outcome of this drama. The Senate Judiciary Committee asserted its prerogative to act as advocate for the system of white racism. In filling this role, the antics of the Committee were described by the chairman as "the process." This process came off as a simple repetitive political ideological contest between Republican and Democratic committee members. The hearings were structured for both groups to collaborate comfortably in the vilification of a black woman. The judiciary committee turned these assemblies into a dramatic farce where the theatrics of senators titillated public opinion.

They used tactics ranging from clown-like entertaining to raw political campaigning to criminal court procedures.

The judiciary committee's actions in dealing with Ms. Hill's presence were demonstrations of excessive malicious adversarial disdain, discourtesy and disrespect. Had she been a less secure person her life could have been made irreparably unstable. Racism and gender bias expressed in the Senators' admonitions, opinions and questions, along with their self-targeted compliments, filled every crevice. Despite the elaborate and profuse explanations voiced, there was a detectable noxious theme of meanness directed toward the supporters of Ms. Hill. The mentors, supporters and strategists for Clarence Thomas are suspected of advising him to assume a charade of blackness. This was accomplished by his describing the unanticipated ramifications of Ms. Hill's testimony as a high-tech lynching. Such an uncharacteristic upsurge of black consciousness on the part of the nominee suggests that a bizarre reservoir of ambiguities, incongruities and anachronisms could fill his life. It must not be forgotten that it was Thomas who did not provide any answers to any inquiries about his political, legal or social concerns. He refused to articulate any awareness or comprehension of matters of common interest, or of serious concern, to persons and organizations throughout the nation. News accounts have repeatedly called attention to the Pin Point Clarence Thomas as a product of whites doing their missionary type things in a run-of-the-mill fashion, where no checks and balances were held by the surrounding black community. Such information now stirs conjectures that the Thomas of today may be burdened with a mendacious spirit and an intellectual shortfall.

Senate and administration contempt for the black population has never been displayed more blatantly. The entire sequence of events is socially flawed by unreceptiveness to input expressing the interests, preferences or concerns of black individuals and organizations. The nomination was an insult to Thomas, Hill, the black population and the American polity. There are more than 750,000 lawyers and judges in this nation. Bush's statement that Thomas was the best choice as a United States Supreme Court nominee is incredible. Questions and challenges voiced by spokespersons representing broad professional, religious, political and social thought sectors of American life were disregarded completely. Through several media presentations, Clarence Thomas was reported as a significant point man in carrying out anti-black, anti-poor and anti-labor policies for the Reagan administration. Some of these accounts were anything but flattering. To modify the effects of these reports, Judiciary Committee members used supercilious rhetorical abrasiveness in what seems an unprecedented hostile intent to erode professional and social compatibility among black men and women.

In acting to preserve a psycho-social history of keeping blacks in their place, the Senate risked trashing the United States Supreme

Court. Customarily and historically, black people's lives are filled with stress, crisis and catastrophe. These are unavoidable for all peoples who live under white racist repression. The extreme racism and chauvinism manifested by Senators during the hearings shook the sensitivities of the nation. Now, from the top levels of global corporate control downward through all branches of government and on into the polity, thinking is more focused on ameliorating some of the abominable, governmentally created disorders rampant throughout the country. Events so vividly reviewed in the hearings should create for some Senators unexpected problems because of their fervor to use the troubled circumstances for some blacks as evidence that a white racist system is forever desirable and preferable.

Throughout the history of this nation, blacks seeking improvements in status were committed to achieving civil rights as a priority. Irrespective of their origins, there was dedicated use of minds, bodies, education, money, organizations, political skills, legal talent, scientific capability, intellectual proficiency, artistic genius, social thought and military propensity. These and more were applied to loosen the white racist choke-hold gripping the black population.

There are no records or reports showing real successes for blacks who attempt to realize civil rights through endorsing or practicing accommodation. Concomitantly, increased elevation of status for oppressed people never occurs solely because of expressions or acts of benevolence on the part of some empathetic members of the dominant population. Struggles of the oppressed must be marked clearly by internal consciousness, social and political. There must be a decisive rejection of racist behaviors, in or out of government, that affirm a devalued human status for any citizens or inhabitants. The history of blacks in America is, in addition to other content, the chronicle of resistance to slavery, exploitation, deprivation and maltreatment.

Civil rights struggles resulted in the eventful presence of a distinguished civil rights advocate and defender, Thurgood Marshall, becoming a United States Supreme Court Justice in 1967. A turnabout in 1991 has a black justice seated on the court through the political machinations of an administration broadly perceived as anti-civil rights. White House strategists and senatorial collaborators are not likely to understand, or care, that dissenting blacks do not seek justice and respect as favors. As a people, we are committed to achieve these despite the continuing criminal and discriminatory actions defended and often fostered by an insensitive government and the culture to which it conforms.